Praise for Promises of Freedom

I am happy to endorse and recommend this book which is very much written in the tradition that Bernard Crick and I set out. In seeking to set out and extend the case for an inclusive, humanistic and optimistic vision of each of the three issues the text concludes with an agenda for action: a set of principles which need to underpin and guide lifelong learning. This will ensure the future development of both citizenship and belonging in a democratic and pluralistic society, against a modern background of the threats of globalisation, risk and increasing insecurity.

Rt Hon David Blunkett, MP

Promises of Freedom is an original and stimulating reflection on the meanings of citizenship and belonging in relation to the realities of lifelong learning. It will be of great value to both practitioners and academics.

Professor John Annette, Pro Vice Master for Lifelong Learning and Engagement and Professor of Citizenship and Lifelong Learning, Birkbeck, University of London

Promises of Freedom
Citizenship, Belonging and Lifelong Learning

R. H. Fryer

Published by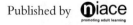

© 2010 National Institute of Adult Continuing Education (England and Wales)

21 De Montfort Street
Leicester
LE1 7GE

Company registration no. 2603322
Charity registration no. 1002775

NIACE has a broad remit to promote lifelong learning opportunities for adults. NIACE works to develop increased participation in education and training, particularly for those who do not have easy access because of class, gender, age, race, language and culture, learning difficulties or disabilities, or insufficient financial resources.

You can find NIACE online at www.niace.org.uk

Cataloguing in Publications Data
A CIP record for this title is available from the British Library

ISBN 978 1 86201 442 8

Cover design by Book Production Services, London
Designed and typeset by Kerrypress Ltd, Luton
Printed and bound in the UK by Page Bros, Norwich

Biographical note

Professor R. H. (Bob) Fryer is Chair of the Campaign for Learning and a board member of NIACE. He recently served as one of the commissioners on the independent Inquiry into the Future for Lifelong Learning that reported in September 2009. Between 2001 and 2007, Bob was the Founding Chief Executive of NHSU (the 'corporate university' of the NHS) and National Director for Widening Participation in Learning and Chief Learning Adviser at the Department of Health. Before that, he was Assistant Vice Chancellor at the University of Southampton and, for 15 years, Principal of the Northern College for Residential Adult Education.

Bob served as the Chair of the Labour Government's National Advisory Group on Continuing Education and Lifelong Learning (NAGCELL) and as a member both on the Moser committee on adult basic skills and on the task group on Skills for Neighbourhood Renewal. He was an Executive Director and board member of Ufi/learndirect and a founding national council member of the Learning and Skills Council.

Bob was awarded the CBE for services to community education in the 1999 New Year's Honours.

For Ann

Contents

Acknowledgements

This monograph owes most to my friends and colleagues at NIACE. First, to Peter Lavender, who originally commissioned me to write a paper on citizenship and belonging for NIACE, which then developed into a briefing paper for the independent commission of Inquiry into the Future for Lifelong Learning, sponsored by NIACE and chaired by Professor Sir David Watson. Secondly, I owe a great debt to my dear friend Alan Tuckett for sharing with me and with many others, over several decades, his encyclopaedic and sensitive understanding of the civilising and liberating virtues of adult education and lifelong learning worldwide. It was Alan, in particular, who encouraged me to develop my original thoughts on the related themes of citizenship, belonging and lifelong learning into the monograph that follows. Alan was ably and enthusiastically aided by Jenny Williams, who led the efficient and hard-working support team for the independent inquiry, and by Tom Schuller, its Secretary, whose thorough grasp of the key issues, political pragmatism and sheer grit were responsible for bringing the Inquiry to successful completion and publication. Sarah Turner and David Shaw have been most supportive editors, encouraging me to turn my papers for the independent Inquiry into this monograph. Through NIACE, I have learned much, too, from the quiet rigour and intellectual sharpness of Stephen McNair, and about the importance of vigilance on all matters concerning public policy for adult learning from Alastair Thomson and Dan Taubman.

My own interest in the politics of freedom and its energising promise, and in the contribution that lifelong learning can make towards its expanding possibilities, has been stimulated by over 40 years of learning with, and teaching of, a huge number of adults, drawn variously from trades unions, community groups, voluntary organisations and from the many so-called 'new social movements'. They, too, were inspired by the clamouring for recognition and liberation by hitherto excluded social groups in the USA, UK and Europe in the 1950s, 1960s and 1970s, by anti-colonial struggles throughout the world, and especially by Nelson Mandela, whose exemplary quest for freedom eventually brought the rights of full citizenship, a long-yearned-for sense of belonging, and a validation of their identities, to millions of fellow Africans.

Through the Workers' Educational Association (WEA) and, especially, in my work at the Northern College for Residential Adult Education, I met many colleagues and students from whom I learned how education could help change and enhance people's lives. At the College I met my close friend and colleague Ed Ellis, alongside whom I worked for a quarter of a century. Ed showed me the contribution to successful learning that can be made by a commitment to excellence in teaching and by the acceptance of nothing short of the highest quality standards for students whose initial experiences of education may often lack both.

When I first went to the Northern College, we were fortunate to count among our academic advisers Raymond Williams and Royden Harrison – both wise, committed and expert adult learning practitioners as well as scholars, and both of whom had been appointed by my immediate predecessor, the illustrious Michael Barratt Brown, founding Principal of the College, a brilliant adult educator and indefatigable pamphleteer in the causes of education, peace and freedom. The writings of Raymond Williams have been a constant source of inspiration for me, as I hope is evident in the pages of this monograph, however inadequately expressed. John Field, also my one-time colleague at the College, continues to inform, educate and impress me with his prolific writing and extensive knowledge of lifelong learning in this country and abroad.

Other colleagues and friends, first made at or through the Northern College, continue to inspire and re-invigorate me with their energy, commitment, ideas, creativity and inventiveness – including, especially, Roy and Val Bailey, Jill and Steve Brunt, Rita and Geoff Britton, Ian Johnson, Pat and Ros Seyd, and Dianne Willcocks, alongside several other former colleagues at Sheffield Hallam University, and many, many more, including tutors, lecturers, governors, students and administrative staff. When we worked together at the Northern College and long after, the late Mo Mowlam tried hard to show me the virtue of turning ideas and learning into action that counted. Colleagues from my days at Warwick University also supported the College, and me as its Principal, acting as thoughtful advisers, provocative speakers, or by serving as rigorous academic assessors – Bob Burgess, Simon Frith, Paul Corrigan and, particularly, John Selby, who, together with his wife Ann, has always spurred me on with his indomitable devotion to widening participation in learning.

It was also at the Northern College, in 1983, that I first met David Blunkett, whose lyrical foreword to the Green Paper, *The Learning Age*, penned when he became a senior minister in the Labour Government, elected in 1997, continues to inspire and to serve as a talisman for me and for thousands of other lifelong learning professionals. I am privileged to have served David as one of his advisers when he was in office, and continue still to benefit from his friendship, commitment to the liberating effects of education, and his own willingness to learn, including from mistakes.

I owe a special debt to the trades union movement in the UK, with which I have worked closely throughout my professional life, for demonstrating to me the importance of understanding the contribution of collective organisation to individual freedom, and of the articulation of both with democracy, participation and accountability. Among hundreds of trades union colleagues, I have learned chiefly from the late Alan Fisher, General Secretary of the National Union of Public Employees (NUPE), and from the dazzling, quirky and genuinely organic intellectual Bernard Dix, also from NUPE. I have benefited greatly, too, from the ideas and practical example in promoting participative democracy of my lifelong friend Rodney Bickerstaffe, from Bill Gilby, Bob Abberley and Paul Haunch, and from Jim Sutherland and Steve Williams, whose quietly effective opening up of a chance to 'return to learn' to thousands of rank and file union members has represented a transformative opportunity for personal and collective improvement.

My other intellectual debts are mostly too numerous to mention by name, but half a dozen deserve special mention. Above all, it was from my father, Harold Fryer, whose own formal education did not extend beyond secondary school, that my two older brothers and I gained a love of learning, poetry, music and the arts, a respect for practical skills (in his case, motor mechanics and engineering), an appreciation of the educative value of experience, and an alertness to the endless possibilities for fun, before his untimely death in my early teens. My mum believed that educational success represented the instrumental ladder up which to climb away from poverty, deprivation and drudgery in working life, and towards social honour – understandably, befitting a woman with her working class roots in the economic and social hardships of the Black Country.

My long-time friend Huw Beynon explained to me and to adult students at the Northern College eager for a return to activism that effective writing could constitute a legitimate and influential form of political intervention; I have striven to follow his exemplary practice in the pages that follow. My erstwhile tutor and subsequent friend Alan Fox introduced me to the insights and excitement of sociology, especially the light that it can throw on the routine experiences of exploitation, managerial control and employment insecurity, coupled with the consolations of fellowship at work that typified the jobs undertaken by my own family and by millions of others like us. Alan's autobiography, *A Very Late Development*, is an enlightening and enlightened testament to the truly liberating powers of education for mature students, as well as to the continuing scope for increased insight that flows from an unflagging devotion to critical scholarship. For me, the exhortations of the radical American sociologist C. Wright Mills for the 'sociological imagination' to show the connection between private troubles and public issues also have direct application to the three related issues of citizenship, belonging and lifelong learning and their promises of freedom explored in this monograph.

Colleagues from our time together at the National Health Service university (NHSu) always do their best to turn my flights of fanciful vision into practical schemes, and I am grateful to them, especially Edward Prosser, Vince Ion, Dave Arnold and Mike Evans, for their untiring willingness to do so. In thinking about the many dimensions and possibilities of learning, I also continue to draw great strength from the Campaign for Learning and from its energetic Chief Executive Tricia Hartley, and from one of her predecessors, Bill Lucas, a widely published writer on learning, and enthusiastic advocate of lifelong learning. Mark Corney serves as a statistically dextrous adviser to the Campaign for Learning on all matters touching the funding of learning, and as a close personal friend and supporter to me.

Last but by no means least, I have learned from my wife, Ann Wheeler, my lifetime's dearest love and constant companion, the serenity and wisdom to be gained from reaching out towards calm understanding, empathy, tolerance and respect for others with their diverse expressions of identity and belonging. Ann strives modestly to exemplify the necessary articulation between everyday personal ethics and an engagement with the wider moral issues, risks and disasters that concern the world at large, whether emanating from human frailty, from political manoeuvring, or from natural causes. It is to her that this volume is dedicated.

Despite all of these valuable and inspirational influences, all of the errors, omissions and oversights in these pages are my responsibility, and mine alone.

Bob Fryer
Ealing
London
June 2010

Preface

This is a timely book which scopes the role of learning for citizenship and belonging – key surely to the achievement of the 'Big Society' that the coalition government in Britain has put at the centre of its social policy agenda. The 'Big Society' idea envisages communities shaped by voluntary activity and mutual enterprise which thrives in meeting local needs; where everyone has the skills, and the confidence needed, to share in identifying how best we can create a world where everyone can fulfil their aspirations; and where everyone shares responsibility for building that society. It is quite a task.

When I first worked in adult education there seemed to be no doubt that education for an informed and engaged citizenship was at the heart of the work. University extra-mural programmes flourished. Trade union studies courses boomed. In Liverpool and London major initiatives in adult and community education explored how best to support working-class communities to use learning to secure social change, and in London we developed popular planning programmes to support people in shaping the future of their local physical environment and communal facilities. The *Russell Report* highlighted the gap in opportunities faced by groups then called the 'educationally disadvantaged'. Meanwhile in Brazil Paulo Freire was writing up his work on literacy as 'cultural action for freedom'.

In the years since then, much of the infrastructure to support adults in understanding change, adapting to and shaping it through learning – to use Raymond Williams' helpful typology – has eroded. A large proportion of university community education programmes have been cut, along with the departments that organised them. In further education a rump of liberal adult education continues to receive public support through the Skills Funding Agency's safeguard. The Workers' Educational

Association and a small number of specialist adult education bodies (mainly in London) continue to thrive, along with the half a dozen long-term residential colleges.

There are, however, some positive signs: the Access course programmes of the 1980s produced a rich vein of curriculum innovation; the trade union learning representative movement has led to a flowering of second-chance education in the workplace; and the environmental movement has been powered by informal learning led by activists. In the last year of the Labour government The Learning Revolution initiative saw the flowering of a wide range of third sector projects – many of which were focused on the citizenship agenda.

Nevertheless, *Promises of Freedom* meets a real need: it offers an overview which captures the dialogues and disagreements central to the contested meanings ascribed to citizenship, identity and belonging; reviews a range of the educational initiatives undertaken to promote them; and identifies a baker's dozen of principles that should underpin a programme of learning for citizenship of the sort needed for a complex industrial democracy like Britain today.

The genesis of the book repays some attention. In part it grew from the work of the independent Inquiry into the Future for Lifelong Learning which NIACE commissioned between 2007–09, chaired by Sir David Watson, and led by Tom Schuller, with Bob Fryer as one of the commissioners. Bob's thematic paper on citizenship and belonging, prepared for the Inquiry, forms the basic building block of the present study. The Inquiry's final report, *Learning Through Life*, described a wide range of measures to promote learning throughout the life course, at the heart of which was a call for a citizen's curriculum built initially around four capabilities – digital, health, financial and civic, together with employability. In this study, Bob expands on the citizenship and belonging dimensions of the Inquiry's work, but he also locates its proposals in the wider history of ideas that led to it.

In this, he has drawn on his distinctive range of skills as scholar, policy maker and teacher. As a distinguished Principal of Northern College, Bob sits firmly in a tradition deriving from the work of Tawney and Temple, Williams, Hoggart and Thompson, to bring to the general audience the fruits of wide reading, and the tools for independent analysis. As a long-term advocate of learning for cultural change, working inside and outside government, it is unsurprising that his book ends with a call for a national debate. It is just over a decade since Bob chaired the work of the National Advisory Group on Continuing Education and Lifelong Learning and was instrumental in the last government's early commitment to lifelong learning. If this government's 'Big Society' is to take flight it will need opportunities for adults to learn or refresh the skills needed to be engaged, active and critical citizens. *Promises of Freedom* offers a recipe book for their engagement.

Alan Tuckett
Chief Executive, NIACE
Leicester, 2010

CHAPTER ONE

Introduction

Focus

This monograph on citizenship, belonging and lifelong learning, and on the relationships existing or posited between them, was originally prepared as a Thematic Review for the independent Commission of Inquiry into the Future for Lifelong Learning (the Inquiry), sponsored by NIACE.[1] It builds on a briefing paper previously prepared for the Inquiry, and readers may wish to consider the documents in conjunction.[2] It also draws on the written submissions provided to the Inquiry by individuals and organisations in response to a call for evidence and on the presentationsand ensuing discussions, at a special seminar on citizenship and belonging convened by the Inquiry. The monograph also includes a review of relevant literature in the field, and of the objectives and implications of recent key public policy initiatives in the UK that touch upon citizenship and belonging. It also examines the aims, publications and behaviour of a range of UK organisations involved with one or other aspect of the matters considered here.

The purpose of this monograph is first to explore the principal ideas and debates in the published literature on citizenship and belonging, and their relationships with lifelong learning, with the aim to acquaint readers with some of the main theories, concepts and arguments pertaining to

---

1 The final report of the Inquiry has now been published. See Schuller, T. and Watson, D. (2009) *Learning Through Life: Inquiry into the Future for Lifelong Learning.* Leicester: NIACE

2 Fryer, R. H. (2008) *Lifelong Learning, Citizenship and Belonging: A Briefing Paper.* Leicester: NIACE. The briefing paper can be accessed on the IFLL website at: www.niace.org.uk/lifelonglearninginquiry (accessed August 2010)

our three linked themes. It is not an an exhaustive account, but one intended to outline some of the most pertinent issues in our time relating to citizenship and belonging, and the promises of freedom that inhere in each of them. Secondly, I want to set all of those discussions in the context of debate about the current and future role, and the appropriate functions and ultimate promise of lifelong learning. Thirdly, building on the analysis in the first two elements of my monograph, and as contribution to the debates initiated by the Inquiry, I set out some principles which I believe should guide the way forward for lifelong learning in enhancing and extending citizenship, and broadening and enriching people's various senses of belonging in the UK.

Much of the published literature on citizenship and belonging consists of theoretical and conceptual argument, policy development, advocacy and assertion. By contrast, the amount of immediately relevant empirical enquiry focused specifically on the themes explored in this monograph, and the relationships between them is relatively limited. In addition, organisations and individuals concerned with either citizenship or belonging are usually interested in only one or the other of these fields. Only a small minority also ventures to make an explicit link between citizenship and belonging, or to spell out the implications of their position for lifelong learning. Where the second of the major themes – belonging – is at issue, discussion is often framed largely through a consideration of 'identity' which, although a significant element of the notion of belonging, is not exactly the same.

Contest and confusion

Citizenship and belonging are both hotly contested issues in the UK today, as well as in other countries currently engaged with programmes to promote one or other of them. Each is the subject of much debate and division in the published literature of both scholarship and policy, especially as concerns the practical implications that follow from conceptual debate.

There is a long-established, vast and rich literature on the subject of citizenship, and a rapidly growing one on belonging (Shafir, 1998; Heater, 1999; Isin and Wood, 1999; Delanty, 2000; Benhabib *et al.*, 2007; Lawler, 2008). The citizenship literature stretches back to what are now regarded as the 'classical' debates and peculiar circumstances of Ancient Greece and the Roman Empire and earlier, and embraces in particular the writings of philosophers and key political figures involved in the European Enlightenment and responses to it (Hampson, 1982). The theme of citizenship also figured strongly in the documents, pronouncements and institutions associated with the quest for, and creation of, American Independence and in the French Revolution (Kettner, 1978; Schuk and Smith, 1985; Gunderson, 1987; Bradburn, 2009).[3]

Many of the ancillary ideas and concepts involved in the debates about citizenship, belonging and lifelong learning are themselves also slippery, unclear, elusive, and even contradictory. Analysis therefore involves grappling with the many ideas and concepts that are associated with both citizenship and belonging, as well as with lifelong learning, which are all equally contested. Some of those regularly deployed – especially the various notions of liberty, freedom, democracy, participation, civil society, community, social capital, social cohesion and, not least, lifelong learning itself – are deeply controversial and subject to intense argument. Hence, the would-be reviewer or policy adviser will inevitably encounter confusion and division over the meaning, validity and appropriate measurement of most of the key concepts and propositions involved. Most notably, debates over the principal topics of concern for this monograph are conducted from a *normative* point of view, concerned mainly with advocacy of a given perspective or criticism of it, rather than being argued on more theoretical or empirical grounds.

These conceptual and theoretical debates are likely to continue, and those engaging with the debates need to ensure that the differences of meaning and emphasis that they encompass are all well understood. This is especially important for those responsible for shaping public policy. As will be illustrated later in this monograph, the various theories and the assumptions that they rest upon have informed deeply the development of public policy in the UK. Even those concerned primarily with the practicalities of citizenship are influenced by theoretical and conceptual argument, and in particular by the assumptions and principles on which it rests.

Turnbull (2002) has suggested that, to be of any analytical and practical use, the concept of citizenship needs to be 'multi-layered', and adequately reflect its local, community, national, international and global

---

3 Revolutionary polities have by no means always constructed citizenship as an open or inclusive category for *all* of the people, for example in early American republicanism and in the creation of the French Republic.

dimensions. This suggestion rightly draws attention to the diverse levels, domains and forms in which modern citizenship can be expressed and developed still further. The problem with such an otherwise sensible approach, however, is that it might consequently require the concept simply to try to do too much. The danger is that the concept of citizenship risks being overburdened and required to capture a perplexing diversity of what are inherently dynamic and fluid social relations, themselves inevitably influenced by the particular historical and cultural contexts in which they are embedded. Such difficulties are only multiplied by what Keogh (2003, p.9) calls the elaboration of 'adjectival citizenships'. One finds, he says 'a veritable A to V of citizenships', notably the core idea of 'active' citizenship.

It is also necessary to consider the many different practical meanings given to citizenship and belonging by different groups of people. For example, the authoritative INCA study of active citizenship in 20 countries (including the four home 'territories' of the UK), commissioned by the Qualifications and Curriculum Authority, reported 'limited exploration of the conceptual underpinnings of active citizenship and, as a result, a distinct lack of clarity and common understanding of where it has come from and what it means' (Nelson and Kerr, 2006, p.6).

Although debates about concepts and their meaning usually proceed in accordance with more or less peaceable rules and protocols, the ensuing differences occasionally spill over into bitter social conflict and, more rarely, into violence. In a perceptive reminder, Amartya Sen has drawn attention to the potentially calamitous consequences of constructing inescapable, and sometimes deliberately exaggerated, identities for individuals and whole social groups.

> (M)any of the conflicts and barbarities in the world are sustained through the illusion of a unique and choiceless identity. The art of constructing hatred takes the form of invoking the magical powers of some allegedly predominant identity that drowns other affiliations, and in a conveniently bellicose form can also overpower any human sympathy or natural kindness that we may normally have. The result can be homespun elemental violence, or globally artful violence and terrorism. (Sen, 2006, p.xv)

Thus, failure to clarify the theories and concepts deployed and to secure at least working agreement on their implications for practice can have serious consequences, not just for debate, but also for how people are treated in the world.

Contrasting notions of citizenship

There is evidence of support for, or opposition to, contrasting notions of citizenship and what constitutes appropriate 'citizenly' behaviour in attitude surveys conducted in connection with the study or advocacy of citizenship. For example, an international study of citizenship, civic knowledge and engagement among 14-year-olds in 28 countries (Torney-Purta *et al.*, 2001) presented a complex picture of conceptions of, and attitudes towards, different aspects of citizenship and citizenship education between the pupils of different states.

Scores for the 'civic competence' of English pupils placed them at about the middle of a scale running from Poland and Finland, whose pupils scored highly, to Chile and Colombia whose pupils' scores were the lowest. English pupils were less likely than the average across the 28 countries studied to rate highly either 'conventional' indicators of good citizenship – such as voting, joining a political party or obeying the law – or 'social movement citizenship'. The countries' pupils who rated both conventional and social movements as indicators of *good* citizenship included Chile, Colombia, Cyprus, Greece, Italy, Lithuania, Portugal, Romania, Slovakia and the USA. Alongside English pupils, the countries rating both measures lower than the average included pupils from Australia, Belgium, the Czech Republic, Denmark, Estonia, Finland, Germany, Norway, Slovenia, Sweden and Switzerland.

English pupils also scored slightly lower than the average on a measure of positive attitudes towards immigrants, where the highest scores were recorded in Colombia, Cyprus and Sweden. The lowest scores on this measure were in Germany, Slovenia and Switzerland, although English girls' scores were higher than those of English boys. By contrast, English pupils' support for women's political rights was substantially higher than the average, scoring the highest measure of support alongside pupils from Norway. The lowest scores on this measure were recorded in Bulgaria, Latvia, Romania and the Russian Federation.

Only a small proportion of English pupils (11–14 per cent overall) expected that they would participate in illegal forms of protest as an adult – such as spray-painting, blocking traffic or occupying buildings – although English boys were more inclined to anticipate such behaviour than were English girls (15–19 per cent, as against 8–9 per cent). (Just by way of contrast, 30–42 per cent of Greek pupils expected to participate in such forms of illegal protest as adults.)

Finally, English pupils reported about average levels of 'citizenly' activity in respect of participating in a school council, taking part in an environmental organisation or engaging in community-based voluntary activities. They were much less likely than the average of the 28 countries surveyed to be in a political party or human rights organisation, but much more likely to have participated in a charity collecting money for a social cause.

These results illustrate just how conceptions of what counts as good citizenship varies considerably between young people from different countries.

Why the interest in citizenship, belonging and their links with lifelong learning?

The reasons for enquiring into citizenship and belonging and their relationship with lifelong learning are multiple. In each case, there are major implications for how citizenship and belonging are conceptualised and how each is manifested, challenged and altered in practice.

First, and above all, each of these three themes has an impact on our everyday lives. Exploring these themes helps us understand better who we are, how we live and learn, and how we can learn to thrive in the world. Reviewing them enables us to conduct a kind of 'audit' of the current workings and challenges of our political arrangements for democracy, with which each of the three themes explored in this monograph is intimately connected.

Secondly, and serving as the main motif for this whole monograph, learning, as well as the extension or enhancement of citizenship and the enjoyment of a complete sense of self and belonging, have all been invoked as principal ways of seeking liberation or as signalling freedom. Emancipation can consist of an escape from ignorance or want, the overthrow of tyranny or oppression, or the challenge to unfairness and inequality (Freire, 1986 and 1998; Green and Janmat, 2006).

In common with so many of the ideas and concepts explored in this monograph, freedom is deeply contested and controversial. Freedom is just as likely to be prayed in aid by the politically conservative right as it is by the radical or revolutionary left, by those in power, as well as by those seeking to liberate themselves from oppression. 'The very universality of the language of freedom camouflages a host of divergent connotations and applications', observes the distinguished American historian, Eric Foner, in demonstrating that its use and meaning can only be understood properly through a rigorous exposition of the context in which it is deployed – in his case, by an examination of the history of the struggle for the emancipation of American slaves (Foner, 1994, p.436). In his critical exposé of the ideology and practice of neo-liberalism, with its adulation of 'free markets', David Harvey opens his analysis with the wry observation that 'freedom's just another word ...' best understood by a close examination of its deployment in the politics of the cold war, right-wing hostility to state intervention in the economy and social life, and in American military actions prosecuted in the wake of the horror of 9/11 (Harvey, 2005).

Freedom is not inscribed in some sort of unbroken narrative or gradually unfolding, smooth path towards continuing enlargement. It is always born and sustained through struggle, vigilance and dogged opposition to the many manifestations of its opposite – 'un-freedoms' of all kinds, wherever they are found. Seen in this way, although the idea of freedom and the conditions necessary for it to flourish are rooted in conceptual debate and analytical argument within political philosophy, it is clear that any understanding of the meaning of freedom and its application in the world makes sense only when understood in terms of the historical, social and political contexts in which the notion of freedom is deployed, constrained, denied, yearned and striven for. This is particularly the case when freedom's promises are articulated in relation to the development of citizenship, the construction of people's sense of belonging, and the contribution that education and learning can make to each.

As Foner remarks, freedom has served as a cause of optimism and a core aspirational value for some, yet as a 'cruel mockery' for others, with its boundaries defined and redefined in epic political, economic and cultural struggles, and through the construction of binary opposites – freeborn and slave, ruler and ruled, state and individual, citizen and serf, hope and despair, confinement and liberation, compliance and dissent, autonomy and control, exclusiveness and inclusion, and, above all, possibility and denial. In these pages, the promises of freedom are offered as constant and inspirational 'resources of hope', to borrow Raymond Williams' unforgettable and wholly relevant aphorism (Williams, 1983 and 1989). Nothing is beyond reach, when ordinary citizens learn, think and act together: as expressed in his optimistic call to arms, 'once the inevitable are challenged, we begin gathering our resources for a journey of hope' (Williams, 1983, p.268).

Thirdly, citizenship, belonging and lifelong learning have all been perceived as having important roles to play in the striving for democracy and in supporting its workings once achieved: characterising it, promoting it and underpinning it. In particular, education often figures centrally in helping to sustain democratic citizenship in the contemporary world and in building people's identities and their tolerance of a plurality of alternative identities (Carr and Hartnett, 1996). As one authority has written: 'not only should education (formal, non-formal and informal) foster the types of awareness, empowerment, and participation that are crucial to active, democratic citizenship, but the *processes* of democracy themselves should be educative, dynamic and ongoing' (Hill, 2006, p.172, emphasis added).

Fourthly, we live in times of rapid and far-reaching changes in the social, economic, cultural and technological organisation of society (Beck, 1992). Where the UK is concerned, very few of its principal social institutions, ways of earning a living, patterns of family life, forms of leisure, social identities and aspirations, means of communication and contours of consumption have remained unchanged over the past 30–40 years (Fryer, 2008). Change seems to have become both ubiquitous and continuous. It behoves us to consider the implications of these changes for citizenship, belonging and lifelong learning and to ask how action on each of these fronts might enable people to deal with these changes to their own satisfaction.

Fifthly, one of the most significant and still only partially understood changes, with marked consequences for all three themes of this monograph, is globalisation in which, increasingly, people, finance, technology, culture, ecology and decision-making do not just cross what once were well defined borders, but also tend to ignore or even transcend them (Held *et al.*, 1999; Held and McGrew, 2003). What are the prospects of citizenship, belonging or lifelong learning being able to measure up to the forces of globalisation? Not surprisingly, the notion of globalisation is yet another arena for definitional struggle and evaluative conflict. As Croucher (2004, p.51) observes, 'globalization, in its economic, technological, cultural and political dimensions has, and continues to have, a significant impact upon citizenship as a form of belonging', eroding it in some regards, but also possibly invigorating it in others.

8

Sixthly, a particular concern that touches centrally upon citizenship and people's sense of belonging is the growth in social inequality, both within and between nations, and the apparent closure of some of the traditional avenues of social mobility (Green and Janmat, 2006; Hills *et al.*, 2009). It needs to be asked whether action on one or more of the fronts of citizenship, belonging or lifelong learning can help counteract these trends, and whether, indeed, any notion of citizenship can be acceptable, unless it is firmly underpinned by a commitment to civil, political and social equality.

Seventhly, and of no less importance, there are numerous signs of increasing tension between different ethnic, faith, cultural and generational groups in a number of countries, the UK included (Benhabib, 2002; Kymlicka, 2007). Is it possible that an exploration of the three themes of this monograph could cast some light on these areas of social conflict, and maybe even suggest ways of easing them? Most importantly, is there any possibility of reconciling the demands for the recognition of, and respect for, legitimate difference advanced by these groups? These differences emphasise distinguishing particularity, potentially at odds with the core values of unity and powerful norms of universality that are essential for binding together any wider community, and are also integral to any coherent notion of human rights, irrespective of the social and political milieux in which people live their lives (Laclau, 1996).

Finally, in the UK over the past decade, as in many other countries, there has been a flurry of activity by governments and other influential bodies introducing major policy initiatives with respect to one or other of the themes addressed in this monograph. Hence, a timely examination of citizenship, belonging and lifelong learning can help understand, evaluate and, if necessary, argue for changes in public policy and its approaches to these aspects of contemporary life. In particular, and in line with much of the analytical thrust of the considerations of citizenship and belonging addressed in the following pages, it is instructive to see the extent to which, if at all, public policies in the UK have sought to open up space for people to enlarge their own capabilities and experiences as citizens, and to engage actively in the shaping of their own identities and sense of belonging, rather than having these matters determined 'from above', by the State or some other central authority.

Education, especially for school pupils and young people, and varieties of schemes to help community development, 'regeneration' and 'renewal', have featured centrally in the construction and implementation of public policy in the UK concerned with citizenship and belonging. In this, certain key figures played a leading part, especially the late political theorist, Professor Sir Bernard Crick, and the senior Labour politician and Minister of the Crown, David Blunkett. Blunkett studied politics at Sheffield University when Crick taught there and, later, wrote jointly with him, before engaging him to lead a series of government-sponsored task groups charged with developing public policy for the promotion of citizenship and the design of citizenship education. Any full account of recent public policy regarding citizenship and belonging in England needs to trace the relationships between each of their writings and policy making and practice.

CHAPTER TWO

Some headline messages

Common humanity; varied experience

Citizenship and belonging, and the various ways in which they both impinge upon lifelong learning, affect our common humanity and our shared experiences of life, although we perceive and interpret the effects in many different ways.

Citizenship concerns every one of us, with its accompanying rights (or lack of them), duties, relationships, obligations, activities and opportunities, to which we enjoy access or for which we strive, or which we feel we lack, or from which we are excluded. We may feel that we fully understand and accept the possibilities and requirements that our citizenship status confers on us, or else we may be oblivious of them or content for them mostly to be ignored. We may campaign or struggle, either to enhance our own rights or to secure them for others who are currently denied them or excluded from full citizenship.

Similarly, we all have our own experiences of a sense of either belonging or of being more of an 'outsider' in different situations. We may feel that we are part of something that is wider than just ourselves, and identify with people whom we feel are 'like us' in terms of their values, beliefs, culture, traditions, language, interests, objectives, locality or aspirations. Thus, we usually think of ourselves 'as members of this family or community, nation or people, as bearers of this history, as sons or daughters of that revolution, as citizens of this republic' (Sandel, 1982, p.179). Or else, we may experience exclusion and face unwanted barriers to inclusion.

Learning is woven into all of these experiences, most significantly and prosaically in a mostly non-formal or informal but continuous way, as

11

an everyday aspect of living and of our involvement in what might be called 'practical citizenship', or in the numerous unreflective expressions of belonging that are manifest in our daily behaviour (Field, 2002; Rogers, 2004). Mostly, these sorts of learning activities are by-products of normal daily life, more adventitious than intentional, often quite unreflective and even largely tacit.

> *Informal learning permeates the lifeworld, often absorbed so fully into daily routines and habits that people do not think of it separately as learning but just as a relatively unquestioned activity that they choose to pursue. (Field, 2002, p.44)*

At the same time, the learning associated with either citizenship or belonging can also be more formal, systematic or organised, or even provided through channels whose principal purposes are education and learning – such as schools, colleges, universities or training centres. All of these different ways of learning matter in considering how our contemporary notions and practices of citizenship and belonging can be examined, strengthened, renewed and enriched.

Emancipation, liberation and freedom

Citizenship and belonging, and especially the learning that they each entail, have also enjoyed long-established, or at least long-claimed, links with liberation and freedom (Fletcher, 2000). President Franklin D Roosevelt, in his annual message to Congress in January 1941, famously declared that freedom consists of four essential dimensions for all people throughout the world: freedom of speech and expression, freedom of religion, freedom from want, and freedom from fear. This was no vision, he declared, of some distant millennium, but was attainable in 'our own time and generation'.

Learning has promised the possibility of escape from the bonds of ignorance, of throwing over the tyranny of oppressors, or of challenging the exclusions of privilege and the perceived unfairness of inequality. Learning has also been suggested as a means of challenging unfair discrimination, opposing exploitation, and starting on the path to citizenship and full recognition of people's particular sense of themselves, their identities and their feelings of belonging (Freire, 1986; Thompson, 2000).

12

The slogans, manifestos and banners of groups and organisations mobilising to increase their freedom, to secure emancipation or to throw off the burdens of oppression, frequently incorporate a central role for education in the cause of liberation or in the quest for more equality in whatever sense. Learning can be a stimulus to initiating such movements – in 'opening the eyes' of the oppressed and un-free; it can be an inherent element of both the processes and outcomes of campaigns and struggles, or it can contribute to them by enhancing wider understanding, by helping the exploration of tactics, strategies and alternatives, or by training the people leading various fights for freedom and greater fairness around the world.

Campaigns and movements around both citizenship and people's sense of themselves and of belonging also often centre on securing recognition and respect for a wider range of identities and patterns of behaviour than previously. In recent decades in the UK (as elsewhere in the world), demands have been raised for increased tolerance, greater acceptance, improved rights, and even for special treatment for different social groups. Over the past half century or so, such claims have been advanced variously on behalf of women, people with physical and learning disabilities, people from a range of different ethnic and racial backgrounds, people from different religious faiths, cultures, sexual orientation, refugees and asylum seekers, and older people.

Democracy and participation

Learning also features centrally in debates about the nature, principles and workings of democracy. The theory and practice of democracy has a long and complex history, being evident in a range of alternative forms, and manifesting great diversity and a whole variety of associated institutions and practices. But, just as there are many instances of people striving for democracy or to improve such democratic arrangements as have already been achieved, so too democracy often finds itself under siege or being criticised. This is what John Keane, in his recent authoritative history of democracy, refers to as 'the brittle contingency' of democracy, at a time when 'there are signs of mounting disagreement about its meaning' (Keane, 2009, pp.xiv–xv).

Keane reminds his readers that democracy is neither some 'timeless fulfilment of our political destiny', nor has it always been with us. Democracy and all of its associated definitions, claims, principles, institutions and practices are always time-bound, related to the context in which

13

they occur. Most importantly, in its many different manifestations stretching back to Mycenae and the other urban settlements of the Peloponnese of the Bronze Age, democracy has meant the 'de-naturing of power'. Throughout its long and contested history, the champions of democracy have thus insisted that 'the most important political question is how to prevent rule by the few, or by the rich or powerful who claim to be supermen'. Democracy centrally embodies a political agenda that ensures that 'who gets what, when and how should be a permanently open question'. As a form of self-government among equals, the core purposes and functions of democracy are, in Keane's memorable adaptation, 'the government of the humble, by the humble, for the humble' (*ibid.*, p.xii).

Most versions of democracy thus also include some consideration of the role of citizens and their place in its various institutions and operations. Given the diversity of political regimes that can, with some justification, lay claim to being some sort of a democracy, it follows that many different versions of citizenship and belonging are also possible (Held, 1987 and 1995). Discussion of different versions of democracy thus embraces the implications for people's rights and obligations as citizens, the various arenas in which they can and do – even should – participate, and the extent to which people's identity and their sense of belonging figures, if at all, in the functioning of democracy.

Contest, conflict and confusion

The three themes examined in this monograph all have their own rich and complex histories and literatures. Each has been the site of contest and struggle, and each, too, is typified by sharp differences and debates about the definitions, meanings and implications of the various concepts involved. Such debates are not only of intellectual interest. Where the implementation of policy or the actions of individuals, groups, organisations or whole communities are based on such differences, whether explicitly or implicitly, the debates not only entail markedly different practices and patterns of behaviour, but can also sometimes lead to sharp confrontation, bitter conflict and, on occasion, violence or even war.

None of these disputes and confusions can be settled definitively or to the satisfaction of all. As a minimum, any analyst of either citizenship or belonging must be prepared to consider the rival schemes of norms and values that invariably sit at the heart of these disputes. Often, such positions are grounded in a particular view of human nature, or of the 'good life', of what constitutes civilised or reasonable behaviour, or what is meant by civic virtue and how best to promote it. Where protagonists neither declare nor recognise that their position or claims rest upon a given theory or set of concepts, mostly they still do, even if the theories are a muddle of many different ideas and propositions. Hence a certain amount of clarification of definitions and concepts is unavoidable in examining both citizenship and belonging, and the same goes for lifelong learning.

Social change

In part connected with such debates, and often used to explain or seek some shift in the character of citizenship or in people's identity, an exploration of learning's links with social change also deserves attention – to understand and explain it, support or criticise it, and, above all, to help people, communities and governments cope with its consequences.

Both citizenship and the various aspects of belonging and identity are inherently dynamic, always liable to modification and revision, even when there are powerful elements of continuity within them. The role of lifelong learning too may take many different forms – to promote change, to explain it, to steer it, or to explore ways in which the changes can be responded to.

In the UK as elsewhere in the contemporary world, we live in an era typified by ubiquitous change and radical transformations in key aspects of our lives. Often the world is also experienced as a kind of 'runaway world' (Giddens, 1999) or what Beck (1999) has termed 'world risk society', characterised by an increasing degree of uncertainty, unpredictability and anxiety (Dunant and Porter, 1996; Elliot and Atkinson, 1999). In a world that constantly threatens change (or promises it), it is hardly surprising that people's standing, their experience of citizenship, and their sense of belonging or of being 'on the outside' are also subject to major shifts.

Whatever its form or purposes, lifelong learning has to try to match the dynamism of social change, even if it aims to cultivate some elements of continuity or to emphasise values that transcend the particularities of new conceptions of citizenship or new expressions of belonging and identity.

Community and social solidarity

In circumstances of rapid or fundamental social change, the traditional foundations for social solidarity and community organisation also often shift or are undermined as industries and occupations rise and fall, and as people move and migrate, as lifestyles alter, or people develop new understandings of themselves or other people (Crow, 2002).

The sources, purposes, consequences and possibilities of community and social solidarity, their absence, or people's exclusion from them, are varied. All touch upon the ways in which citizenship is demonstrated or how belonging is expressed and experienced. When we experience or sense a strong or pervasive 'sense of community', especially as an active participant rather than as an observer, it is rarely in a purely cognitive or intellectual manner. 'Community' is something that we engage in as part of normal living, and maybe something that we come to appreciate (or resent) more and more as we recognise the influences of that community on our lives and in helping to shape our sense of ourselves. Many subtle meanings and signals give shape to communities and to our own sense of belonging – of being part of the community – and identity.

Feelings of community are not simply 'given' but are gained through gradual accumulation, reflection, reinforcement and challenge – in other words, through learning. Such learning may be solidified through all sorts of rituals, signs and symbols, as well as being manifested through the everyday practices of the community. The learning is also often marked by a growing understanding of the community's main operating principles and of the sorts of routine opportunities and obligations which membership of the community involves, including what frequently become the sheer normalities of mutuality, reciprocity and solidarity among community members.[4] Of course, we may even experience this sort of community – especially where it constitutes an unwelcome pressure towards stultifying conformity – as restrictive and oppressive. In any case, depending in part on our feelings of commitment, continuing involvement or influence, we come to understand how the community has helped to make us who we are.

---

4 Raymond Williams illustrated perfectly this pervasive sense of 'community' and its everyday experiences of mutual support in declaring to world-weary fellow students and academics in Cambridge that he fully understood from his upbringing and from subsequent learning the potentially rich meanings of the notion of 'neighbourliness'. (Williams, 'The Importance of Community', in Williams, 1989: pp.112–115.)

The role of learning in contemporary solidarity, or its apparent absence, can also vary. Traditional foundations of solidarity – such as work, family and community structures, religious beliefs and practices, culture or a sense of place – all embrace diverse kinds of learning. When the foundations of solidarity change or collapse, it is likely that the learning embedded in them is altered too, but not always in predictable ways. In such processes, learning may serve as explanation, representation, understanding or mobilisation – or, indeed, all of these. Some argue that profound and rapid social change also calls for entirely new ways and new locales of learning – what they term 'tertiary' learning – 'a kind of learning which our inherited educational institutions, born and matured in the modern ordering bustle, are ill prepared to handle' (Bauman, 2001, p.127).

Globalisation, state and nation

Globalisation and its consequences now figure centrally as major forces in social change. As finance, information, culture, people, technology, environmental pollution, knowledge and decision-making increasingly transcend or simply ignore the once-dominant boundaries and jurisdictions of independent nation states, so there are significant implications for citizenship and identity (Albrow, 1996; Held and McGrew, 2003; Croucher, 2004).

However, the impact of globalisation on citizenship and belonging is by no means the same everywhere, nor always in the same direction of apparent erosion and diminution. As Sheila Croucher shrewdly observes, 'the very same elements of globalization often shape, simultaneously, both the demise and the invigoration of citizenship' (Croucher, 2004, p.70). What is more fruitful, Croucher suggests, is to consider the *reconfiguration* of both citizenship and people's sense of belonging in a globalising world. At one level, reconfiguration may mean that the traditional and often purely national rights of citizens, and their associated expectations and opportunities increasingly count for less. At another level, people may feel that they are increasingly committed to a kind of 'global citizenship', either as an expression of not being attached to any particular nation or state, or in order to engage with (and with the intention of helping to shape) these new forces, or as a signal of accepting a share of responsibility for tackling social, ethical, political or environmental issues that necessarily transcend the traditional boundaries of place and time.

Another response to globalisation and the apparent erosion of national identity and national action is to emphasise that the only practicable and effective way to connect with, make sense of and materially influence the forces of globalisation is to focus action locally. Whatever the case, learning may play its part either as a basis for people's understanding of the dynamics of globalisation, or as a prompt for their affiliations and actions. Not surprisingly, there is plenty of scope for voicing conflicting conceptions of citizenship and belonging in all of this, and for learning to be part of that conflict as well as seeking to comprehend it.

Public policy: the definition, support and practice of citizenship and belonging

Citizenship, belonging and lifelong learning have all featured in a range of recent public policy initiatives in the UK, sometimes with all three yoked together. These initiatives have centred not only on the usual domains of education (schools, colleges, universities and training centres), but have also been concerned with political participation, civic and neighbourhood renewal, migration and immigration, political refuge and asylum, crime and disorder, community and economic regeneration, and social cohesion.

One apparently urgent example of public policy in respect of citizenship and belonging concerns giving people born in other countries residence in, and possibly citizenship of, the UK when they come to find employment, join families, or seek refuge or asylum. Following the terrorist attacks in New York in 2001 and in the UK in 2005, the British Government instigated a number of measures aimed at reinforcing border security and tightening access to full citizenship for people unable to claim it through either of the traditional routes of consanguinity or co-location.

The issue of national security has also become entangled with controversy about the numbers and provenance of immigrants into the UK, and with questions about their loyalties and affiliations, their cultures and identities. This is especially so where the Islamic faith or some of its adherents' practices are singled out for questioning following the UK Government's involvement in the invasion of Iraq and the war against the Taliban in Afghanistan.

These concerns, and especially Government's response to them, partly explain the creation of new rules and procedures for granting British citizenship, including the requirement for applicants to pass a citizenship test to demonstrate knowledge of British history and culture, and the introduction of ceremonies for people becoming British citizens. There has even been talk of some sort of citizenship 'passing out parade' for all young people in this country. To some observers, this is evidence of a shift to a more 'regulatory' and disciplinary conception of citizenship, and constitutes a marked diminution of more generous conceptions of inclusive democracy and greater tolerance – celebration even – of diversity (Delanty, 2003).

Public policy reports and initiatives also often include a particular vision of what in the UK is usually termed 'active citizenship'. This usually rests upon, or sometimes explicitly invokes, some notion of 'ideal' or 'appropriate' behaviour, as well as advancing propositions about how education or lifelong learning, organised in conjunction with such activism, can support policy. The analysis of social problems and the recommended programmes of action regularly refer to such contentious notions as participation, involvement, reciprocity, democracy, social cohesion, social capital, renewal, accountability, autonomy and identity. In each case, conflicting meanings and interpretations may be given to such concepts according to the point of view of those advocating or opposing a particular idea. Typically, learning of some kind is inscribed in such policy initiatives – either explicitly and inherently in their design – from the launch or else developed subsequently to promote or support them. The learning involved also often manifests great diversity of mode, type and location.

Some critics of this kind of learning argue that it represents clear enough evidence of governmental attempts at greater regulation and the control of citizens, especially in circumstances where matters of national security are given heightened importance, or where there is controversy about access of newcomers or non-native citizens to a nation's social benefits and other advantages of citizenship (Delanty, 2000). Critics suggest that certain public policies for learning constitute little more than one-sided, ideologically driven views of the world and models of how to act and live in it, rather than seeking to enhance the lives of citizens or enable them to make sense of the world (Martin, 2000 and 2003).

Education and learning for citizenship

In the world of formal education, particularly in schools and further education, energetic change has occurred recently, mostly in respect of the teaching and learning of citizenship in the UK. Over more than ten years a series of influential Government-sponsored reports and curriculum reform initiatives have sought directly to affect the education of school pupils and young adults in further education in the UK and its devolved administrations and governments. Part of this has included an enthusiasm for promoting and enabling volunteering, especially among young people at school, college or university.

Although most of the curriculum innovation in schools and colleges around citizenship in the UK dates only from the last decade or more recently, it is nonetheless instructive to examine the views of teachers and education inspectors about its early roll-out. One of the most striking features is that these developments have had to fight for space with greater pressure on students to pass formal tests and examinations, achieve higher grades and demonstrate the achievement of nationally determined 'targets'. The evidence suggests that despite the importance the government and educational regulatory authorities have attached to the teaching and learning of citizenship, it has sometimes been difficult for staff to access the necessary time, resources and training to enable them to engage satisfactorily with the new tasks.

In addition to formal education about citizenship and belonging, citizens have opportunities for all sorts of informal and non-formal learning, and for the acquisition of tacit understanding and knowledge from family and friends and in their daily lives. Learning *for* as well as *about* and *through* citizenship is embedded in the occasions and institutions of 'civil society', although not always in a self-conscious way, and rarely in such a fashion to ensure that such experiences are open equally to all.

A framework of principles for lifelong learning

The final 'headline message' of this monograph concerns lifelong learning itself, and its potential role in relation to both citizenship and belonging. The topic of lifelong learning has become an arena of increasing debate in recent years, both in the scholarly literature and in its deployment in the promotion of public policy, especially in the UK. Some critics of the notion have suggested, first, that the apparent emphasis upon the 'learning' element, while possibly representing a welcome shift of focus towards the interests and perspectives of the learner, sometimes seems to lose sight of the wider roles of education, teaching and knowledge in the development of individuals, groups and communities and, in particular, in helping to cast critical light on such contentious matters as citizenship, identity and belonging. This is undoubtedly an important matter, but the debate need not detain us further, save to affirm that the kinds of lifelong learning advocated in this monograph embrace all that is best in both teaching and learning. It includes learning in all its manifestations, ranging from the most formal to the least, and extends to a wide range of skills, capabilities, competence, knowledge and understanding.

Problems arise when it appears that the ideas and promise of lifelong learning have been appropriated, especially by governments and other authorities, to serve narrow and more restricted purposes. Critical and creative learning throughout the whole of life can engage with all aspects of the life course and in a rich mix of forms and locales. The difficulty is that, as governments have given greater prominence to the achievement of economic and business goals, so their deployment of lifelong learning has centred more on its role in helping to develop work skills and competences and in the promotion of 'flexible' labour markets (Leitch, 2006). Few doubt the importance of learning at, for, or through work; however, such a policy focus often suggests that the learner is the one element in the work environment that especially needs to adapt, respond or 'fit in' with the requirements of employers, of changing technology, or of competition. It is also sometimes clear that, although governments claim to seek to enlist lifelong learning in the cause of community development or renewal, in practice the learning focuses much more on regulation, control or the elimination of certain sorts of 'undesirable' behaviour than on enabling individuals and communities to challenge the limiting and exploitative aspects of their lives.

Conceiving of learners largely as the *objects* or *targets* of learning and placing them in positions of passivity and assumed subordination is in stark contrast to the conception of lifelong learning that stresses learners' capacity for debate, critique, reflection, creativity, innovation and even transcendence, and for action according to their own needs, values and priorities. It is the latter approach which informs the perspective adopted in this monograph and which underpins the principles that I advocate in the concluding part for enriching considerations of citizenship and belonging in twenty-first-century Britain. The promise of the kind of lifelong learning endorsed by this monograph is precisely that envisaged

21

over 50 years ago by Raymond Williams, when he wished that we should 'recognize that education is ordinary: that it is, before everything else, the process of giving to the ordinary members of society its full common meanings, and the skills that will enable them to amend those meanings, in the light of their personal and common experience' (Williams, 1989, p.14).

CHAPTER THREE

Citizenship

The promise

Our first promise of freedom consists of the development, consolidation and extension of *citizenship*. It would be through a modern and relevant version of citizenship, apt for the twenty-first century, that individuals and a variety of mutually respectful groups would enjoy increasing opportunities and display the essential capabilities for leading satisfying, self-governing lives, in an interlocking multiplicity of institutions and situations in which everyone would be resourced to participate, if they so desired. Under the beneficent panoply of this promise, all citizens would be committed to the widest possible conception of the good life for themselves and for their fellow citizens, including its aesthetic and spiritual dimensions. The promise would also embrace a broadening of equality, diversity, tolerance and pluralism within a determination to construct and continue to refine a common narrative describing and celebrating the character, purposes and benefits of shared citizenship.

Citizens of this kind would not be diminished by a narrow, self-regarding descent into a selfish concern only for the destinies of those enjoying the same rights, opportunities and responsibilities as themselves, but would also accept that their willingly acknowledged obligations included duties to engage with the challenges, uncertainties and risks facing fellow people across the globe. This would include the issue of worldwide social justice, as well as environmental issues and the strategic deployment of science, technology, information, manufacture and trade in the interests of progress.

The self-evident fact that such a promise manifests all the typical characteristics of utopianism would not mean that it should be dismissed as unachievable. On the contrary, the promise should not only constitute an ideal constantly to be striven for, but also a template against which achievements and improvements in contemporary citizenship, and what Eric Olin Wright (2010) refers to as progress towards 'real utopias', should be measured. In 'envisioning real utopias', Olin Wright sets out the principal tasks of what he terms 'emancipatory social science'. First come diagnosis and critique – identifying the various ways in which social institutions and social structures harm people and, conversely, what would be entailed in a radical, democratic and egalitarian version of social and political justice.[5] Secondly, emancipatory social science should develop 'a coherent, credible theory of the alternatives, incorporating desirability, viability and achievability'. The third task is to elaborate 'a theory of social transformation' or what Olin Wright describes as a journey from the present to a possible future. Such a theory of transformation would embrace four main elements: a theory of social reproduction – how current blocking mechanisms work and interact; a theory of the gaps and contradictions within the process of reproduction; a theory of the underlying dynamics and trajectory of unintended social change; and, finally, a theory of collective actors, strategies and struggles (*ibid.*, pp.10–29).

Two traditions

Conventional analysis divides approaches to citizenship into two broad camps (Turner, 1993; Beiner, 1995; Heater, 1999; Shafir, 1998). On the one hand, in the *liberal tradition*, stand those who seek to restrict the idea to a concern with questions of the status of the citizen and the bundle of legal and political rights and minimum obligations associated with that status. On the other sits the model of *civic republicanism*. Civic republicanism emphasises the active participation of citizens in the life and governance of their communities and, thereby, the core principle of citizens having regard for the good of the community as a whole.

---

5   Olin Wright defines 'radical democratic egalitarianism' as 'an encompassing moral conviction that challenges all social and cultural practices which generate inequalities in access to the material and social conditions for human flourishing, and challenges all obstructions to equal access to the conditions for real individual freedom and collectively empowered democracy. These include structures of power and privilege linked to gender, race, ethnicity, sexuality, nationality and citizenship' (Olin Wright, 2010, p.33).

Both traditional versions of citizenship are concerned with the wider issues of liberty and freedom, and each carries different implications, both for individuals and for the role and responsibilities of the State.[6] In Isaiah Berlin's famous distinction, the first approach centres on maximising freedom from undue constraint, interference and restriction imposed by others (what he terms 'negative' freedom), the second stresses the freedoms to engage, participate and take responsibility – to be a 'subject' rather than an 'object' ('positive' freedom). As Berlin put it, positive freedom entails a 'wish, above all, to be conscious of myself as a thinking, willing, active being, bearing responsibility for [my] choices and able to explain them by reference to [my] own ideas and purposes' (Berlin, 1969, p.131).

The liberal tradition

From a traditional liberal perspective, the principal concern is to defend the citizen's precious rights and essentially limited obligations. According to this model, the rights and duties of citizens – those minimally required for compliance with the law, respect for the rights of others, and the duty to defend the State itself – should be secured against (additional) impositions placed on the citizen by a higher authority such as Government or State. The role of the State, in classic liberal theory, should be restricted principally, in Locke's succinct characterisation, to that of a beneficent 'night watchman'. Classical liberal theory fits well with contemporary political ideologies of 'neo-liberalism', resting on the assertion that it is best for individuals, as well as for society, for free markets to operate with the minimum of constraint and regulation, commensurate with liberalism's core tenets.

The late political theorist Professor Sir Bernard Crick explained the implications of the liberal model of citizenship for the respective responsibilities of the State, individual and, especially, education. Crick had played a central role in the formulation of public policy on citizenship in England and the wider UK, alongside his sponsor and former student the

---

6 Not all political theorists subscribe to the idea that liberalism, civic republicanism and communitarianism constitute fundamentally different perspectives. 'It is not now much disputed that the so-called 'liberal-communitarian debate' was nothing of the sort ... Once we see that any liberalism must be simultaneously communitarian and individualist, we can work out more delicately in what sense ... persons would not have selves at all but for the ways they have been shaped by their backgrounds and upbringing' (Ryan, 2001, p.189).

senior Labour Government Minister David Blunkett. As Crick put it:

> *It has been an axiom of liberal theories about the relationship between government and the governed that the only way to maximise freedom must be to minimize the extent to which public demands can legitimately be made on our private lives. In other words, the modern liberal democracies give us freedom within the laws and we need only stir our stumps when these laws are violated ... (Crick, 2002b, p. 12)*

Although liberalism allows the possibility of designating 'the good life' to which people might aspire and direct their energies, it is wholly agnostic, or at least neutral, as to what should be the key characteristics of such a life. Liberalism's task is to ensure that all are equally free to envisage, explain or enjoy their own particular version of the good life, provided always that, in doing so, nobody infringes anybody else's freedoms to do the same. In particular, in classical 'minimalist' liberalism, it is not for the State or any other authority, however well meaning, to impose its conception of the good life on its citizens.

Where belonging is concerned, the purely liberal conception of citizenship may mean that any sense of commonality between people will be limited to those categories of person sharing the same status, legal position and rights. It would certainly not include any necessary moral commitment to a common identity or even shared sense of belonging, except by being subject to the same minimal legal regulation; the stress is on the individual's 'self-ownership', with inviolable control over the disposition of those rights (Nozik, 1974).

Over the past three centuries or so, British citizens have accrued important legal, civil and political rights, and, eventually, employment rights: freedoms of speech and assembly, rights concerning the ownership of property and the extension of the franchise, protections against the consequences of accidents at work, and, eventually, some limits to the risks of arbitrary dismissal from employment – often achieved as a result of bitter struggles and long campaigns. In each case, learning has contributed both to attaining these rights and realising them in practice. More recently, these rights have been enhanced by the incorporation of human rights legislation into British law.

The various struggles and movements to secure citizenship in Britain and Ireland have been significant not only in achieving rights before the law, but also in politics for people hitherto denied them. They have also contributed significantly to the twentieth-century growth of the 'social' rights of the citizen, documented by T.H. Marshall after the Second World War. In Marshall's distinction, citizenship can be divided into three elements: 'civil, political and social'.

> *Civil rights came first, and were established in something like their modern form before the first Reform Act was passed in 1832. Political rights came next, and their extension was one of the main features of the nineteenth century, although the principle of universal political citizenship was not recognised until 1918. Social rights, on the other hand, sank to vanishing point in the eighteenth and early nineteenth centuries. Their revival began with the development of public elementary education, but it was not until the twentieth century that they attained to equal partner- ship with the other two elements in citizenship. (Marshall and Bottomore, 1992, p. 17.)*

Social rights

The social rights of citizens derive from broadly egalitarian principles, according to which the policies formulated aimed to secure the minimum core necessities of modern life for all citizens, institutionalised in the development of the modern welfare state.[7] For Marshall, this commit- ment to the progressive attainment of equality clearly marks off citizens' social rights from circumstances in which people's life chances are determined predominantly by the inherent inequalities of social class. As far as Marshall was concerned, in the twentieth century, citizenship and the capitalist class system were 'at war'.

> *Citizenship is a status bestowed on those who are full members of a community. All who possess the status are equal with respect to the rights and duties with which the status is endowed. There is no universal principle that determines what those rights and duties shall be, but societies in which citizenship is a developing institution create an image of an ideal citizenship against which achievement can be measured and toward which aspirations can be directed. The urge forward along the path*

---

7   Stedman Jones (2004) argues that the origins of proposals to create a universal framework of social security date back as far as to the writings of Condorcet and Paine, associated with the American and French revolutions.

thus plotted is an urge towards a fuller measure of equality an enrichment
of the stuff of which the status is made and an increase in the number of
those on whom the status is bestowed. (ibid., 1992, p. 18)

One of the most significant examples of the extension of social rights captured by Marshall's revisions was the formation of the National Health Service in 1948. The NHS, as its recently revised constitution affirms, still rests on the core principle of equal access to treatment for all according to health need – healthcare provision depends not on the ability to pay or on privileges afforded to particular people, either of which would breach the common right. At the same time, contemporary policy recognises persistent inequalities in access to healthcare facilities and good health, and the necessity of promoting healthier living, not least through education for the whole population, including the necessary targeting of social groups or localities requiring particular attention.[8]

As Marshall observed, reforms of public education in the UK also represent potent instances of the continuing struggle to extend social citizenship (Carr and Hartnett, 1996). This struggle is exemplified today, for example, in the push for 'inclusive learning' – strategies for those young people traditionally excluded from mainstream education by virtue of various learning difficulties and disabilities (Barton, 1996; Tomlinson, 1996). It manifests itself, too, in successive government policies to raise the 'learning leaving age' for school pupils and for those in continuing education, and, especially, in the attempts to widen opportunities for participation and achievement in education, including access to higher education, irrespective of students' social background or ability to pay (Dearing, 1997; Kennedy, H., 1997; Duke and Layer, 2005; Layer, 2005; Watson, 2005a and 2005b).

Citizenship: equality and reality

As Marshall correctly observed, echoing an earlier conclusion by Jean-Jacques Rousseau, at its heart, the liberal theory of citizenship must contain at least the aspiration for a kind of equality between all who hold the same status as 'citizen'. However, citizenship does not secure for all the

---

8   See the key role given to education, and especially to community-based education, in the major policy document guiding the improved promotion of public health in England, *Choosing Health* (Department of Health, 2005).

same *formal* rights and entitlements; the various social, economic, cultural and political barriers make for a more limited *substantive* reality. In some cases, there are gradations of citizenship. For example, in the UK, the British Nationality Act defined five categories of citizen, each with quite different civic rights, in the following order: British citizens, British dependent territories citizens, British overseas citizens, British subjects, and British protected persons. Nor does such apparent differentiation always make clear who qualifies for what. Heater quotes an 'eminent British lawyer' to the effect that many of the provisions of the 1981 Act 'are so obscurely drafted that they are unfit to be in the statute book'. (Heater, 1999, p.81)

Heater suggests that it is possible to distinguish five different levels of citizen within different nation states. 'At the top of the ladder are the full and also active citizens, those, depending on the society we are examining, who have the most complete set of rights and who most fully discharge their civic duties.' Heater stresses the importance of not forgetting this second element: if equality is good for rights, it must also hold good for responsibilities. He continues his analysis through the following four categories: citizens who are 'apathetic by virtue of their non-activity'; then 'second-class' citizens, who suffer hostility and discrimination; next is the so-called 'underclass', who, despite their formal citizenship, are severely deprived both economically and socially; finally there are those non-nationals who are granted resident rights and a limited number of the rights of full citizens (*ibid.*, 1999, p.87). There is no need to accept the whole of Heater's analysis, or even some of his possibly dubious categories; nevertheless, the marked differentiation among citizens in 'citizenship in practice' affects the sorts of belonging that may be associated with different categories and brings different challenges for lifelong learning.

The critique of liberalism

Ever since the publication of Marshall's analysis, widely acknowledged as an advance in the understanding of the modern dynamics of citizenship, his thesis (together with its distinguished forebear, the liberal theory of citizenship) has met a series of serious objections.[9] These have ranged

---

9   For an excellent collection of papers expounding some of the major criticisms of the liberal model, see Shafir (1998) and Delanty (2000).

from those that criticise the distortions arising from its obvious Anglo-centric focus (historical developments have not followed the same trajectory elsewhere), to its inadequate recognition of the exclusion from full citizenship, or at least from some of its core elements, of key social groups such as women, married women, children, minority groups and migrants.

Over the 25 years or so following the publication of Marshall's lectures, successive criticisms were mounted that his version of the liberal model of citizenship failed to differentiate adequately between *formal* and *substantive* rights, and that its implied acceptance of the separation of the *public* and the *private* spheres of life overlooked the disadvantaged and exploited position of (especially) women and others. It was criticised in that, insofar as it generally reflected an altogether excessively gendered and white man's experience of citizenship, as well as not dealing adequately with diversity and difference, it also tended to play down questions of social conflict and division. Again, as a key plank of twentieth-century improvements in citizenship of the kind described by Marshall, education also continues to be as much an arena for the *reproduction* and *distribution* of social inequality as it is a site for its obvious manifestation, as well as serving as a platform for subsequent upward social mobility for some people.

If critics suggest that Marshall and other liberal theorists have been over-optimistic about the effectiveness of theories of citizenship in promoting social equality, protagonists of the liberal perspective are also charged with having overlooked the decline of some core aspects or institutions supportive of twentieth-century citizenship, such as those manifested in strong independent trades unions and tight-knit working class and local communities. In short, Marshall and others are accused of having seriously under-estimated the marked, and in some cases widening, empirical gap between the range of rights, freedoms and entitlements which citizens can claim, and their enjoyment in practice.

Similarly, in many instances, the growth of capitalist enterprise or even its mere survival appears to have entailed serious damage to local communities, depriving their members of any sense of a 'right to work', transgressing any respect for people's identities or sense of belonging, and resulting in their social exclusion. In circumstances of rapid and widespread change – for example, the wholesale collapse of local communities traditionally organised around industries such as coal mining, dock work, railways or shipbuilding, following mass closures – citizens' rights alone, including social rights, at best provide some minimum protection through 'due process'. They do not stave off, let alone repudiate, the disaster itself (Fryer, 1973a and b).

In their historical preoccupation with matters centred on the achievement of formal and legal equality for all, traditional versions of the liberal model of citizenship are criticised in particular for a failure to give sufficient recognition to the politics and culture of difference and diversity, especially where gender, ethnicity, sexuality and disability are concerned. More recently, it has been suggested that new dimensions of citizenship are urgently required to meet challenges such as those arising from the threat of environmental degradation or globalisation (Giddens, 1999). For some authors, that means abandoning or at least downgrading some of the classic liberal principles of citizenship, and the rights and responsibilities of citizens, in favour of consumption and the role of the consumer in providing meaning in the contemporary world. Others have simply suggested new modalities: 'global' citizenship, 'cosmopolitan' citizenship or 'radical' citizenship (Mouffe, 1993; Delanty, 2000; Mayo, 2005).

From within the ranks of liberalism itself, neo-liberals single out for attack Marshall's third dimension of 'social' citizenship. For the neo-liberal, attempts to secure even rough equality in the social sphere of life, in parallel with what has been achieved in the formal legal or political arena, is a fool's mission. These critics maintain that inequalities between people are simple and unavoidable facts of human existence, and argue that no amount of intervention can overcome such 'naturally' occurring attributes. Moreover, they say, such efforts are contrary to the core tenets of liberal philosophy. Increasing state provision of benefits and other social services not only undermines the independence and private world of the individual, it also requires a large, expensive and necessarily intrusive public bureaucracy, eroding both individual liberty and self-sufficiency. By requiring some citizens to fund the social benefits of others, principally through taxation, the State also limits the freedom of those taxpayers while creating a kind of 'something for nothing' ethic for the recipients. What is more, say the neo-liberals, social provision to some citizens undermines the efficient operation of free markets.

There is an element of validity in each of these criticisms, although some have been, at least in part, repudiated or tempered (see, for example Macedo, 1990; Heater, 1999). For this monograph, what is especially striking is that some of the most vibrant examples of lifelong learning, and some of the most innovative approaches to its pedagogy, are associated precisely with those aspects of citizenship that are cited as being underdeveloped in, or wholly absent from, liberal models – including that of Marshall. In addition, some of these same arenas of social life, said by critics to be inadequately engaged by classical liberal models of citizenship, are also the ones to which those involved declare a deep sense of belonging and from which they derive significant aspects of their identities.

In summary, although Marshall's extension of the understanding of rights undoubtedly constituted a valuable addition to the contemporary conception of citizenship, it was more useful as a way of making sense of developments in the UK in the first half of the twentieth century than as an adequate framework for understanding the possibilities and promise of the liberal conception of citizenship, and of its continuing weaknesses, in the twenty-first century.

Civic republicanism

The second approach to citizenship is 'civic republicanism'. In this second camp are those writers and activists who emphasise the opportunities for, and duties of, citizens to actively engage in decision-making and governance more generally in their communities. This second perspective links citizenship directly with matters of politics, democracy and participation, where citizens have responsibility to participate and share actively in government, thereby demonstrating commitment to their fellow citizens and to the common good. Thus, the civic republican perspective entails that citizens reach beyond the narrow and selfish preoccupations of the personal sphere and shift their attention more to the realm of the public (Oldfield, 1990 and 1998).

Modern civic republican theorists trace their origins back variously to Machiavelli, Montesquieu, Rousseau[10] and de Tocqueville. Rousseau, in particular, stresses the virtue of citizens' participation, as well as participation as a duty. Rousseau's ideal system, argues Schugurensky (2003, p.2), was 'designed to develop responsible, individual social and political action through the effect of the participatory process itself'. Carole Pateman underlines three virtues in such participation. First, it

---

10 Carole Pateman has suggested that Rousseau could be considered 'the theorist *par excellence* of participation' (Pateman, 1970, p.22).

develops citizens' responsible, individual social and political action, including education. Secondly, it enables decisions taken through such a process to be more easily accepted by those who participated in them, and opens the way to consensus. Thirdly, participation increases individuals' feelings of belonging in their community (Pateman 1970, pp.24–27).

In civic republican theories of citizenship, participation in public life for the benefit of wider community is both its principal characteristic and its chief virtue. For both Aristotle and Cicero, two of the key founding philosophers of the civic republican ethic, good citizens were those who were committed to engaging in the public sphere of the *polis* for the common good. For Aristotle, such participation was the only authentic route to discovering one's true, full humanity. Citizens' involvement in politics thus constitutes a public good of the very highest order. As Cicero put it, 'a worthy and truly brave citizen, and one who deserves to hold the reins of government … will give himself to the service of the public, as to aim at no power or riches for himself; and will so take care of the whole community, as not to pass over any part of it …' (from *De Officiis*, quoted in Heater, 1999, p.47).

Citizens who manifest civic republican virtue do so classically in being equally willing to engage in the processes of ruling as they are in accepting that they should be ruled. The full life of the citizens consists precisely of a willingness – more, a wholesale acceptance – to be involved in the public life of the community to the benefit of all. Thus, both duty and service figure prominently in most versions of the civic republican model. Duty towards fellow citizens, duty to serve the community, duty to protect and uphold the republic itself, duty to become involved in the political processes, duty to accept and promote moral responsibilities and, not least, duty to keep a watchful eye on governments and the operations of the State. The civic republican model holds that such behaviour fosters not just a proper sense of mutuality and reciprocity, but also provides the only effective guaranteed protection of individual freedom and the preservation of democracy, with its central stress on the accountability of those who govern. In addition, theorists and adherents of the civic republican ideal underline that the same processes of participation and involvement are simultaneously educative of the understandings, shared sense of community and very identities of citizens (Pateman, 1970; Mill, 1982).

Civic republicans resolve the dilemma of how citizens can both submit to being ruled and retain their basic freedom, by emphasising the centrality to their model of *legitimate* government in which citizens engage simultaneously in governing and being governed. As Jane Mansbridge (1995, p.4) summarises it, 'by genuinely willing what is good for all, human beings can take up a new identity as part of a larger whole, and can experience laws that result not as coercion, but as emanations from the better part of their beings'. Citizens participate in shaping the common rules and then willingly submit themselves to the rules that they have helped to fashion. Optimally, this means that citizens should know each other both as individuals and as members of the same community, and all should have opportunities for participation in its affairs. All of this is upheld by a shared commitment to friendship and to the conduct of collective decision-making in a spirit of mutual respect. In order to preserve freedom and sustain the republican state, citizens must thus themselves live in the republican style of upholding a sense of community based on the Aristotelian virtue of 'concord'.

Thus, by contrast with the essentially legal, political and economic formalism of liberal perspectives on citizenship, regarding it as *a largely private matter*, civic republicanism stresses the engagement and *active participation of citizens* in the social institutions, organisations, processes and networks of *public society*. In part, the apparent renewal of interest in the civic republican version of citizenship also represents a rejection of the perceived excesses of extreme individualism and the increased 'marketisation' of social relations evident in much recent political debate and the formation of public policy according to the tenets of 'neo-liberal' and 'neo-conservative' thinking (Harvey, 2005). Thus 'the renaissance of civic republicanism represents a reaction against the individualism of the liberal citizenship paradigm that has dominated contemporary political life' (Lister, 1997, p.23).

A learning citizenry

In ancient Greece, the *polis* constituted an educational community in its own right, expressed by the Greek term *paideia*, and involvement of the citizenry in politics was about more than the admittedly important matters of regulating or ordering the affairs of the community; it also constituted a kind of 'school' for living, a 'curriculum' for life. Thus the purpose of civic engagement, political life, was the self-development of the citizens for the public good and for the benefit of the community.

Where Rousseau makes little reference to *collective* deliberation as a core feature of educative democracy (while emphasising active participation's undoubted educative value for individuals), de Tocqueville has no doubts. For him 'town meetings are to liberty what primary schools are to science; they bring it within people's reach, they teach men (*sic*) how to use and how to enjoy it' (de Tocqueville, 2003, Book I, Chapter 5). For de Tocqueville, people's involvement in voluntary associations also produces commitment to the common good through an appreciation of the arguments made by other members as 'feelings and opinions are recruited, the heart is enlarged, and the human mind is developed by the reciprocal influence of men upon one another' (*ibid.*, Book II, Chapter 5).

John Stuart Mill, too, argued that participation in representative government, or democracy, should be undertaken both for its educative effects on participants and for its substantive beneficial political outcomes. Even if elected or appointed officials can perform better than citizens, Mill thought it advisable for citizens to participate 'as a means to their own mental education – a mode of strengthening their active faculties, exercising their judgment, and giving them a familiar knowledge of the subjects with which they are thus left to deal'. In Mill's view, the development of the person can and should be undertaken in concert with an education for citizens. The 'mental education' he describes is:

> *The peculiar training of a citizen, the practical part of the political education of a free people, taking them out of the narrow circle of personal and family selfishness, and accustoming them to the comprehension of joint interests, the management of joint concerns – habituating them to act from public or semi-public motives, and guide their conduct by aims which unite instead of isolating them from one another.* (Mill, 1982, p. 181)

More recently, Robert Putnam has also made the point that voluntary associations and community groups are precisely 'places where social and civic skills are learned – schools for democracy'. In bonding together in their various bodies, people learn about, and how to 'do', organisation, public speaking, campaigning, communication and debate. People are able to engage 'in thoughtful deliberation over vital public issues', while also 'learning civic virtues, such as active participation in public life' and the value of high trust relationships and reciprocity (Putnam, 2000, pp.338–340).

Citizenship as action

Oldfield insists there are two key tests for genuine civic republican citizenship that clearly distinguish it from liberalism's individual moral autonomy; both are of central concern to this monograph. The first is that citizens should engage principally because 'citizenship is an activity or a practice, and not simply a status, so that not to engage in the practice is, in important senses, not to be a citizen'. The second is the recognition that, unsupported and left to their own devices, individual citizens cannot be expected to participate: they need to be encouraged, helped and given incentives and motivation to engage.

For Oldfield, matters of shared identity and belonging are not merely about sentiment or vague nostalgia for a supposedly lost world of community-based mutuality. Nor is shared identity simply the sharing of a common language or history, important though they are. Instead, social solidarity and social cohesion are a question of politics: they involve a self-consciously recognised and acknowledged common identity, born partly out of common experiences, shared ambitions and hardships, and working through difficult problems and challenges together and for each other. 'If one of the identities to which duties are attached is that of citizen, then one of the forms of collective life is the political community' (Oldfield, 1998, p.78).

> *In a political community, what is shared is identity, born in part from self-determination and in part from common history, or language or continued occupancy of the same territory. Political solidarity and cohesion result from the equality of shared identity, which is at least in part self-determined and chosen ... And it is as 'active citizens' that we choose (ibid., p.80)*

There is a danger that both protagonists and critics may present the civic republican world of active citizenship and community involvement as a world typified by a vague 'love-in' style of philosophy and intellectual sloppiness where more or less anything goes. Oldfield, however, believes:

> *Civic republicanism is a hard school of thought. There is no cozy warmth in life in such a community. Citizens are called to stern and important tasks which have to do with the very sustaining of their identity. There may be, indeed there ought to be, a sense of belonging, but that sense of*

belonging may not be associated with inner peace and, even if it is, it is not the kind of peace that permits a relaxed and private leisure, still less a disdain for civic concerns. (ibid., p. 79)

Strong, developmental and deliberative democracy

There is, however, plenty of variety within the civic republican perspective. For example, the American political theorist and activist Benjamin Barber (2004) draws a sharp distinction between 'strong' participative democracy, in which citizens actively engage in a wide range of civic institutions and activities, which he advocates, and the 'thin' purely representative democracy of traditional liberalism. Thin democracy, based largely on episodic electoral activity and party involvement for a minority, is characterised by political alienation and poor accountability, and affords only a 'precarious foundation (on which) no firm theory of citizenship, participation, public goods, or civic virtue can be expected to arise' (Barber, 2004, p.4). Others, similarly, have distinguished between 'thin' and 'thick', or 'maximal' and 'minimal' conceptions of citizenship and democracy (Walzer, 1983 and 1994). Stokes (2002) suggested that 'developmental democracy' and 'deliberative democracy' both constitute more expansive versions of civic republicanism.

Developmental democracy envisages citizens engaged in public activity and the determination of the common good based on 'reflection, discussion and argument over a proposed course of action'. Citizens, within developmental democracy, demonstrate 'capacity for criticism and self-criticism' and consider the possibility of extending democratic participation into other sites of experience, beyond the realms of conventional politics' (*ibid.*, p.37).

Deliberative democracy goes still further, especially with regard to the possibilities of autonomy and self-governance, in which dialogue and communication rather than people's prior status, role or identity underpin public decisions (Stokes, 2002, pp.39–41; Gutmann and Thompson, 2004). Within deliberative democracy, citizens willingly open themselves to the possible revision of their opinions and preferences, showing the moral strength to accept decisions reached through discourse 'in which participants strive to reach agreement solely on the basis of the better argument, free of coercion and open to all competent speakers' (Bohman, 1996, cited in Stokes, 2002, p.41).

From this point of view, the authenticity of democracy depends upon evidence of all sorts of instances and arenas in which citizens can engage in 'argument, rhetoric, humour, emotion, testimony or storytelling, and gossip' in debate and reflection in the determination of collective preferences (Dryzek, 2000, p.1). This is democratic decision-making forged out of what Dryzek calls a 'contestation of discourses'. Dryzek goes further and seeks to establish a distinction between deliberative and what he terms 'discursive' democracy. He sees the latter as a form of democratic consideration that 'should be pluralistic in embracing the necessity to communicate across difference without erasing difference, reflexive in its questioning orientation to established traditions (including the tradition of deliberative democracy itself), transitional in its capacity to extend across state boundaries into settings where there is no constitutional framework, ecological in terms of openness to communication with non-human nature, and dynamic in its openness to ever-changing constraints upon and opportunities for democratization' (*ibid.*, p.3).

There is not space here to examine these large claims in any detail. The champions of discursive democracy must, however, respond to the powerful reservations about its efficacy which suggest that discursive exchange based on the mobilising of argument, stories, imagery and the deployment of rhetoric risk privileging those who are able – by virtue, for example, of their background and character – to dominate debate and to overwhelm those less prepared to engage effectively and equally as citizens. In other words, even in the idealised world of discursive democracy, the risks of distortion through hierarchy, domination and power are still present.

What's wrong with civic republicanism?

Although critics of the civic republican model of citizenship will acknowledge its compelling vision of participative democracy as an ideal, many see it as impractical, unrealistic, and socially and politically naive. Some critics of the conventional civic republican model also charge it with not fully recognising the distinctiveness of certain social groups in its assumptions of universalism and commonness. Some even go so far as to suggest that the model of participation advanced by civic republicans now constitutes yesterday's solutions to tomorrow's problems as the forces of globalisation shift the locales of action and authority beyond its compass. The restless 'shakers and movers' of the new transnational scene deny their attachment to any particular domain, or at best regard such commitment as no more than purely transitory (Bauman, 1997, 2001 and 2002).

First, there are the related problems of the size of the political community and people's remoteness from the real seats of power and decision-making in the contemporary world, which makes effective participation by all citizens a practical impossibility – even using the Internet. In any case, say the critics, the vision is unrealistic: most people are either too busy, too uninterested in the processes and subject matter of politics, too lacking in information or in the skills and confidence to make participation effective, or just plain cynical about the way politics operates.

> *Citizenship is not an easy life; it requires conscientious application. Most people lead a very full life with their family commitments and employment – above all, employment, for we are not Greeks with slaves to work for us. Yet the republican citizen must, in addition, allocate time, summon up the energy and generate commitment to an involvement in public affairs … How many individuals are prepared to make that adjustment? (Heater, 1999, p. 73)*

Secondly, critics point out that even when there is widespread opportunity for citizens' involvement in public affairs, some citizens' and some groups' opinions always hold more sway. Some voices dominate debate. Some people seem to be better connected to decision-makers, and others are more adept at negotiating the pathways of authority. What is more, critics argue, it is all a matter of power, the unequal distribution of resources and the systematic 'mobilisation of bias' in setting agendas and determining outcomes (Bachrach and Baritz, 1962; Lukes, 1974 and 2004).

Thirdly, from the point of view of women, and especially when viewed through the critical prism of feminist politics and scholarship, civic republicanism is only marginally more acceptable than the liberal perspective on citizenship. Feminist critics hold that, within the classical civic republican perspective, there is still an excessive dependence upon an abstract, gender-neutral conception of citizenship that both overlooks the many barriers to women's full engagement in the established institutions of political and institutional life and discounts the insights and experiences of their lives that could substantially enrich what is meant by politics and citizenship (Phillips, 1991; Young, 1995 and 1998).

Thus, where women and their full recognition and inclusion in citizenship are concerned, the charge is fundamental. Some feminists have contended that 'in Western political discourse, citizenship remains defined as an activity practiced in an androcentric field of action and represented through the codes of phallocentric discourse'.

> *Not only do women lack the full complement of 'rights' included in citizenship, but also the conceptualization of citizenship in these systems – the characteristics, qualities, attributes, behaviour, and identity of those who are regarded as full members of the political community – is derived from a set of values, experiences, modes of discourse, rituals and practices that both explicitly and implicitly privileges men and the 'masculine' and excludes women and the 'female'. (Jones, 1998, p.221)*

Although, as we shall see later, there are many different strands and variations in feminist critiques of citizenship, and much controversy between them, there are four main issues to address: the formal changes that are still needed to extend full civil, political and social rights to women (to use Marshall's distinctions); the changes required in the social, economic and cultural organisation of societies to overcome the barriers to women's full and equal enjoyment of citizenship status in practice; the task of blurring or even transcending the traditional boundaries between the public world of citizenship and the private sphere of mostly 'domestic' life; and, most challenging of all, the radical redefinition of citizenship to embrace what are deemed to be characteristically 'feminine' experiences, perspectives and priorities. As Heater puts it, 'the institution of citizenship needs a more complete association of women as much as women need to be complete citizens' (Heater, 1999, p.94).

Similar arguments can be heard from ethnic and linguistic minorities, from migrants and from those seeking within existing sovereign states to (re-)establish their claims for recognition of distinctive national traditions and identities. In the first instance, this has been a matter of demanding that due recognition and respect be afforded to differences of ethnicity, language, cultural practices and religious affiliation. But even minority groups themselves may not regard claims for this sort of 'multiculturalism' as sufficiently nuanced to do them justice. As Yasmin Alibhai-Brown (2001, p.48) observed in a radical commentary that rejects 'old multiculturalism' as a response to ethnicity claims based on diversity in contemporary Britain: 'our national identity is in a state of flux and is causing endless anxieties'. One of the main challenges is that 'where once people of colour were happy to call themselves black, we are now Asian,

Hindu, Caribbean, African, Muslim, Shia Muslims, Kashmiris, Khalista-
nis. This gives them a platform for making demands which are not only
positive, but also negative, against other groups ...'

Finally, when it comes to education for civic republican citizenship,
there are the two problems of being accused of too much timidity and
adherence to the established order of things on the one hand, and of
attempting indoctrination and a kind of brainwashing on the other.
Sheldon Wolin expresses the risk thus: 'The inherent danger ... is that the
identity given to the collectivity by those who exercise power will reflect
the needs of power rather than the political possibilities of a complex
collectivity' (Wolin, 1989, p. 13). For some totalitarian regimes – fascist
or communist, for example – this is not a danger at all but, instead, the
very purpose of their forms of civic education.

Communitarianism

For some observers, the growth of *communitarianism* in the 1980s and
1990s represented a third approach to citizenship and belonging. For
others, it constituted an extension and modification of the core ideas of
civic republicanism in an era when the size and complexity of the State
and the inadequate operation of representative democracy rendered
unlikely the chances of most citizens taking an active part in national
politics. Protagonists of communitarianism also deliberately opposed
their conception of citizenship to what they dismissed as the atomised
rights of asocial individualistic approach promoted by neo-liberalism
(Sandel, 1982; Walzer, 1983; Taylor, 1989). As Delanty observed, the
philosophy of 'liberal communitarianism' places the promise and positive
functions of 'community' at the centre of its critique of both the theory
and practice of existing citizenship.

> Community has appeared to many to hold out the promise of a utopia
> destroyed by both society and the state. Rather than retrieve the state
> project, communitarianism seeks to recover a lost dimension of commu-
> nity, the utopia that modernity promised but restored. Communitarians
> can be seen as liberals disenchanted by liberal individualism. (Delanty,
> 2000, p.25)

Thus, in communitarianism, the principal focus shifts to the dynamics of
the family, school and local community (including, sometimes, the

'community of communities' – the nation state) and to people's obligation to act to maintain and strengthen the moral order, shaped by the
particular history, values and standards of a given locality or shared set of
interests. Amitai Etzioni, the leading sociological theorist and chief
advocate of communitarianism, indicated the benefits and consequences
of extensive involvement in public and civic affairs by well informed,
virtuous citizens operating within 'bounded autonomy'. 'Once citizens
are informed, they must make it their civic duty to organize others locally,
regionally, and nationally to act …' (Etzioni, 1993, p.244).

According to the core tenets of communitarianism, families, local
communities, schools and public education generally all need to contribute to the social formation of citizens and to the construction of society's
overall moral order. People's true sense of belonging and most expressive
form of citizenship, and indeed their identities and real sense of themselves, thus consist of accepting responsibility in their families and the
community, and in acting always in a self-denying and public-spirited
fashion. With such emphasis, communitarianism constitutes largely a
powerfully *moral* conception of citizenship, or even of its need for what its
principal adherents regard as the *renewal* of citizenship's threatened or lost
dimensions.

There are many different versions of communitarianism (Delanty,
2000). Although Etzioni became its best-known public advocate, his
intellectual work in this field has been criticised for not having the level of
scholarly rigour that characterised his earlier academic work in economic
and industrial sociology, or that of other distinguished political theorists
who have written on this topic (MacIntyre, 1985; Avinerni and de Shalit,
1992; Demaine, 1996; Miller, 2000; Crow, 2002).

In one of the most celebrated communitarian contributions to the
debate on citizenship, the philosopher Charles Taylor (1994) traced the
connection between people's conception of themselves and 'others', in
which their identities are formed in a kind of 'dialogic' encounter
through a shared language, culture and array of symbols, amounting to
what Delanty calls a 'discourse of recognition' (Delanty, 2000, p.26). For
Taylor, within an overall liberal commitment to equality, affording recognition to people's identities requires acceptance of differences and people's
diversity of feelings of belonging. This is especially important where the
maintenance of the cultural life of majorities and their relationships with
cultural minorities are concerned.

Problems with communitarianism

Among the many criticisms of communitarianism, the principal ones include: its relative neglect of power in general and of the State in particular; its underdeveloped analysis of social inequality; its failure to adequately respond to shifts in sexual politics and the politics of the family; its somewhat 'retro' tendency towards romantic and conservative moralisation; and its excessive voluntarism and its reification of 'community'. Indeed, even this central core of the communitarian argument – the pivotal idea of 'community' – remains both unclear and, to the extent that it has been refined, somewhat narrow and exclusive. Whilst communitarianism's various representations of community enable it to track its provenance within classical conceptions of citizenship, 'the concept of community in communitarian discourse is the community of the dominant culture which is officially recognized by the state' (*ibid.*, p.27). Minorities, incomers and those who stand outside the dominant culture therefore need either to adapt to it or, if allowed, to join it, in order to participate fully in cultural, social and political life.

The moral values espoused by some versions of communitarianism, perhaps especially those extolled by Etzioni, are also deeply contentious, particularly where they touch upon the implications for family life, for parenting and for the roles of women. In some respects, communitarianism suggests the desirability of rowing back on some of the 'social' achievements of the welfare state, and re-emphasising instead the twin importance of self-help and voluntary contributions, reminiscent (in the UK at least) of so-called 'Victorian' values. Underlying this stress on moral renewal and citizenly responsibility, some critics also detect a lurking authoritarianism.

For all its welcome opposition to rank liberal individualism and its noble aim of reversing the loss of a shared common morality, many critics have thus noted communitarianism's tendency to ignore, or at best be agnostic about, social, economic and political inequalities. They argue, too, that communitarianism smacks too much of conservatism, of adherence to the status quo, of middle-class morality and of a tendency to be stifling in its limitations and repressive of fundamental or radical dissent. Thus, they suggest, communitarianism masks the reality of pressure towards insidious conformity with an illusionary emphasis on choice and voluntarism. Moreover, the stress placed on the importance of unity as a binding ethic of community overlooks the ways in which vigorous debate among citizens can do more to create a strong sense of communal mutual respect and social solidarity than can comfortable but superficial and unthinking consensus.

'New Labour' and communitarianism

A number of authors have noted the ways in which some of the core themes and arguments of communitarianism have been echoed in New Labour's political programme for 'modernisation' after its general election victory in 1997, and, especially, in the construction of a politics of the 'third way' (Prideaux, 2005; Hale, 2006; Hoban, 2008). There are clearly some common elements between New Labour and communitarianism. These include: ideological and moral opposition to the politics of the neo-liberal 'new right' with its uncritical celebration of the virtue of untrammelled markets, individualism and deregulation; a determination to update social democratic analysis and policy direction; and a 'reinventing' of democratic politics, with renewed emphasis on the importance of shared ethical values (Giddens, 1998 and 2000).

Within this 'new' politics, supporters of communitarianism and 'third way' advocates both centre on paid work and volunteering for fostering vibrant, 'inclusive' citizenship. They champion a drive towards civil and local 'renewal' and emphasise the importance of balancing rights with responsibilities. There is also in both (especially third-way perspectives) an attempt to develop policies and ways of working that comprehend the direction of travel of global, cultural and community politics (Miliband, 1994; Giddens, 1994 and 1998; Driver and Martell, 2006).

Critics of these variants of 'New Labour communitarianism' claim that much of their language and analysis acts as an ideological fig leaf for what they suggest is, in reality, much closer to an uncritical acceptance of key elements of neo-liberal philosophy.

Postmodernism, citizenship and belonging

Critics of postmodernism reject the idea of the 'grand' or 'meta' narrative in general theories such as the liberal or civic republican models of citizenship, with their origins in the enlightenment-inspired search for overarching 'truths' and the scientific route to 'progress'.

> *Postmodern corrosives eat away at the foundations of grand schemes of the Enlightenment, the expansive spread of Westernization, and the optimistic dreams that made modernity bearable if not enjoyable. All lie exposed*

as fictions, the super-stories of progress. As Lyotard says, they are no longer believable; 'incredulity towards metanarratives is the order of the day' … Escaping the shackles of modernist assumptions and expectations, (some) postmodernists relax in a playground of irony and irreverent pastiche, where pluralism and difference contrast with the older 'terrorism' of totalizing discourses. 'Here's to heterogeneity!' might be its slogan …Ecstasy, enthusiasm and even emancipation are promised in the postmodern. (Lyon, 1994, p.75)

Rejecting the modernist emphasis on scientific objectivity and its ultimate manifestation in the imposed controls of managerialism and 'performativity' – which have increasingly impacted upon such key areas of social life as education and citizenship, as well as the world of work and production – postmodernists advocate a radically different approach to knowledge. This approach abandons 'the separation of the cognitive, normative, and aesthetic spheres and the division between fact and values or knowledge and politics' (Seidman, 1994, p.17). Such a perspective has far-reaching implications for both citizenship and learning, in particular in its rejection of generalised theories or programmes of action divorced from specific circumstances and situations. As Ichilov (1998, p.22) questions, how are some of the key issues entailed in discussions of democracy, citizenship and morality even possible where analysis emphasises 'partiality, relativity, uncertainty, the absence of foundations, incommensurability, pluralism, fragmentation and poly-culturalism'? We are left with the irresolvable postmodern puzzle of how, if at all, can order, meaning, legitimacy and morality exist once certainty, foundations, commensurability, unity and the prioritised self are deconstructed?

Embracing – celebrating even – 'chaos' and uncertainty, postmodernism holds out the prospect of a different conception of identity, belonging and emancipation. In this, it posits 'a view of identities that are plural, unstable, situationally enacted, and sites of social contestation for which we would need a postmodern language of self and society. Thus we might learn to speak of 'composite' rather than unitary, additive identities, of selves simultaneously positioned along multiple social axes …' (Seidman, 1994, pp.17–18). The challenge then for the social theorist as advocate is to embrace a new moral standpoint that draws not on generalised 'truths' about citizenship, freedom, democracy and learning, but which is entrenched in and respects specificity and locality.

45

Just as an individual's identity mix is varied in innumerable ways, his or her experience of self as empowered or dis-empowered will be similarly varied and multidimensional. We need to shift from an essentialist language of self and agency to conceiving of the self as having multiple and contradictory identities, community affiliations and social interests. (ibid., p.133)

In a similar fashion, Edwards and Usher (2001), while acknowledging that adult learning's location 'within a postmodern landscape has been, and continues to be, a troubled one', nevertheless see in the emergence of a range of discourses about lifelong learning the opening up of increasingly varied forms and places of learning. 'Under the sign of lifelong learning,' they remark, 'institutionalized education at all levels is becoming increasingly diverse in terms of goals, processes, organizational structures, curricula and pedagogy.' Moreover, under conditions of postmodernisation, institutionalised educational authority is simultaneously being challenged and de-centred, opening up the 'boundlessness of learning' without 'predetermined outcomes, formal institutions, and epistemological control'. Consequently, as Edwards and Usher observe, 'once learning starts to become recognized as located in a variety and diversity of social practices outside the institutional, a greater multiplicity of activities is seen as involving learning and hence can be deemed educational' (*ibid.*, p.276). In this sense, they conclude, lifelong learning itself is *part of the postmodern condition* as much as being shaped by it, in the midst of attempts, not least by governments, to regulate, discipline or control it.

Postmodernism's cul-de-sacs

There can be little doubt that postmodern critics' hostility to some of the more grandiose claims and schemes of citizenship, belonging, identity and democracy is a useful corrective to what might otherwise loom as excessively all-embracing, fixed and universal certainties, when in reality there is plenty of evidence of diversity, ambivalence and change. At its best, postmodernism challenges absolute values and emphasises multiplicity, cultural relativism, the vacillations of desire and even transgression. Indeed, even in its emphasis on the potential for inventive initiatives with regard to people's lives as citizens and in their identities, postmodernism has drawn attention to the inherent dynamism and to some of the

46

possibilities in what is meant by citizenship and belonging in the contemporary world.

However, there is no need to accede to all of the iconoclastic assertions of postmodernism in order to accept the validity of these points. In particular, it is postmodernists' refusal to engage with some of the core issues at the heart of serious considerations of citizenship and belonging – such as the inherently 'big' ideas of justice, freedom, human rights or equality – in a seemingly ahistorical insistence on the autonomy of the subject that limits postmodernism's contribution to the debate. As Terry Eagleton has (ironically!) observed, postmodernism's reluctance to embrace the liberal notion of liberty as self-determination means that 'it is forced to fall back on the modern or negative notion of liberty as doing your own thing free of external constraints ... however, it presses this freedom to the point where the subject risks imploding upon itself, leaving nothing much to experience the freedom in question' (Eagleton, 1996, p.87).

Moreover, the problem is that, if liberty, according to postmodernism, entails the complete dissolution of the unified subject, then, logically, there is no possibility of freedom at all: all that the subject can be free of is its own self. In such circumstances, there would be no point in exercising the sorts of choices or expounding the kinds of values that are essential for the expression of both citizenship and belonging of any kind. Against this, Eagleton posits the case expressed by Charles Taylor:

> *To know who you are, is to be oriented in moral space, a space in which questions arise about what is good or bad, what is worth doing and what is not, what has meaning and importance for you and what is trivial and secondary. (Taylor, 1989, p.28, cited in Eagleton, 1996, p.24)*

CHAPTER FOUR

Identity, belonging and 'difference'

The promise

The second promise of freedom – that of belonging – is no less utopian than the first. It consists of a vision of expansive social, cultural and political circumstances in which all individuals and a rich diversity of groups and nations feel able fully to express their identities, and can do so in ways that confirm in them a sense of belonging and enable them to benefit from their free association with other similar people. In this world it would be normal for people to manifest many different sorts of identity and happily admit to feelings of belonging to a variety of communities of common interest (social, cultural, political, etc.) with their associated rights, obligations and loyalties.

The only limitation on such diversity would be that, in freely pursuing their own expressions of identity and belonging, people would be required to adhere to one of the core principles of liberalism: that in so doing they did not render unviable the enjoyment by others of their own legitimate versions of difference. Thus, in bearing free and joyful witness to their own identities, and living according to its openly declared norms and values, such individuals and groups would show respect for manifestations of identity different from their own, deepening such mutual understanding through greater knowledge and insight bolstered by critical learning of all kinds.

In this ideal world, such multiplicities of identity and diversities of belonging would be bound together by overarching principles, standards and values which would not only regulate the relations between legitimate expressions of difference, but would also serve as bonds of wider unities, whether at the level of organisations, communities or nation states, or in the acknowledgement of shared humanity.

A sense of self

Although often intertwined, identity and a sense of belonging are not the same. At the level of the individual, 'our inner personal identity seems to be based on an awareness of persistence through time: it expresses the individual's psychic continuity across the years', although that personal narrative may encompass many subtle shifts of orientation and changes in self-expression throughout life (Maier, 2007, p.67). Our identities, particularly when an expression of our own sense of self, are rarely fixed or projected in the same way in all situations, shifting through both time and space, even when founded on some core characteristics or underpinned by relatively persistent principles. Moreover, although analytically distinct, any sense we may have of ourselves – the 'I' in identity – necessarily depends upon what other people also make of, and the extent to which they validate the identities which we seek to project – the 'Me' (Jenkins, 2004). In this way, the identities by which we strive to be known result from a constant dynamic between the internal and the external through both time and space. The balance between constancy and change, between acceptance and repudiation, and in the salience of different aspects of our identities for our behaviour, are matters of empirical circumstance.

In opening her sociological review of the concept, Lawler declares that identity 'is a difficult term: more or less everyone knows more or less what it means, and yet its precise definition proves slippery' (Lawler, 2008, p.1). Part of the problem with the term, she suggests, 'derives from difficulties of defining it adequately'. Bauman goes further: ' "identity" is a hopelessly ambiguous idea' (2004, p.76). In noting that 'the term "identity" is made to do a great deal of work', Brubaker and Cooper (2000, p.8, cited in Jenkins, 2004, pp.8–9) go so far as to suggest its abandonment for the purposes of serious social analysis.

For Isin and Wood (1999, p.17), 'the concept of identity is troublesome'. For Zygmunt Bauman, identity is a sword brandished by opposing sides in 'cultural crusades' to establish their respective preferred versions of what deserves primary loyalty. When it comes to the expression of cultural preferences, Bauman observes, there is 'more disruption and antagonism than unity; conflicts are numerous and tend to be bitter and violent' (Bauman, 2004, p.82).

Identity, let us be clear about it, is a 'hotly contested concept'. Whenever you hear that word, you can be sure there is a battle going on. A battlefield is identity's natural home. Identity comes to life only in the tumult of a battle; it falls asleep and silent the moment the noise of the battle dies down (ibid., p. 77)

At its core, the construction and sustaining of identity, or its alteration, is a matter of meaning – of the interpretations of who and what we are and the sense that we and others make of the various ways in which we signal that meaning. In that necessary transaction and interaction with others, identity is entwined in a complexity of 'agreement, and disagreement, convention and innovation, communication and negotiation' (Jenkins, 2004, p.4). In this way, identity always has, at least latently, the potential to develop; learning and understanding the communicative feedback from significant others plays a key part. Our sense of identity helps us understand and convey to others just exactly who we are, the kind of person we want to be seen as by other people, and, if necessary, what we stand for. Thus a person's definition of self can be seen 'as an individual's sense of her or his own particular identity, constituted vis-a-vis others in terms of difference, without which she or he wouldn't know who they are and hence wouldn't be able to act' (*ibid.*, p.27).

One important way in which we each construct and explain our identities and where we feel we fit in, or do not, is through narratives (Lawler, 2008). Narratives are stories which we tell, re-visit, revise and re-tell to ourselves and to others, and that give meaning to our lives. Of necessity, the generation and authoring of the narrative, like the writing or telling of any story, requires selection and omission from the myriad experiences, memories and inherited stories that make up our lives; episodes need to be stitched together to produce some kind of coherence or to make a point about who we are and how we became as we are, including the interpretation of apparent success, suffering and failure. To this extent, as Lawler explains, 'identity is not something foundational and essential, but something produced through the narratives people use to explain and understand their lives' (*ibid.*, p.17). The stories which we relate – with their cast of characters, their plots and contexts – embed the meanings that we give, and that we want to be given by others, in the unfolding nature of our being. The resources on which we can draw in shaping our life narratives include not just our personal recollections and interpretations, but also those given to us by cultural institutions, by oral and written histories, in formal educational settings, and in a multitude of informal and non-formal learning encounters and conversations that typify everyday life. It is through the sharing and exchange of such narratives, too, that we are able to construct a sense of belonging or, alternatively, of being excluded or not wanted.

Thus, identity also enables us to recognise, join with and value others whom we perceive as being like ourselves, and among whom we thus 'belong' and feel secure. One special case of belonging is that of being part of a shared political community. Andrew Mason provides a useful definition:

> *A person has a sense of belonging to a polity if and only if she identifies with most of its major institutions and some of its central practices, and feels at home in them. When a person identifies with those institutions and practices, she regards her flourishing as intimately linked to their flourishing. (Mason, 2000, p.127)*

When a person endorses particular institutions and practices, he or she will not only be comfortable with those institutions and practices, but will also feel free to participate in them according to personal preferences. Nor do people need necessarily need to agree with the outcomes of the workings of those institutions and practices, but only to believe that the operation of them does not deny to the people in question the opportunities of realising their goals and priorities in life, or of expressing openly their cherished values and aspirations. Thus a sense of belonging to a political community does not necessarily mean that all who belong need also to express that belonging by sharing the same 'history, religion, ethnicity, mother tongue, culture or conception of the good'. Seen in this way, belonging to a political community can be distinguished from the idea of people belonging together in a broader sense (Mason, 2000, p.127).

Nevertheless, collective identities and a shared sense of belonging depend upon 'the symbolic construction and signification of a mask of similarity, an umbrella of solidarity under which all can shelter' where communal membership is both imagined and a potent and real influence on people's lives (Jenkins, 2004, p.110). Even so, the degree of homogeneity captured by these various 'masks' and the extent of coverage of these different umbrellas can be expected to vary. In some circumstances, there is little scope for the expression of differences within the overall commonality for fear of breaching the implied unity; in others, opportunities abound for people to manifest some plurality within an overall and binding sense of similarity. In any case, as sociological research has demonstrated, in even the most straitened circumstance of autocratic or bureaucratic control, people are remarkably inventive at finding ways to express their individuality.

We can also endow our experiences and the milieux and institutions in which we express ourselves with their own identities. Hence apparently identical institutions, even those that share the same names and same main characteristics, can be expected to vary between different times and places. In this way, the precise meaning given to such identities can change. Just think, for example, of what elementary school and schooling – major locales in the formation of identities – meant to a working class child in the cotton towns of nineteenth- or early twentieth-century Lancashire or London's East End, as against the experience of going to a progressive, modern secondary school or public school in the twenty-first century. Mary Stuart (1995) explains the connection between individual identity and the changing identities of the institutions that help to shape us:

> *By identity, I mean an agreed sense of who we are as individuals. Individuals develop a sense of themselves and will behave in ways which they feel reveal the 'type' of personality they have. Socially we also create an identity for our institutions. For example, we have a shared knowledge in our society of what the 'medical profession' is, or what 'school' is like. In other societies these 'identities' will have different meanings. These identities are not simply fixed, they are shaped and altered by a variety of social forces, and change over time. (ibid.)*

Individual identities are also partly formed by people's sense of place: where they were born or brought up, and went to school; where they live, work, and so on. The salience of a particular place across the lifespan will depend on the significance of the experiences associated with each in the mind of the individual. Moreover, the influence of a given place will probably vary over time. The 'shape' of place as an influence will also be influenced by geography, topography, architecture and, not least as far as governments are concerned, territoriality (Maier, 2007). In the designation of place as territory, the marking of boundaries often carries with it other implications, not just for people's identity, but also for their status, including whether by virtue of living within the designated boundaries they qualify as citizens.

Clarification and, if necessary, amendment or reinforcement of identities is usually something that happens at their borders, on the boundaries that differentiate the identity of one individual from another, of a group of people in comparison with another – the essential integrity of 'me' and 'you', of 'us' versus 'them'. In some cases, these boundaries are policed with the eagle-eyed vigilance of militant border guards; in others, there are those who cross borders with ease, or who succeed in occupying both camps, and who are able facilitate mutual understanding between different identities or to assist in the processes of accommodation between them.

Social groups and collectivities

Identity and collective life

Analytically speaking, although an almost wholly individualised, *liberal* conception of citizenship can underpin key aspects of a person's identity, especially in granting either the legal rights or political status that constitute inclusion of a *formal* kind, it is in the realm of collective actions, reciprocity and social interaction that more *substantive* notions of shared identity and belonging are forged. Indeed, for Rousseau, one of the virtues of citizens' participation is that it enhances individuals' sense of belonging and of their identification with fellow members of the political community in which they are engaged.

By contrast with individual identity and the personal meanings with which we endow our experiences, 'group or collective "identity" is constructed out of a synchronic web of affiliations and sentiments. It expresses individuals' sense of belonging within a society or community' (*ibid.*, p.67). When people feel that they belong, however, they often get together with other people or groups with whom they feel they share some important characteristics – attitudes, experiences, values, origins, aspirations or goals. People thus join with others who are like themselves, with a common sense of history or culture, or who adhere to the same religious beliefs, speak the same language or dialect, or who feel they face the same sorts of adversity.

This link between individual identity and group affinity was under-lined by the late Iris Marion Young in her defence of the importance of recognising difference and of compensating for disadvantage among different groups.

A social group involves first of all an affinity with other persons by which they identify with one another, and by which people identify them. A person's particular sense of history, understanding of social relations and personal possibilities, his or her mode of reasoning, values and expressive styles are constituted at least partly by her or his group identity. (Young, 1998, p.272)

Naturally, there are all sorts of different ways of belonging to different groups, and it is likely that different individuals will manifest differing levels or intensities of identification with the various groups to which they are affiliated. What matters is that the nature of that affiliation and of that sense of belonging will help to shape and explain their behaviour as well as both contributing to the character of the social groups to which they belong and being, in turn, partially shaped by them. In many respects, that is a matter for empirical enquiry: neither individual behaviour nor organisational pattern can be simply 'read off' from belonging.

Everyone belongs, though some people belong to some groups with more intensity and often less choice than others belong to any other. Such belonging matters not only as a subjective state of mind – not only insofar as it feels either good or bad to individuals. It matters also as a feature of social organization. It joins people together in social relations and informs their actions. Without it, the world would be a more chaotic place. (Calhoun, 2007, p.286)

Whatever the basis of their shared identities – be it, for example, occupation, class, gender, religion, ethnicity, or shared goals or disadvantage – people express their identities in a wide range of different ways and in different sorts of organisations and patterns of behaviour. People may express their identities in a voluntary organisation or community group, in a religious or faith group, in a campaigning body or self-help organisation, in a political party, or indeed, by wanting to bear witness as a fully fledged citizen of a given country or nation, accepting the rights and obligations that go with such a status. People also announce their shared identities and their sense of belonging by display – by the clothes that they wear, by sporting badges and other symbols, or by the use of slogans, songs and a common idiom. In these ways, a sense of belonging and of sharing identity reflects people's standing and underlines their feelings of being together with others as either insiders or outsiders.

54

Membership

Expressing or securing a sense of commonality with a particular group – a nation state, an ethnic or religious community, or a social club – is often demonstrated by membership. 'Full' members are those accepted by others in the group as insiders, able to take advantage of the rights of membership, to participate in the inner life and symbolic practices of the group, but also to be subject to the rules and behavioural norms of the group. Citizenship is an excellent example of this sort of exclusive group membership: 'membership lies at the heart of citizenship. To be a citizen is to belong to a given political community' (Bellamy, 2008, p.52).

Membership – of a group, a team, an organisation or a political institution – usually has consequences. Where we elect to join, or where the aims and ways of working of the body or institution of which we are, or become, a member are benign, then the consequences of membership and inclusion are beneficial, advantageous, enjoyable and may help to reinforce or strengthen our commitment. In such circumstances, membership may carry with it benefits that are not available to non-members, such as the right to vote, to stand for election, to own property or to qualify for certain pecuniary benefits. Where membership is forced on us by others or by the unavoidable circumstances of our lives – say incarceration in prison, allocation to an outcast or despised group, or being of minority and excluded status – the consequences may be negative or convey a powerful sense of disadvantage and unfairness. But even in such circumstances, all may not be lost, and learning may play its part in helping people understand better how membership constitutes disadvantage. Learning can contribute to raising people's awareness of their condition and how best to challenge and change it, and it can help educate others about the unacceptability of such conditions in a society which, for example, subscribes to the values that emphasise fairness, equality, opportunity and human rights, and that sit at the core of most contemporary versions of citizenship.

Needless to say, all of this requires that those who subscribe to a common sense of identity or to a shared sense of belonging need to be able to communicate their feelings to themselves and others, as well as to other groups whose identities may equally call for understanding and a knowledge born of some degree of mutual recognition. To that extent, and perhaps paradoxically, the imperative of a strong sense of belonging has inscribed within it the potential for realising that others with quite different identities are equally likely to make claims for recognition. Of course, that does not necessarily bring mutual tolerance, respect or (especially) celebration of such differences. However, these matters of clarification, communication, increased knowledge, recognition and understanding – and even the more challenging possibility of reciprocal acceptance – are the very stuff of lifelong learning, of discussion, dialogue, critique and reflection.

A shared sense of exclusion, of being on the outside, can provide the foundations of a common identity for individuals and groups. As Parekh (1991, p.192) remarks in an analysis of the dynamics of British citizenship, cultural difference and the experience of Asian communities, 'difference draws attention to oneself, intensifies self-consciousness, singles one out as an outsider, and denies one the instinctive trust and loyalty extended to those perceived to be "one of us" '. Reciprocally, one profound effect of exclusion, by reinforcing people's strong sense of difference, may be to heighten their feelings of 'belongingness' with others who are similarly excluded, thus helping to create a sense of identity based on a shared sense of difference, but also possibly on powerful feelings of inequality and a lack of justice.

Thus other people, groups and, most importantly, powerful institutions also contribute to identity formation and to people's sense of belonging – of being in significant ways the same as others or of being somehow different.

> *Any identity depends upon its difference from, its negation of, some other term, even if the identity of the latter term depends upon its difference from, its negation of, the former. Identity is thus formed not against difference but in relation to difference. (Isin and Wood, 1999, p.16)*

Group formation also depends, in part, on the deployment of social capital within networks, on exchanges and a range of social obligations and reciprocities that help define boundaries and create a sense of belonging through what Bourdieu described as the 'unceasing effort of sociability' (Bourdieu, 1986, p.250; see also Ball, 2003). For Shotter, this means that we have to grasp the processes of identity formation and sense of belonging as essentially *socially constructed meanings*, negotiated with others through what he terms a 'political economy of ontological opportunities'. That is possible only where people not only enjoy rights and entitlements but are also 'actively involved in regulating and sustaining the shape of that community' (Shotter, 1993, p.129).

56

Culture

Debates about belonging and identity – particularly with regard to the politics of ethnic, religious, sexual or physical difference – often also invoke the notion of 'culture' of particular groups to explain differentiation or inter-group relations. These matters have been raised as much by social movements as in intellectual debate, where groups and individuals have been struggling to define and gain recognition for their distinctive identities. This is especially true where claims of particular identity promise the opportunity of mobilising special interests and demands that the individuals concerned – or more likely groups – argue have been overlooked, denied or suppressed by dominant interests.

Culture, of course, is another of those slippery and overworked concepts, or rather notions, that is deployed in a different and sometimes contradictory way (Williams, 1989). For some, culture means that unique combination of signs, symbols, images, meanings, myths and actions – often captured in specific language and idiom – that expresses the identity of an individual, group or whole community. For others, the idea of culture is best reserved to describe all forms of artistic production (including, for example, music and literature). In some cases, culture becomes imbued with assumptions of 'high' examples of those modes of action usually followed by an elite. (By implication, its opposite, 'low' culture, is associated more with the generality of people.) More loosely, 'culture' is deployed to describe the whole way of life of a group of people and the many institutions, relationships, structures and traditions that govern their behaviour. Whatever the case, we need to understand the particular meaning that is being given to the word when accounting for people's identity or sense of belonging.

Raymond Williams's assertion that 'culture is ordinary' offers clarification and possibilities for human agency, learning and everyday democratic creativity.

> *A culture has two aspects: the known meanings and directions, which its members are trained to; the new observations and meanings, which are offered and tested. These are the ordinary processes of human societies and human minds, and we see through them the nature of a culture; that it is always both traditional and creative; that it is both the most ordinary*

common meanings and the finest individual meetings. We use the word culture in these two senses: to mean a whole way of life – the common meaning; to mean the arts and learning – the special processes of discovery and creative effort. (ibid., p. 4)

Williams concludes his groundbreaking essay with three wishes, each pertinent to the principal topics addressed in this monograph. First, 'that we should recognize that education is ordinary: that it is, before every-thing else, the process of giving to the ordinary members of society its full common meanings, and the skills that will enable them to amend these meanings, in the light of their personal and common experience'. To this end, he asks for 'a common education that will give our society its cohesion, and prevent it disintegrating into a series of specialist depart-ments, the nation become a firm' (*ibid.* p.14). Secondly, Williams wishes for funding and for more active public provision for the arts and for adult learning, including for libraries, museums, galleries, orchestras and com-munity education – all principally for their own sake. Thirdly, that shorn of the vast and wasteful income derived from advertising, news media – 'our common services' – should in future be funded in ways that 'will guarantee proper freedom to those who actually provide the service, while protecting them and us against a domineering minority whether political or financial' (*ibid.*, p.17).

Choice

In the contemporary world, where many individuals are able to make some sorts of choice, at least about lifestyle options, people may also seek to free themselves from what they experience as the limiting constraints of an overwhelming definition of self or the confining boundaries of an identity-endowing community or culture, forging an individual or at least quite different identity, and possibly shifting any consequent sense of belonging from one milieu to another (Giddens, 1991). In its most pronounced form, this argument suggests that individuals in contempo-rary times need to be increasingly engaged in reflexively (re)writing their own, unique biographies (*ibid.*; Beck, 1992).

We live in an age in which the social order of the national state, class, ethnicity and the traditional family is in decline. The ethic of individual self-fulfilment and achievement is the most powerful current in modern

58

society. The choosing, deciding, shaping human being who aspires to be the author of his or her own life, the creator of an individual identity, is the central character of our time. (Beck and Beck-Gernshein, 2001, pp.22 and 23)

Making a choice may also result in a decision *not* to join, *not* to be part of the broader 'we' or the 'us'. Individuals may even prefer not to be regarded as belonging to any particular group, preferring instead to 'bowl alone' (Putnam, 2000). They may reject the life of 'community' or 'society' as being altogether too fixed, insufficiently flexible and unacceptably confining or restrictive.

Bauman has drawn attention to the demise of the traditional notion of 'society' that dominated European thought for nearly five hundred years, and the intellectual discipline of sociology to which it gave rise, with its associated connotations of 'proximity, togetherness, a degree of intimacy and mutual engagement'. What is disappearing, he avers, is a 'solid', once familiar world in which there is a common experience of 'the "we will meet tomorrow" feeling, the sense of consistency and continuity suggesting a thinking, acting, quarrelling yet cooperating company cemented by a shared purpose and joint planning'. In its place, as we have seen, is consumption, 'an experience of life as a series of consumer choices made in response to the attractions put on display by competing shopping malls, television channels and websites' (Bauman, 2002, p.42 and 45).

Reflexivity and biography

Against laments for the disappearance of older forms of solidarity and social cohesion, some commentators have argued that these changes create the possibilities and inherent challenges of greater openness and opportunity, and the promise of freedom from traditional constraints. They also emphasise the virtues and veritable excitement of choice, stressing the possibilities of greater individuation and reflexivity, the widening of people's horizons and experiences, the huge expansion of access to information afforded by the Internet, and the chance of people 'surfing' life and its risks much as they might surf the World Wide Web and its virtual realities.

Emancipation and freedom from traditional forms of exploitation, inequality and oppression may open up possibilities of a new 'life politics':

enhanced life chances, new lifestyles, and greater choice in constructing a narrative of self-identity (Giddens, 1991). Living a life of one's own thus requires the continuous creation and re-creation of one's own biography. It entails the demanding processes of reflexivity, a capacity to sift and respond to a plethora of often conflicting information.

The principal ethic in such a world is that of individual self-fulfilment and achievement (Beck and Beck-Gernshein, 2001). As the individual is increasingly dis-embedded from the traditional influences and obligations of social life, so the emphasis switches to the person as creator, chooser, and essentially actor and agent. Such new emphasis on both choice and responsibility sometimes leads to more fanciful notions of people becoming the designers, jugglers and stage directors of their own biographies in a continuously changing world of risk and uncertainty.

Those, including governments, who emphasise the potential benefits and challenges of such changes not infrequently underline the importance of people seeking to make the most of such benefits and challenges and, in order to thrive, needing not just initial education and continuing learning. They also require the navigational and intellectual skills necessary to operate successfully in a knowledge-rich and increasingly knowledge-driven world where digital confidence and competence can open up a range of new kinds of interaction and community and make possible novel forms of identity and belonging, including opportunities for virtual experimentation in 'second' lives.

Multiplicity of meanings and multiple identities

It is clear from the above that identity and belonging share a significant characteristic with citizenship and lifelong learning: that is, their potential for multi-dimensionality. Many commentators have drawn attention to the fact that, perhaps especially in a late modern world marked by increased mobility and less ascription of roles, citizens may easily claim multiple identities, refusing to be restricted to a single one, moving comfortably and with ease from one environment of potential belonging to another. The possibilities here are extensive: just to give a limited example, people may not only happily admit to dual nationality, or feel that they belong simultaneously both to, say, England and the UK, but also see themselves as Liverpudlians and supporters of the Everton Football club, and so on. That would by no means exhaust their range of identities: to continue the same made-up example, the same person may identify as being Black British, or male, or as a dad, or disabled, or as a trades unionist, or as a lifetime Labour Party supporter.

Exactly which identity comes to the fore at any given time will partly depend upon context, the strength of the person's feelings and those of others, of the issues in hand, or the stage in people's life, and so on. In reassuring readers that he perceived no crisis of belonging in the UK, Lord Goldsmith's 2008 review of citizenship in Britain recognised the legitimacy of such multiplicity: 'people can and do have multiple feelings of belonging. Being British is not an *alternative* to other feelings of belonging. It provides a shared sense of identity and not an *exclusive* one. People can feel British as well as feeling a strong sense of attachment to a local community, a faith, another nationality, or even to all of these' (Goldsmith, 2008, p.88, emphasis added).

With many potential identities available (but not infinite numbers, of course), and with those aspects of identity that are in the gift of the State possibly declining in significance, citizenship as traditionally conceived faces the challenge of whether and how it can continue to constitute an overarching, universalising source of meaning. In this, there is no need to succumb to the absurdist position of suggesting that people are free simply to take up or discard any identity that they fancy or to declare a sense of belonging to any community or movement of their choice. Although there will thus always be an element of constraint as well as of opportunity, it is evident that assuming excessive fixity in people's identities and senses of belonging may also do mischief to the unfolding character of their lives or to the variety of circumstances in which they find themselves.

Different versions or elements of citizenship, different aspects of identity, and a range of different types of belonging struggle for dominance in this scenario of choice and options; each is also fluid and subject to change and modification (although, again, the scope for unilateral shifts in any or all of these should not be exaggerated). Alongside the prospect of potentially profound differences of identity and different sites of belonging and meaning for different groups and individuals, there is also the possibility of shifts in identity and the prospect of the impermanence of some sorts of belonging, or at least their attenuation by multiplicities of identity. The images and metaphors of surfing and shifting, and what Bauman describes as the 'slicing and spicing' of life – not necessarily with any deep sense of commitment or involvement –

capture some of these possibilities graphically. Where any notion of citizenship or learning is entailed in such lifestyles, its transience and lack of fixity once more comes to resemble more the dynamics of the learner or citizen as consumer rather than as engaged participant.

One of the most demanding implications of the multiplication of identities, sites of belonging and instances of citizenly behaviour concerns the time, resources and repertoires of the individuals and groups who are required to move between these milieux. People need to demonstrate versatility, adaptability, wide-ranging skills of presentation and communi-cation, and not a little energy.

> *Modern citizens must wear so many civic hats that, if they accept the proper burden of citizenly responsibility, they cannot but feel a variety of strains. Multiple citizenship presents the demands of multiple under-standing, multiple identities, multiple loyalties, multiple rights and multiple duties. (Heater, 1999, p. 149)*

To repeat, not all options are always open to free choice by individuals or groups, whatever the people wanting to express that choice may desire – perhaps a desire to be included or accepted. Comprehending the limits and possibilities, making sense of the opportunities and restrictions, is not just a matter of perception, but also of learning and of translating understanding into action. Moreover, as Calhoun has rightly noted (2007, p.300), first, it is rarely the case that individuals are able to choose or choose not to be members of certain groups, social relations or cultures, free of material, psychological, social, legal and political con-straint or incentive: in a sense, it partly 'happens' to them. Secondly, 'the idea of individuals abstract enough to be able choose all their "identifica-tions" is deeply misleading'. Individuals or groups may be deliberately or coincidentally excluded from belonging to a particular group or to the special category of 'citizen' or 'naturalised' person. Exclusion may be formal or informal, even in defiance of the rules. For example, the formal award of the legal status of 'citizen' or the admission of people into an organisation as 'members' may depend upon the decision of the admitting body rather than the applicant. In turn, the body with the power to determine the outcome may set criteria for admission or insist on particular rituals before admission is deemed complete. This is what the UK Government is seeking to do in response to current political pressures over immigration. In such circumstances, one of the aims of the receiving body is to foster a greater sense of belonging and may, as again in the UK citizenship case, use education in that cause.

Thus it is that a key and sometimes overwhelmingly powerful element of becoming a citizen relates to the decisions about a person's identity made by authorities. The State has the authority to restrict, suspend, refuse, or even strip people of formal identities, including their citizenship or claims to it. 'Negotiation' with the State alone creates the prospect of an uneven and potentially brutal contest. Claims for recognition of particular affiliations, group identities, and senses of belonging that rest on difference and differentiation are best tackled in the wider hurly-burly of civil society. There, in the everyday, commonsense and tumultuous world of 'multitudinous diversity' and 'continuous transactions', people are best able to participate in shaping and re-shaping their identities and lives in what Shotter, after (Bakhtin, 1965), celebrates as a ' "great carnival" of different ways of socially constituted being in which everyone can have a voice' (Shotter, 1993, p.131).

The 'politics of identity'

The emergence of a range of social groups with claims for recognition has been described as constituting a new global 'politics of identity'. Crucially, for some, this new politics represents a challenge to traditional approaches to democracy and citizenship, entailing calls for 'special' measures to overcome perceived disadvantage. Such claims are frequently voiced in circumstances of controversy and social conflict: new claims frequently represent a challenge to established interests, and to traditional ways of life, attitudes and thinking (Isin and Wood, 1999; Kane, 2002; Kenny, 2004).

> Our contemporary condition is marked by the emergence of new forms of identity politics around the globe. These new forms complicate and increase centuries-old tensions between the universalist principles ushered in by the American and French Revolutions and the particularities of nationality, ethnicity, religion, 'race' and language. (Benhabib, 2002, p.vii)

In this tension – the challenge of reconciling claims for recognition of difference and receiving 'special' treatment with the universalistic assumptions of common citizenship – the demands of certain groups

63

feature most prominently. These groups are women, ethnic groups, migrants (both 'legal' and illegal'), adherents to different faiths, lesbians and gay men, people with disabilities, and national and regional 'minorities'. Moreover, even within such groups, claims are made for further differentiation.

Thus, for example, it is suggested that not all women can be assumed to fall under what Ruth Lister (2000, p.35) calls the 'false universalism of the category "woman"'. Indeed, it was principally the renewal of the women's movement from the 1960s onwards, and the flourishing of the associated feminist scholarship, that drew attention to misleadingly simplistic conceptions of difference. Anne Phillips points out that 'the most innovative of feminist writing moves beyond a binary opposition between male and female towards a theory of *multiple* differences ... and group identities and group specifics are increasingly regarded as part of what must be represented or expressed' (Phillips, 1995, p.288, emphasis added).

In this regard, noting the leading role played by black feminists in articulating such claims, Lister cites the words of the poet June Jordan: 'every single one of us is more than whatever race we represent or embody and more than whatever gender category we fall into. We have other kinds of allegiances, other kinds of dreams' (Lister, 2000, p.35). In other words, in recognising the claims to difference by certain groups, there is a danger of assuming that all people who share some of the core characteristics of such groups – in terms of physical or social attributes – will share the same interests.

So where are the limits to differentiation, or are there no ways of determining the boundaries of identity while sustaining an overarching commonality that embraces legitimate diversity? Kenny (2004) observes two main anxieties in attempts both to construct unity and to accord recognition to difference at the same time. The first is that 'the commonality and unity of purpose that citizenship requires may be imperilled if citizens are overtly aware of group differences', and the second is that centring on the different identities of groups threatens to blur unhelpfully 'the relationship between the political and non-political spheres of life' (*ibid.*, p.43). Against this, suggests Kenny, the advent of groups and movements pursuing the 'politics of identity' illustrates the 'inherent contestability of the boundaries of politics'.

By no means all observers are content with infinite claims for the recognition of difference, not least because they fear that the consequences risk breaking up any idea of a common sense of belonging or shared identity. Porter (1987, p.128), for example, emphasises that 'the organization of society on the basis of rights or claims that derive from group membership is sharply opposed to the concept of society based on citizenship'. According to this view, if citizenship is constantly differentiated, the hope of any larger commonality will have to be abandoned. Amartya Sen (2006, p.178) has also expressed the worry that if the emphasis is on 'uniquely hardened categories' where cultural differences result in the 'illusion' of the 'solitarist belittling of human identity', difference can easily be exploited for fomenting division and inter-group strife. Richard Dagger (1997), too, draws attention to the risks of an infinite fragmentation of group identities, to the central problem of who and by what criteria claims of legitimate difference are to be set (is no group's claim 'beyond the pale'?), and the dangers of social paralysis inherent in giving groups the power of veto over policies that they claim affect their interests.

The problem is that a wide range of differences, within as well as between groups, may not only constitute dilemmas and conflicts for the individuals or groups caught up in them. There is, too, the risk that some instances of these differences will actually be, or be regarded as being, at odds with the core values, common formal rights and standard obligations that constitute the defining features of citizenship and belonging in a given society.

An infinite number of particularisms?

Thus, it is one thing to proclaim the virtue of a cultural and political environment in which a myriad of social groups can both claim legitimacy for and enjoy their declared differences, and through that achieve a fuller sense of themselves and of the integrity of their peculiar identities. It is quite another to know whether there should be any limits to an otherwise potentially infinite registration of such claims: what or who should set the criteria for the determination of legitimacy and, most importantly, in what relation to the rest of the wider community (which, in any case, will embrace other such groups insisting on their own versions of difference) should any group stand? Aside from the threat of a successive fragmentation of any broader sense of unity, as the philosopher

Ernesto Laclau has forcibly argued, 'an appeal to particularism is no solution to the problems we are facing in contemporary societies'. When faced with a profusion of particularisms:

> *The assertion of pure particularism, independently of any content and of the appeal to a universality transcending it, is a self-defeating enterprise. For if it is the only acceptable normative principle, it confronts us with an unsolvable paradox. I can defend the rights of sexual, racial and national minorities in the name of particularism; but if particularlism is the only valid principle, I have to accept the rights to self-determination of all kinds of reactionary groups involved in antisocial practices.* (Laclau, 1996, p.26)

What is more, all of these different groups will also, at least potentially, voice competing claims. In such circumstances, there will have to be a wider framework of principles applicable to all, or some postulated overall unity or harmony, against which the virtues of conflicting claims can be judged. In addition, as Laclau points out, a further paradox of insisting solely on difference – where frequently a key aspect of that difference is the group's differential access to power or its suffering at the hands of powerful others – is that 'if the particularity asserts itself as mere particularity, in a purely differential relation with other particularities, it is sanctioning the *status quo* in the relation of power between the groups' (*ibid.*, p.27).

The danger that Laclau identifies is that affirming the right of the various cultural and ethnic groups to assert only their differences and their separate development opens up the 'route to self-apartheid' consisting of the 'mere opposition of one particularism to another'. That way risks that relations between groups asserting only their differences will descend into mutual antagonism or even war. Moreover, such claims are also often made in association with the unsustainable assertion that 'Western cultural values and institutions are the preserve of white, male Europeans or Anglo-Americans and have nothing to do with the identity of other groups living in the same territory' (*ibid.*, p.32). As Laclau continues, it is one thing to declare that the universalistic values of the West are the preserve of its traditional dominant groups; 'it is very different to assert that the historical link between the two is a contingent and unacceptable fact which can be modified through political and social struggles' (*ibid.*, p.33).[11]

Blending the particular with the general

In practice, few claims for difference and for particularity are made without reference to wider sets of values or norms in order to justify a group's claims. More often than not, demands for recognition of new expressions of identity also make appeals to the universalistic canons on which citizenship rests. Indeed, to the extent that claims are met, either the group achieves inclusion within the previously existing conception of citizenship that sanctioned their demands, or else the group succeeds in expanding the accepted boundaries of citizenship and of the bonds that tie groups together in shared citizenship. As Laclau concludes, any claim to the right to express difference needs to be addressed in a community of some kinds of overarching common values – 'that is, within a space in which that particular group has to coexist with other groups'. Such coexistence is possible only with 'some sense of belonging to a community larger than each of the particular groups in question'.

Claims to legitimate difference, the search for common rules and principles of coexistence, and the consequent potential re-conceptualisation of citizenship, can thus manifest the proper inter-weaving of the particular with the general, especially in generating social solidarities and the active practice of self-government (Walzer, 1995). Seeing citizenship and identity as inherently antithetical 'makes sense only if we neglect the degree to which the latter invokes universalizable norms and understate the social particularities through which citizenship is mediated' (Kenny, 2004, p.62).

In a discussion of the challenges of establishing contemporary 'democratic citizenship' that bears centrally upon identity, Hayward (2007) depicts the challenge as one of finding some way of reconciling issues of 'binding' with those of 'bounding'. The particular strength of the 'ties that bind', to use Will Kymilcka's powerful invocation, may depend upon the firmness and clarity with which boundaries are drawn, so that

---

11 To illustrate this, Laclau observes that 'when Mary Wollstonecraft, in the wake of the French Revolution, defended the rights of women, she did not present the exclusion of women from the rights of man and citizen as a proof that the latter are intrinsically male rights, but tried, on the contrary, to deepen the democratic revolution by showing the incoherence of establishing universal rights which were restricted to particular sectors of the population' (Laclau, 1996, p.33).

only restricted groups have access to a given identity. For such persons to seek to give up their separate identities or to submerge them into a wider inclusive identity, or for others (such as governments) to urge them to do so, may be impossible without weakening the bonds that link them meaningfully to others like themselves.

The challenge that remains is to find some pragmatic reconciliation between the claims of individuals and social groups who argue that their particular interests or identities have been overlooked or systematically discriminated against, and who therefore demand recognition, respect and perhaps special consideration over and above that accorded to the rest of the population, and all other citizens. In this, argument, debate and the deployment of evidence in the context of mutual respect for divergent points of view – all characteristics of vibrant lifelong learning – at least offer the prospect of the challenge being given a fair and proper airing. This truly is the terrain for active, deliberative citizenship.

We shall return later in this monograph to the vexed issue of how particular identities, cultures and senses of belonging can be related to wider generalities, and the prospects of groups claiming difference engaging with a common set of principles for all citizens within a given community. We shall do so when we consider the specific responses in the UK to 'multiculturalism' in circumstances of heightened anxiety about the apparent orientations of certain Muslim groups.

CHAPTER FIVE

The politics of citizenship and belonging

Emancipation and diversity

Emancipation, liberation and freedom all bear directly upon conceptions of citizenship, on people's sense of belonging, and on the possible contribution of learning to each of them. As already mentioned, heroic strivings for freedom are evident in the various efforts of those involved in the struggle for legal, political and organisational rights over the past 200 years (Thompson, 2000; Hanley, 2007).

In more recent times, liberation and emancipation have continued to be common themes in the advocacy of citizenship or its strengthening, and as individuals and social groups press for recognition, tolerance, respect or representation. In what Giddens (1991, Chapter 7) describes as the 'emergence of life politics', the 'politics of emancipation' centre on combating exploitation, inequality, unfairness and oppression. This usually entails combining efforts not only to throw off current restrictions, but also to open up new opportunities for (increased) autonomy. As Giddens (*ibid.*, p.213) summarises it, 'if there is a mobilising principle of behaviour behind most versions of emancipatory politics, it could be called the principle of autonomy'.

Campaigns for liberation in the UK

Struggles for liberation, to challenge corrupt authority and for a broadening of citizenship, based on an extension of education and increase in knowledge for the common people, figured centrally in the campaigns of the Chartists and early trades unions in nineteenth-century Britain. Their demands powerfully invoked the promise of emancipation for the people. Emancipation would be achieved through a combination of an extension of people's learning with a marked improvement in their material circumstances, captured in the slogan 'Bread, knowledge and freedom'. As David Vincent's 1981 analysis of nineteenth-century working class autobiographies shows, there was among these (usually) autodidactic authors a deep yearning to liberate working people from the perceived tyrannies of superstition, ignorance, drunkenness, intellectual deference and scientific unawareness, and the associated daily subordination and unfeeling exploitation by employers that they likened to slavery. As Vincent observes, such men (and the great majority of the writers were indeed male) 'were convinced that book knowledge could be used to transform the quality of their own lives and that of their class as a whole' (Vincent, 1981, p.195). A notable illustration of this is found in the writings of William Lovett, one of the leaders of the Chartist movement in the 1830s and 1840s, when imprisoned in Warwick gaol for his part in the movement.

> *Imagine the honest, sober and reflecting portion of every town and village in the kingdom linked together as a band of brothers, honestly resolved to investigate all subjects connected with their interests, and to prepare their minds to combat with the errors and enemies of society ... Think you a corrupt Government could perpetuate its exclusive and demoralizing influence amid a people thus instructed? Could a vicious aristocracy find its servile slaves to render homage to idleness and idolatry to the wealth too often fraudulently extracted from industry? Could the present gambling influences of money perpetuate the slavery of the millions, for the gains or the dissipation of the few? Could corruption sit in the judgement seat – empty-headed importance in the senate house – money-getting hypocrisy in the pulpit – and debauchery, fanaticism, poverty and crime stalk triumphantly through the land if the millions were educated in a knowledge of their rights? No, no friends; and hence the efforts of the exclusive few to keep the people ignorant and divided. Be ours the task, then to unite and instruct them; for be assured the good that is to be must be begun by ourselves. (Lovett, 1840)*

Invocations of emancipation, the struggle for liberation and the promise of freedom have also figured in the campaigns, slogans and imagery of British trades unions since the nineteenth century, alongside affirmations of the need for working class unity, solidarity and the emancipatory value of learning. The invocations feature in key speeches, motions to union and political conferences, in union leaflets and pamphlets, in trades union rules and constitutions, on union posters and lapel badges, and, especially, on trades union banners (Gorman, 1973 and 1985). For example, echoing the influence of pre-First-World-War industrial syndicalism, the banner of the Rickmansworth branch of the National Union of Railway-men carried the declaration 'Liberation of the working class is the act of the workers themselves' underneath an image of a worker shackled by the ball and chain of capitalism. Similarly, the back of the banner of the 'Shamrock' branch of the National Builders' and Labourers' and Con-structional Workers' Society (formed to organise Irish migrant workers in the building industry in the Edgware Road area in London after the First World War) bore the slogan 'Freedom, fraternity, equality', while the front depicted images of a man, woman and child – 'romantic symbols of flourishing union strength' – underneath the declaration that 'The cause of labour is the hope of the world' (Gorman, 1973, pp.132 and 133).

In January, 1894, *Liberty*, 'a journal of anarchist communism' first appeared'(Gorman, 1985, p.138). The second issue carried an article by William Morris (who was opposed to the physical violence endorsed by many anarchists, which, he felt, would 'bring nothing but disaster to the cause of liberty') on 'why I am a Communist', later published as a pamphlet by the Liberty Press.

Appeals to freedom also underpinned women's demands for changes in their legal status, for their rights to own property, for greater educa-tional opportunity, and for their full inclusion in suffrage (Rowbotham, 1973 and 1997; Brown *et al.*, 1998; Purvis and Holton, 2000). Thus, writing in 1792 in the wake of the French Revolution and after Tom Paine's publication of his declaration of the *Rights of Man*, Mary Woll-stonecraft challenged women's continued subordination to men, arguing that only when women and men enjoy truly equal freedom, and woman and man are equally dutiful in exercise of their responsibilities to both family and State, can there be true freedom for all. For Wollstonecraft, education was the key to women's emancipation and their attainment of full citizenship. Moreover, an extension of the opportunities for increas-ing women's rationality and their achieving virtue through knowledge, rather than threatening marriage, argued Wollstonecraft, would prove to be a sounder basis for a true partnership between men and women.

71

> *Contending for the rights of women, my main argument is built on this simple principle, that if she be not prepared by education to become the companion of man, she will stop the progress of knowledge, for truth must be common to all, or it will be inefficacious with respect to its influence on general practice. (Rowbotham/Wollstonecraft, 2010, p. 4)*

Wollstonecraft was not, however, naive in assuming that education was free of the wider impact of established power, conventional relationships and the mores of the age: all of these would need to be challenged if education was to fulfil its promise of leading to emancipation.

> *Men and women must be educated, in a great degree, by the opinions and manners of the society they live in. In every age there has been a stream of popular opinion that has carried all before it, and given a family character, as it were, to the century. It may then fairly be inferred, that, till society be differently constituted, much cannot be expected from education. (ibid., p. 28)*

As Wollstonecraft outlined in the introduction to *A Vindication of the Rights of Women*, it was because men had constructed a 'false system of education' that women's aspirations were so limited. Instead of considering women as 'human creatures', the men responsible for designing the education of women had been:

> *... more anxious to make them alluring mistresses than affectionate wives and rational mothers; and the understanding of the sex has been so bubbled by this specious homage, that the civilised women of the present century, with a few exceptions, are only anxious to inspire love, when they ought to cherish a nobler ambition, and by their abilities and virtues exact respect. (ibid., pp. 10 and 11)*

According to John Stuart Mill, women's position in the third quarter of nineteenth century Britain was still to be the bondservant of husbands, suffering under the same sort of lack of freedom as slaves did, and in the reign of a female monarch at that! Part of the solution, he asserted, was to afford women full political suffrage: 'all human beings have the same interest in good government; the welfare of all is alike affected by it, and they have equal need of a voice in it to secure their share of its benefits' (Mill, 1861, *On Liberty*, Folio Edition, 2008, p.242).

More recently, again in the name of women's liberation, women have pushed for equal treatment in the labour market and at work, for an end to sexist behaviour and male violence, against sexist imagery and pornography, and for greater control over their own sexuality and fertility (Mitchell, 1966; Rowbotham, 1969, 1973 and 1989; Rees, 1992; Lister, 1997). A distinctive element of the 'new wave' feminism dating from the late 1960s was a focus on raising women's awareness of themselves and of their potential (Sarachild, 1978). Feminism set out to challenge conventional female imagery and identities in the news media and popular culture, in art and literature, and, most importantly, in women's own heads. A plethora of seminars, weekend schools, day conferences, self-help courses and publications, organised by different groups, were aimed at raising women's self-esteem, developing their self-confidence and assertiveness, and generally heightening their consciousness, both of what women continued to suffer and of the possibilities offered to them by their liberation.

Since the first UK women's liberation conference, organised by Ruskin College Oxford in February 1970, British feminism has both flourished and fragmented – theoretically, organisationally, politically and in the everyday struggles and practices of women in all walks of contemporary life. All of this would need to be properly assessed in any serious analysis of women's citizenship and identity in late twentieth-century and early twenty-first-century Britain, and the contribution made by learning both to challenging conventional categories and to opening up alternative possibilities.

The quest for women's real equality in politics and in citizenship, argues Anne Phillips, is far from having been accomplished. Not least, this requires that the chief assumptions of political theory and its core concepts be challenged. With the continuing emphasis on the formation of women's identity, and their prime interests and influence being confined to the *private sphere* of home and the family, the essentially *public arena* of politics remains the domain principally of men.

I see the conventional assumption of a non-gendered, abstract citizenship as something that does indeed operate to centre the male. In denying the pertinence of gender, previous democratic theorists have reinforced the position of the sex that is historically dominant; in identifying politics with (a very particular definition of) the public sphere, they have made

73

democracy coterminous with the activities that have been historically associated with men. (Phillips, 1991, p. 6)

In similar fashion, over more than half a century in the UK, the main areas of struggle for black and ethnic minority people seeking to enhance their citizenship have been against racism in housing and in the labour market, in schooling, in their portrayal in the media, in political representation and participation in elections, and in relation to their treatment by the police and law courts. In short, black and ethnic minority people continue to seek emancipation from what they experience as unfair and unwarranted restrictions upon their rights and opportunities. They perceive that they do not yet enjoy full and equal citizenship (Rex and Moore, 1967; Rex, 1991; Modood *et al.*, 1997; Anwar, 1998; Fletcher, 2000).

People of different faiths, or who follow distinctive religious practices or want to express their own cultures peacefully, have also sought recognition and tolerance of the social and cultural diversity that they represent (Brown, 2006; Cooper and Lodge, 2008).

There have also been successful mobilisations by people with disabilities and learning difficulties, for wider acceptance of the life choices made by lesbians and gay men and, most recently, for the legal endorsement of same-sex civil partnerships (Butler, 1990; Cruikshank, 1992; Munt, 1998; Lawson, 2001; Riddell and Watson, 2003). Their various fights have been to secure recognition of the legitimacy of their needs and interests, for improved rights and opportunities, for an end to perceived unfairness and hostility, and for shifts in the attitudes and behaviour of fellow citizens generally and those in positions of power and authority (Benhabib, 2002; Benhabib *et al.*, 2007).

Mobilisation in such campaigns has frequently entailed some engagement with the main theoretical and conceptual debates about citizenship and belonging, sometimes changing their meaning or the understanding of their implications. Leaders and organisations at the heart of these campaigns have also often envisaged that education and learning would make a contribution to them, even where that education might require challenge and transformation. Learning can help raise public understanding and awareness of the issues, win wider support for the campaigners' objectives, challenge established stereotypes, bolster participants' self-confidence and self-awareness, and contribute to building on any changed status and rights achieved (Lawton, 1977).

Of course, not everyone welcomes any changes achieved. As already observed, any serious examination of struggles to achieve full citizenship or secure recognition for identity encounters conflict. Some who oppose new rights for certain social groups, or greater acceptance of social diversity, genuinely fear that it will lead to social fragmentation or the loss of a sense of the shared narrative of identity and common feeling of belonging that bind people together. Only the most optimistic (and disingenuous) of educational enthusiasts would argue that learning's contribution to such struggles is always regarded as positive.

What all of these different struggles for emancipation and liberation have in common, even when voiced in terms of demands for 'equality', is that all were aimed at enlarging or transforming what had been, up to the point of their voices being raised, the accepted and prevailing domains of people's rights, citizenship and feelings of fair treatment. True, some more that others constituted a more fundamental challenge to the *status quo*. Equally, success for some would require that the rights, or rather privileges, that their oppressors had enjoyed hitherto, often at the expense of those seeking to throw off their shackles or transcend their subordination, would be curtailed or even reversed, if the campaigns acheived their objectives. In every case, success would entail a re-casting of citizenship and what it meant to be a citizen, freed from the oppresions identified by the various leaders, activists and supporters of the different struggles.

Autonomy

Essentially, people's struggles in these domains are concerned with the attainment or increase of autonomy, both as individuals and collectively, in order to lead 'self-governed' lives – often declared to be the principal function of all learning (Giddens, 1991; Held, 1995; Dagger, 1997). Another way of putting this is that people striving for liberation or freedom are seeking inclusion in a fuller conception of citizenship, including peaceable acceptance of, and respect for, the distinctiveness of their various ways of life.

Held (1995, p.149) comments that, although the prospective outcome of autonomy did not feature in Rousseau's conception of active citizenship, the principle of autonomy sits at the core of the modern liberal democratic project. This, he argues, is concerned with the 'capability of persons to determine and justify their own actions, with their ability to choose between alternative political programmes ...' Autonomy consists of four key elements, all of them central to the issues of citizenship, belonging and lifelong learning considered in this monograph. These elements are: protection from the arbitrary imposition of political authority and coercive power; citizens' involvement in the determination of the conditions of their association; the creation of the best circumstances for citizens to develop their nature and express their diverse qualities (including through learning); and the expansion of economic opportunities for citizens to increase their resources.

Democracy, participation and pluralism

According to Martin (2002), we cannot speak of citizenship without speaking also of democracy. There are, as observed above, many versions of what democracy means and which people or categories of citizen have the right or indeed duty to participate in making it work (Held, 1987; Keane, 2009). As McGrew (2001) observes, 'The history of democratic theory is the successive re-imaginings of the democratic project to fit in with new historical circumstances'. In literal terms, democracy implies government 'by the people', a notion surrounded by a host of definitional and qualification criteria. At least since the writings of Machiavelli and, later, Rousseau, and certainly since the French and American Revolutions, modern conceptions of democracy have usually inscribed the ideal of some kinds of 'active' participation by the citizenry in their main principles, institutions and practices (Pateman, 1970; Heater, 1999; Shafir, 1999; Delanty, 2000).

In modern large-scale societies, democracy is rarely found in its most direct form – active participation in the innermost workings of government by all who are subject to its authority. With the development of systems of 'representative' democracy in nineteenth century Europe and America, formal participation in the institutions of government by those citizens meeting the relevant criteria was limited mostly to taking part in elections as candidates or by voting (Held, 1987; Crick, 2002b). This marked a decisive shift in the opportunities for direct engagement in formal politics by the citizenry, as well as in what was required of citizens to enable them to feel fully involved in some of the key decisions affecting their lives.

From classical antiquity to the seventeenth century, democracy, when it was considered at all, was largely associated with the gathering of citizens in assemblies and public meeting places. By the early nineteenth century, in contrast, it was beginning to be thought of as the right of citizens to participate in the determination of the collective will through the medium of elected representatives. (Held, 1995, p. 11)

The theory and practice of modern democracy rest on the other ways in which people who are subject to authority, especially the policies and decisions of government, give their consent to it. Although some commentators suggest that people give a kind of 'unspoken assent' by not participating in democratic arrangements or in their political apathy, they usually do so by some sort of indirect contribution to the deliberations of government. They do so not only through the various mechanisms of voting – by plebiscite, referenda or the election of representatives – but also by lobbying or by mounting pressure through public debate or protest. Some of the resulting forms of association may also seek to mobilise influence on governments to secure support for their particular interests or points of view (Dahl, 1961 and 2000; Lukes, 1974 and 2004).

Thus modern democratic participation and debates about its strength or weakness have turned as much on people's involvement in the organisations and activities that constitute 'civil society' as on an assessment of their participation in electoral politics (Gellner, 1994; Keane, 1998; Chambers and Kymlicka, 2002; Birch, 2007). Whatever the chosen mechanism, the expectation is that such actions will have some chance of affecting government policy and decision-making, and that, in turn, the decisions made and the policies pursued will bear directly upon the lives of the people, preferably to their advantage. In this sense, modern democracies typically manifest pluralism.

There is a second aspect to this notion of pluralism: citizens both subscribe to certain common rights, responsibilities and identities and, within a defined and overarching shared commonality, accord respect and opportunities for the legitimate expression of a variety of cultures, beliefs and ways of life. This second dimension of pluralist democracy manifests itself most in notions of mutual tolerance, respect for difference, and the shared celebration of diversity.

While a commitment to pluralism of this second type constitutes recognition that different groups may have different legitimate interests and should be allowed to pursue them, the risk always is that it may be at the expense of the expression of common concerns. Moreover, claims for difference are often couched in the language of universality, not infrequently by appealing to the principles of common human rights'

(Bellamy, 2008). In other words, and perhaps paradoxically, the existence of political or cultural pluralism inevitably raises the challenge of how to form and sustain unity and to treat all citizens equally (Kenny, 2004; Laden and Owen, 2007). For Chantal Mouffe (1993), the issue of pluralism – and how to ensure both the application of appropriate rules against which to measure claims to legitimacy by diverse social groups, and their inclusion in a more comprehensive and authoritative unity or commonality – is central to the viability of contemporary liberal democracy.

As will be shown later, in some schemes for strengthening or renewing democracy, learning helps to secure citizens' participation in the dimensions and institutions of democratic society, and their commitment to its values and practices, including the opportunity to develop the skills and habits of dialogue, deliberation and critical watchfulness. For some writers, it is partly through education and learning that citizens develop and refine their sense of 'civic virtue'. In some schemes for democracy, or for its extension or increased effectiveness, learning even features as a prerequisite: only those of a given level of educational attainment are accorded access to the full range of democratic rights and activities.

Autonomy, democracy and communication

Autonomy rests on people's opportunities for, and capability of, debating, deliberating, thinking critically, reflecting and deciding for themselves – all of them central to the tenets of liberal, independent and humane lifelong learning.

> *'Autonomy'… connotes the capacity of human beings to reason self-consciously, to be self-reflective, and to be self-determining. It involves the ability to act, in principle, as the author or maker of one's own life, in public and in private realms. (Held, 1995, p. 151)*

Much the same could be said, as Giddens (1991) suggests, of Habermas's attempt to develop a framework for emancipatory politics and discursive democracy in terms of a theory of communication. According to Habermas (1996), there are, broadly speaking, two spheres of political communication in which issues of autonomy may be both manifest and addressed. The first, which is informal, consists of all of those opportunities and interactions that constitute the vibrancy of civil society, and that are not designed principally for reaching decisions or have not been formally incorporated into the public processes and apparatus of politics. In these diverse arenas, people associate, express views and opinions, discuss, listen, make compromises and reach understanding with their fellow citizens. This is where, if civil society is working as it should, people can both express and expand their own versions of their autonomy as they form opinions and shape their own will. In contrast, formal milieux are where decisions are taken, policies are agreed, and rules and laws are enacted and promulgated in a range of governance arrangements – in local authorities and councils, in parties and representative assemblies, and in parliaments.

The overall political system of democracy is functioning well, according to Habermas, when the various topics discussed within the informal sphere are able to influence formal decision-making, and when the institutions of formal authority are open to the ideas and preoccupations of the informal, thereby enhancing the autonomy of citizens. In this interpretation, Habermas combines the insights of both liberal and civic republican theories of citizenship. The first underpins the individual and private domain of civil and human rights and a realm of autonomy within which individuals are free to reach their own conclusions and pursue their own interests, insofar as this does not inhibit the same freedoms for others. In the second, autonomy both consists in and derives from the public discourse of ideas, preferences and decision-making in which the public good is a product of an active and engaged citizenry. In this, 'popular sovereignty can be construed as the idea that the members of a political community are free to the extent that they can regard the laws that govern them as the expression of their own values' (Finlayson, 2005, p.111).

> *Popular sovereignty is not embodied in a collective subject, or a body politic on the model of an assembly of all citizens, it resides in 'subjectless' forms of communication and discourse circulating through forums and legislative bodies. (Habermas, 1996, p.136)*

Cohen and Arato also perceive in Habermas's theory of discourse ethics a possible route to overcoming the potential contradiction between the thrust towards universality and autonomy emanating from a rights-based conception of citizenship, on the one hand, with its emphasis on individualism, and the virtues of active participation, plurality and differentiation, on the other, that both characterise the civic republican tradition and may give rise to claims of social difference. These authors have in mind the possibility of establishing a universal 'regulative principle of a discursive process in and through which participants reason together about which values, principles, needs-interpretations merit being institutionalized as common norms' (Cohen and Arato, 1994, p.21). Such an approach, they suggest, would constitute actual rather than hypothetical or abstract dialogue, and would not require participants to abandon their concrete interests in order to engage in a shared testing of principles, but rather would encourage participants to express fully their interests during debate.

For Cohen and Arato, such a process would have the additional advantage of embedding in civil society significant elements of both private, individual rights, on the one hand, and associational, public involvement on the other that, together, would secure communicative action between individuals and groups in both the public and private spheres, independent of state control. Thus, Cohen and Arato (in common with a growing number of commentators) envisage more of a combination of, rather than opposition between, aspects of both liberal and civic republican traditions than previously deemed possible. This opens up the opportunity for suggesting a way forward for modern citizenship other than the false dichotomy between either seemingly increasing bureaucratic and paternalistic public interventions, or else the brutal predations of the marketplace. Needless to say, perhaps, there is plenty of scope for lifelong learning to help foster such deliberation and, in so doing, to engage with the multiple instances of civil society that are central to Cohen and Arato's vision for the future of democracy.

Learning can also increase the protagonists' own understanding of their situation, promoting what Paulo Freire calls their 'conscientisation'. This is a continuing and always unfinished and inherently dynamic learning process, 'a requirement of our human condition ... one of the roads we have to follow if we are to deepen our awareness of the world, of facts, of events, of the demands of human consciousness to develop our capacity for epistemological curiosity' (Freire, 1998, p.55).

Electoral politics

One of the principal contemporary manifestations of citizenship still resides in the right of individuals to vote in free elections for political parties and political representatives of their own choosing. The securing and extension of this right has often involved long and bitter struggles and, on its achievement, been the occasion for great celebration and the expectation of consequential changes and benefits, as instanced by the successful campaigns for women's political suffrage in this country and the defeat of apartheid in South Africa.

There has been much anxiety lately in the UK, at least before the 2010 general election, over an apparent decline in people's interest – especially young people's interest – in voting, in joining mainstream political parties and in electoral politics more generally. This is not only in respect of local government or European Union political representation, but also with regard to participation in general elections in the UK and other democracies. As a 16-country study of citizenship education put it, 'There is growing concern in many countries about the attitudes of young people and, in particular, with the signs of their increasing lack of interest and non-participation in public and political life' (Kerr, 1999, p.26).

Some commentators go so far as to suggest that, where there have been reductions in turn-out at elections, this is symptomatic of a deeper malaise in the body politic, of mistrust of politics and politicians, of cynicism regarding political processes, and a general pessimism about the prospects of ordinary citizens making any impact on the political decisions that affect them.

The study of political attitudes and behaviour by the Hansard Society (2008) provides limited evidence to support this pessimistic point of view, although the data reveal quite marked differences between age groups, between the regions and countries of Britain, and between ethnic groups. Overall, only just over half the population (53 per cent) were certain that they would vote in any immediate general election, but this proportion rose to 69 per cent among 55- to 64-year-olds and to 78 per cent among 65- to 74-year-olds; it fell to 23 per cent among the youngest group, the 18- to 24-year-olds. There were also marked differences between social classes: while 66 per cent of 'ABs' (senior managers and professionals) said that they would be certain to vote, only 34 per cent of 'DEs' (semi- and un-skilled) gave the same answer.

In the same study, 44 per cent of respondents surveyed claimed to know a great deal or a fair amount about politics, but only 16 per cent of 18- to 24-year-olds claimed this. By contrast, whereas only 12 per cent overall reported that they knew nothing at all about politics, the proportion among 18- to 24-year-olds rose to 29 per cent. Whereas people from social classes A and B claimed to know a great deal or fair amount about politics, only 20 per cent of those from classes D and E made the same claim.

Against these indicators of low levels of political interest and knowledge, particularly among young and working class British citizens, other signs suggested the position was mixed. On the Hansard Society's own simple measure of political activism (participating in three out of eight activities in the last two to three years), 12 per cent overall were deemed to be political activists, whilst 48 per cent reported taking part in none of the eight activities. (The eight political activities from which respondents had to choose were somewhat conventional.) On the other hand, 40 per cent reported that they had signed a petition, 19 per cent had boycotted a product for political, ethical or environmental reasons, 16 per cent had urged someone to contact their political representative, and 15 per cent had done so themselves. Almost one-third of respondents thought that, if people 'like themselves' got involved in politics, they could make a difference. Another survey confirmed that people from black and ethnic minority backgrounds were more likely than whites to think that they could make a difference both locally and nationally.

The European Commission's six-country project on education and training for active governance in Europe noted similar concerns in a range of European countries. The project made a plea for citizens to be actively re-engaged and equipped with the skills and capacities to become so.

> *Across Europe, there is clear evidence of declining engagement in traditional democratic processes, with governments, companies and other organisations considered to be remote, and insufficiently accountable to their stakeholders. Yet, it is also widely believed that globalisation calls for new, and more devolved kinds of political and social structure, in which individual citizens will play a more active part ...People need to be re-engaged as 'active citizens'... However, many people are both disengaged and lack the skills, knowledge or understanding to do so ...*
> *(Holford et al., 2003, p. 1)*

82

The project aimed to fill a gap in research evidence, exploring 'the potential role of lifelong learning, including less formal learning' in four domains of engagement in collective activity, namely the State and formal politics, the workplace, civil society, and the private domain. In the final report of the project, its senior authors conclude that, notwithstanding governments' recent increasing attention to the topic of lifelong learning, 'the potential of civil society as a site of learning is generally underestimated by governments'.

> *Learning of citizens in the domain of civil society appears to be under-resourced by comparison with similar learning in the workplace, and as a result, work to develop citizenship skills in civil society tends to be short term, less systematic and less sustainable. Those who suffer most from this are those who are already most vulnerable to social exclusion and least likely to become active citizens in any context. (ibid., p. 6)*

Active citizens, the same researchers report, 'usually learn their citizenship skills through trying to solve a problem or to fulfil a mission, rather than by setting out to "learn to be good citizens". Learning and citizenship itself emerge as a consequence of this primary motivation.' Consequently, learning needs to be embedded in these processes of problem-solving and engagement, combining the best of both formal and informal or non-formal learning, although the researchers conclude that this latter form of learning 'remains seriously under-researched, and the educators we interviewed were less confident about how to stimulate and support informal learning than formal and non-formal modes' (Holford et al., 2003, p.8).

Globalisation

For more than a decade now, perhaps the most striking arguments and most far-reaching implications for citizenship, people's sense of belonging and even lifelong learning have been those that centre on the phenomenon of globalisation. Yet again, this is an analytical perspective that excites much controversy and produces sharply conflicting interpretations of contemporary developments in politics, economics, technology and culture. Writing 15 years ago in a wide-ranging survey of the literature (which has since hugely increased), Waters observed that globalisation had already become 'the buzzword of the 1990s in the analysis of social change' (Waters, 1995, p.38).

As Sheila Croucher puts it, 'Globalization has thrust citizenship squarely into the spotlight. Citizenship now figures prominently on policy agendas and in political debates of countries around the world' (Croucher, 2004, p.79). What is clear, however, is that the notion of globalisation is not only contested and greatly different according to social, cultural and political context, but also that it is inherently dynamic: 'any predictions about its future configuration are necessarily speculative' (*ibid.*, p.80).

In both the scholarly literature on the subject and in more popular accounts there has been heated debate about the meaning, extent and impact of globalisation. For Roland Robertson, whom Waters credits with initiating the current discussion and the first serious deployment of the concept, globalisation can be epigrammatically summarised as 'both the *compression* of the world and the *intensification* of consciousness of the world as a whole' (Robertson, 1992, p.8, emphasis added). Similarly, Tony Giddens, in stressing the importance of the *local* dimensions of globalisation, observed that 'globalisation can thus be defined as the intensification of world-wide social relations which link distance locali-ties in such a way that local happenings are shaped by events occurring many miles away and vice-versa ... Local transformation is as much a part of globalisation as the lateral extension of social connections across time and space' (Giddens, 1990, p.64). In his analysis of the distinctiveness of globalisation, Giddens identifies three inter-related and mutually rein-forcing characteristics: time–space 'distanciation' (liberation from the tyrannies of time and space); the dis-embedding of social relations from their local context; and reflexivity – the constant flow of information and analysis which is utilised to revise and update social actions and social relations.

As Steger (2009) has pointed out, the term 'globalisation' is variously used to depict a process, a condition, a system, a force and an age. In any case, it seems sensible to differentiate between the various historical and social processes and changes that together may be deemed to add up to an overall shift to the new social condition that Steger prefers to denote as 'globality'. Different authors and protagonists describe the various dimensions and possible implications of globalisation in markedly differ-ent ways. As Steger has observed, 'scholars not only hold different views with regard to proper definitions of globalization, they also disagree on its scale, causation, chronology, impact, trajectories, and policy outcomes' (*ibid.*, p.11). For Martin Albrow, the 'global age' is differentiated from modernity by five key characteristics: the global environmental consequences of aggregate human activities; the loss of security, where weaponry has global destructiveness; the globality of communication systems; the rise of a global economy; and the reflexivity of globalism, where people and groups of all kinds refer to the globe as the frame for their beliefs (Albrow, 1996, p.4).

Summarising what they depict as the 'globalist' perspective, Held and McGrew identify a group of 'deep drivers' of the emergent processes of globalisation. The drivers are: 'the changing infrastructure of communications linked to the IT revolution; the expansionary logic of capitalism and the development of global markets in goods and services, connected to the worldwide distribution of information; the end of the Cold War, and the diffusion of democratic and consumer values across many of the world's regions ...; and the growth of migration and the movement of peoples, linked to shifts in patterns of economic demand, demography and environmental degradation' (Held and McGrew, 2007, p.9).

Most globalists agree that the phenomenon embraces an increasing tendency for once apparently secure boundaries and well established limitations – whether physical, legal, moral, economic or religious – to be ignored or effectively abolished by the contemporary forces of capital, trade, finance, brands, technology, travel, communications, population movement, pandemic infection, international terrorism, and changes in climate and ecology. The 'victims' of this, as portrayed in the more dystopian accounts of globalisation are: nation states, legislatures and other political or traditional religious authorities; the shared controls once exercised by federations, alliances and associations; and the customary influences and limitations of cultures, conventions and habitual ways of life (Held, 1995; Hobsbawm, 1997; Jarvis, 1997 and 2007; Stiglitz, 2002 and 2007; Held and McGrew, 2003 and 2007).

'At the turn of the millennium,' wrote Sheila Croucher, 'globalization is in full swing, yet in ways that bear witness to the continuing, and perhaps surprising, power and pervasiveness of identity and belonging' (Croucher, 2004, p.185). The contemporary impact of globalisation, she avers, gives both urgency and a decisively new set of twists to debates about the formation and expression of identity and belonging, as people's material, cultural, political and psychological circumstances alter, often in ways that are beyond their immediate understanding or control. Once more, however, although globalisation's effects are to be observed around the world, its precise manifestations in terms of identity, belonging and the meanings of citizenship still vary considerably: 'it must and does work through, with, and around an array of distinct local, state, and regional contexts – all of which shape and reshape the otherwise uniform patterns and processes of globalization in particular ways' (*ibid.*, p.186). Paradoxically, 'many of the aspects of globalization that tear at the very fabric of citizenship simultaneously raise the stakes of having access to it or not', as globalisation results in a heightened sense of insecurity on behalf of individuals, communities and even whole nation states (*ibid.*, p.80).

Many critical observers regard such developments with a mixture of horror and awe. Only a limited number of winners can thrive: international and transnational corporations in search of ever cheaper production and continually expanding and novel markets, and deracinated individuals who cheerfully shed attachments and loyalties in order to relish their alignment with nothing other than their own self-interest and the satisfaction of their appetites. At the same time, this is a world in which decisions affecting all aspects of people's lives are taken by remote and seemingly unaccountable authorities, and with little reference to local needs.

For some critics, especially those on the political left or of a Marxist persuasion, the current concern with globalisation is only the most recent version of capitalism's tendency towards ever-wider realms of exploitation and appropriation, including the transcendence or destruction of all boundaries which threaten to frustrate its ruthless, expansionist thrust, whether these be social, cultural, political, economic, material, spiritual or physical.

> *Capitalism is a novel mode of life (or culture) whose novelty consists in its necessarily totalizing expansionary dynamic. This dynamic is necessary because capitalism is governed by the law of value, or it requires the production of objects which are both exchangeable and useable. This requirement has now resulted in the constitution of the globe as a totality, or, as one division of labour consisting in a contradictory unity of diverse, spatio-temporally separated parts. It is contradictory in the sense that these necessary parts tend to 'forget' their place and function in the totality, thereby generating crises of various kinds. (Dean, 2003, pp. 42 and 43)*

In such a world, education becomes a key site of struggle between the forces of capital and the State that seek to train labour to adapt to the skills needs and drive for flexibility required by global capitalism, including labour migration, and those that seek to make workers more fully aware of their exploitation and the possibilities of challenge and eventual emancipation (Burbules and Torres, 2000).

Risk and uncertainty

Ulrich Beck characterises the changing world of globalisation as the emergence of 'risk society' (Beck, 1992, 1997, 1998, 1999 and 2000). This is a world in which uncertainty, unpredictability and the threat of un-sustainability are the dominant features. In what Beck terms a 'political economy' of risk, 'an ever larger number of men and women are compelled to treat the future as a threat, rather than as a shelter or a promised land'. At the centre of the new power-play tussles between 'territorially fixed *political* actors (government, parliament, unions) and non-territorial *economic* actors (representatives of capital, finance, trade)', what stands out most starkly and simply is that 'capital is global, work is local'.

> *All around the world, at the same time, fragile work increases rapidly, that is part-time, self-employed work, limited-term jobs and other forms for which we have barely found descriptions. If this dynamic continues, in ten to fifteen years about half the employable population of the West will work under conditions of uncertainty. What used to be the exception is becoming the rule. (Beck, 1999, p. 11)*

Zygmunt Bauman (1997, 2001, 2002, 2005 and 2007) stresses what he calls the increasingly 'liquid' nature of the late-modern globalising world, with its essentially transient solidities and unreliable certainties for people's status, relationships, experiences and identities. His pessimistic account of emerging society stresses not just its inherent volatility and characteristic unpredictability, but also the fatal risks that individuals or whole communities run by investing too much hope in their skills, careers or rights.

> *No jobs are guaranteed, no positions are foolproof, no skills are of lasting utility, experience and know-how turn into liability as soon as they become assets, seductive careers all too often prove to be suicide tracks. In their present rendering, human rights do not entail the acquisition of a right to a job, however well performed, or – more generally – the right to*

87

care and consideration for the sake of past merits. Livelihood, social position, acknowledgement of usefulness and the entitlement to self-dignity may all vanish together, overnight and without notice. (Bauman, 1997, p.22 and 2001, p.86)

In these circumstances, people risk losing their 'anchor points in the lifeworld' and, buffeted by life's vicissitudes and events over which they feel they can exercise no control, there is a danger for them that 'the loss of meaning, the erosion of solidarity and moral uncertainty produce various psycho-pathologies in personality formation'. The resulting confusions lead those affected to 'thrash around rather desperately to make sense of their everyday troubles, suffering, problems, let alone figuring out why the world beyond the vulnerable self seems so dangerous and risky' (Welton, 2005, p.186).

Winners and losers

Edward Luttwak, once consultant to the United States Office of the Secretary of Defense and State Department, has depicted the new world of globalisation as being driven by 'turbo-capitalism', which benefits a small global elite, but requires most to adapt to constant change or suffer the consequences. In what Luttwak judges to be a kind of disruptive turbulence at odds with normal human behaviour – 'a fantastical departure from normal human proclivities' – individuals should, ideally, 're-examine their options twice a day, to decide whether to remain in the same trade, profession or job, or promptly switch to whatever alternative offers higher rewards, perhaps in a different locality, country or continent' Luttwak, 1999, p.223). Although supporters of turbo-capitalism prefer to describe it simply as the effective operation of the free market, they agree its defining characteristics with Luttwak.

What they celebrate, preach and demand is free enterprise liberated from government regulation, unchecked by effective trade unions, unfettered by sentimental concerns over the fate of employees or communities, unrestrained by customs barriers or investment restrictions and unmolested as little as possible by taxation. (ibid., p.27)

What these free-wheeling, globally oriented, free-marketeers demand is 'the privatization of state-owned businesses of all kinds, and the conversion of public institutions, from universities and botanical gardens to prisons, from libraries and schools to old people's homes, into private enterprises run for profit' (*ibid.*, p.27). In addition to entailing the rapid and 'creative' destruction of jobs, whole industries and communities, turbo-capitalism also results in a serious 'loss of individual authenticity' and widespread de-personalisation of human relations, including the adoption by its leading advocates (including supporting politicians) of routine manipulations and deceits, consisting of 'meretricious images in place of substance – indeed, as substance' (*ibid.*, p.224).

The emergent world, depicted by Luttwak, is one in which individuals are both required to shape their own identities – with all that such a destiny promises by way of self-actualisation, excitement and discovery, free from the restrictions of ascribed status and inherited position – and, at the same time, to understand that everything encountered and every relationship entered into has a provisional, transient character. The ensuing globalising world of threatened chaos, while probably invigorating for a minority, condemns most to a persistent state of worry in which they are comforted only by the weasel reassurances of advertising, consumption and the illusion of choice (Bauman, 2001). Nobody dare invest any part of their experience, any skill or any partnership with any sort of commitment or expectation of continuity, lest all be swept away by events beyond their control. Endemic precariousness of this kind – what Bauman depicts as a 'kaleidoscopic world of reshuffled values, of moving tracks and melting frames' – breeds anxiety and fear, and yet demands of individuals a willingness to submit entirely to the insistent but unpredictable *zeitgeist* of the age: flexibility.

> *Rational conduct in such a world demands that the options, as many as possible, are kept open, and gaining an identity which fits too tightly, an identity that offers once and for all 'sameness' and 'continuity', results in the closing of options or forfeiting them in advance.* (ibid., p.148)

Some commentators, seeking to provide a more 'balanced' and perhaps tentative account, perceive a mixture of plusses and minuses in this emergent world. In itself, they suggest, globalisation is neither wholly good nor wholly bad. On the positive side, they welcome the breaking of some of the old boundaries and commend the breaching of traditional restrictions. At the same time, they urge caution where the loss of old certainties seems to render futile all planning for the future, whether at the level of the individual, family, business, community, country or even – at worst – all of humanity.

Others take a quite different line. Some say, first, that the processes of globalisation are by no means as recent as is commonly supposed – they can be traced as far back as medieval Europe (Robertson, 1992). Others suggest that the trends identified are much exaggerated, far from universal, do not necessarily all tend in the same direction, or are not wholly disadvantageous or damaging. Rather, they say, aspects of globalisation open up exciting opportunities for people to access new ways of thinking, working, living, consuming, communicating, linking, participating and influencing in the world, and, at the same time, enlarge their fields of pleasure and enjoyment.

Doubters

Among those who doubt the validity of claims and assertions announcing the (impending) triumph of globalisation – globalism sceptics or deniers – are commentators who point to the continued importance of nation states, the watchful maintenance of the security of their borders, the pursuit of their independent foreign policies, and their distinctive national political cultures, heightened since the events of 9/11. 'Sceptics argue that it (globalisation) has been oversold in at least three senses: as a description of social reality, as an explanation of social change and as an ideology of social progress (a political project)' (Held and McGrew, 2007, p.7). In particular, argue those who doubt the irresistible march of globalism, there is scant evidence of independent nation states being willing to forego their monopoly of legitimate violence internally or of the external use of military violence against designated foes (Hirst, 2001; Rosenberg, 2005; Held and McGrew, 2007, Chapter 4).

Act locally

Much of the debate about the effects of globalisation centres on the shifting contours of politics and the consequent potential weakening of democracy threatened by its alleged demarche. National governments appear to be increasingly unable to subject affairs wholly to their own sovereign control, or even their influence (Held, 1995; Stiglitz, 2007; Reich, 2008). Against this, there are countervailing forces and powerful ideologies driving an increased focus on the *local* as an arena of relevance, identity and action in globalising society, captured in the popular slogan 'think global, act local', as likely to be the watchword of the marketing departments of global corporations as the talisman for environmental campaigners[12] (Kraemer and Roberts, 1996; Cantle, 2008). Kellner, writing of the implications of a globalisation that is inflected by neo-liberalism, with its emphasis on dismantling aspects of the welfare state, and liberalising markets for finance, trade and labour, also looks to local action from new social movements to serve as a counter-tendency.

> *In opposition to the globalization from above of corporate capitalism, I would advocate a globalization from below, which supports individuals and social groups in struggle using the new technologies to create a more egalitarian and democratic society … This requires teaching new literacies such as media and computer literacy, as well as helping to empower students and citizens to deploy new technologies for progressive purposes.*
> *(Kellner, 2000, p.316)*

Thus, in 2003, the Scottish Executive published a community development policy document entitled *Think Global, Act Local,* aimed at promoting international education through community learning and development. Not all commentators agree that the most effective and meaningful milieu for action is local. Joseph Stiglitz, formerly of the World Bank, takes the opposite view: 'to make globalization work there will have to be a change of mindset: we will have to think *and act* more globally' (Stiglitz, 2007, p.278, emphasis added).

There are, potentially, far-reaching implications for the rights, obligations and focus of citizenship, and for the prospects of fostering any shared sense of belonging or loyalty, whether through learning or otherwise. For some, globalisation simply renders older forms and expressions of citizenship and belonging inappropriate, or at least less potent and less likely to give people a sense of who they are and how they might best affect the circumstances of their lives. At the very least, with the growth of internationalisation, trans-nationalism and globalisation, and with the often-associated increasing incidence of people moving across borders for business or pleasure, the assumption of a likely coincidence of place, citizenship, identity and sense of belonging is no longer safe.

---

12 There are many claimed origins of the slogan. For example, it is said to have been coined in 1969 by David Brower at the foundation of Friends of the Earth.

Radical and cosmopolitan citizenship

For some authors, the challenges of differentiation, calls for separate recognition, different levels and sites of attachment and identification, and of trying to reconcile the demands of particularism with universality all suggest adopting in response one of two related approaches to contemporary citizenship, considered at some length by Delanty (2000), or even a combination of them. These are *radical citizenship* and *cosmopolitanism*.

Radical citizenship is located neither entirely within the State nor within a largely depoliticised notion of civil society. Rather it is about the articulation of problems around matters of 'voice, difference and justice', in which radical democratic participation becomes 'an identity politics, a politics of enhancing a society's capacity for communication and dialogue' (*ibid.*, p.46). This approach conceives of modern citizenship as a kind of emergent process towards transformation rather than simply a settled status, and owes something to Habermas's later theory of communications and discursive democracy, itself based on informed public debate and responsive to an active citizenry. 'Only after the public "struggle for recognition" can the contested interest positions be taken up by the responsible political authorities, put on the parliamentary agenda and, if need be, worked into legislative proposals and binding decisions' (Habermas, 1996, p.314, cited in Delanty, 2000, p.42).

For Chantal Mouffe, establishing the possibilities of radical democracy 'needs an idea of liberty that transcends the false dilemma between the liberty of the ancients and the moderns and allows us to think individual liberty and political liberty together' (Mouffe, 1993, p.19). Rejecting what she sees as the inevitable individualism of classical liberal theory and its assumption that differences can be resolved by the application of rationality in the forging of consensus, and drawing on a mixture of ideas from Machiavelli, the branch of civic republican communitarianism associated with the writings of Charles Taylor and Michael Walzer, the ideas of political philosopher Quentin Skinner, and the insights of post-modernism, Mouffe sets out to delineate a 'new political philosophy' of radical democracy. This is an approach to democracy that can encompass a multiplicity of contemporary struggles for recognition and will require that a number of conditions be met that go beyond 'establishing a mere alliance between given interests but of actually modifying the very identity of these forces'. Hence, the aim of radical politics, according to Mouffe, will be to construct a different formation of the 'we' that always

92

inheres in the notion of citizenship; a 'conception of citizenship which, through a common identification with a radical democratic interpretation of the principles of liberty and equality', to establish, the new 'we'. This would be based on a 'chain of equivalence' whereby the various demands and struggles of different groups created a new articulation between them that would open up innovative forms of citizenship and what may constitute 'the good life' – 'a common political identity of persons who might be engaged in many different purposive enterprises and differing conceptions of the good' (*ibid.*, p.70).

In what she denotes as the new '*respublica*' of radical politic*s*, citizens would still need to submit to common rules governing the *manner* of seeking their goals, and would also be bound together by 'common recognition of a set of ethico-political values' (*ibid.*, p.69). So, while she accepts that it is important 'to recover notions of civic virtue, public-spiritedness, common good and political community', Mouffe rejects the idea that this can be achieved by the application of 'neutral' procedures in which the citizen figures as a kind of political consumer acting under the supposed neutrality of the State. Instead, she calls for the debate around such central and substantive features of political democracy to be reformulated in ways that both render them compatible with the defence of individual liberty and with 'the ethics of the political. By that, I understand the type of interrogation which is concerned with the normative aspects of politics, the values that can be realized through collective action and through common belonging to a political association' (*ibid.*, p.113). What this would mean in radical politics is the 'political creation of a unity through common *identification* with a particular interpretation of its political principles, a specific understanding of citizenship' (*ibid.*, p.115, emphasis in original).

For Mouffe, the construction of such politics with its potential for a diversity of conceptions of the good life, and the prospect of a radical conception of citizenship – building on, but markedly different from, both liberal and civic republican ideals, and going beyond them – will also render it 'indispensible to develop a theory of the subject as a decentred, totalizing agent, a subject constructed at the point of intersection of a multiplicity of subject positions between which there exists no *a priori* or necessary relation' (*ibid.*, p.12). To some extent, this will entail challenging some of the assumptions inherent in the Enlightenment's conception of democratic universalism. This is necessary, she suggests, in order for the new radical politics to be able to encompass 'the particular, the multiple, the heterogeneous – in effect, everything that had been excluded by the concept of Man in the abstract', thus forging a new articulation between the universal and the particular (*ibid.*, p.13).

All of this means that, in the sort of radical political communities envisaged by Mouffe, there is always likely to be an element of matters being unfinished and never finally resolved. But this is both unavoidable in modern pluralistic and radical politics and a reason for celebration. 'It is this aspect of non-achievement, incompleteness and openness that makes such a regime particularly suited to modern democratic politics' (*ibid.*, p.110).

By contrast, the notion of cosmopolitan citizenship is concerned with neither the geographically defined nation state nor with the various struggles for recognition beneath the State. Cosmopolitan citizenship, according to Delanty, is driven by four main trends: internationalisation, trans-nationalism, globalisation and post-nationalism. In the theory of cosmopolitan citizenship, people would be 'citizens of their immediate political communities, and of the wider regional and global networks which impacted on their lives. This cosmopolitan polity would be one that in form and substance reflected and embraced the diverse forms of power and authority within and across borders ...' (Held, 1995, p.233). There exists a variety of means and milieux in which citizens who adopt a cosmopolitan perspective can engage. Citizens may engage through their involvement in, and frequently critique of, those cultural movements and influences that increasingly bear little relation to any particular nation state, political establishment or geographical area.

Instead, cosmopolitanism finds expression in citizens' engagement with global issues that transcend traditional boundaries and have implications for the whole of human kind, such as ecology, climate change, environmental degradation and nuclear politics. Cosmopolitanism also inclines citizens to focus on current and emergent elements of world governance, in both formal and official institutions such as the United Nations, World Bank, International Monetary Fund or European Union, and in the many non-governmental organisations and informal networks concerned with matters that extend beyond the boundaries of particular countries, for example work around the relief from sudden famine, actions to lessen the impact of natural or man-made disasters, alliances to counteract the trafficking of women or children, campaigns to reduce poverty, and, indeed, movements to challenge the processes of globalisation itself.

Needless to say, these manifestations of radical and cosmopolitan citizenship constitute quite different notions of contemporary citizenship and provide quite different bases for people's identities and their sense of belonging. Usually, a cosmopolitan outlook entails people regarding themselves as 'citizens of the world' with a primary orientation towards the needs of human beings in the world at large, irrespective of nationality, especially those deemed to be suffering from the damaging effects of globalisation. Similarly, the sorts of lifelong learning entailed in such orientations also usually reflect these global agendas in terms of content, objectives, pedagogy and modes of operation. In particular, varieties of cosmopolitanism encompass a great deal of non-formal and informal learning and recognise especially the value of learning through practice.

Echoing Hamlet's agonising self-questioning, Beck has suggested that, in a world where local and national affiliations increasingly count for less in determining people's life chances, 'to belong or not to belong, that is the cosmopolitan question' (Beck, 2003, p.45, cited in Calhoun, 2007). However, as Benhabib insists, these are not necessarily antithetical orientations: cosmopolitan citizenship for most people without some anchorage in more local, meaningful involvement would be an empty aspiration, if not a fantasy. 'A global civilization that is to be shared by world citizens will need to be nourished by local attachments; rich cultural debate; contestations about the identity of the "we"; and a sense of democratic experimentation with institutional design and redesign' (Benhabib, 2002, p.184). In this, citizens would, argues Delanty (2000, p.140), have 'multiple alliances and identities' and, for Held, cosmopolitan democracy would also entail the radical democratic reform of existing international institutions and the creation of new ones to facilitate participation by the citizenry.

Care needs to be taken not to assume that the opportunities for developing or expressing a cosmopolitan mentality are equally open to everyone. Nor is cosmopolitanism always regarded as a benign ideal to be striven for by all. First, some groups, or even nation states, demand such commitment and conformity that any individual attempts to transcend their boundaries are strictly limited. Similarly, some individuals or groups will, by the very circumstances and context of their lives, lack the power and resources to become cosmopolitan citizens or to contribute to the activities of transnational or cosmopolitan institutions. Such people may draw strength or confidence from the solidarity of a group identity which then denies them the chance of expressing cosmopolitanism.

> *Many advocates of liberal cosmopolitanism treat nationalism, religion, and at least strong versions of ethnicity as the 'bad others' to cosmopolitanism. They neglect social solidarity in favour of analyses framed in terms of individuals and the universal, and they underestimate the implications of inequality – including the inequality that empowers some to approach the world effectively as individuals, neglecting the social bases of their own efficacy, while others are all too aware of the limits of their individual capacity and are clearly in need of collective support in relation to the challenges the world throws at them. (Calhoun, 2007, p.287)*

Finally, there is the accusation that those who speak loudest of the possibilities of cosmopolitan citizenship do so in tongues that have a decidedly European and white inflection. They are thus said to be influenced more by the traditions of Western conceptions of democracy and civic engagement than truly reflecting the quite novel demands of responding to the challenges and depredations of contemporary globalisation. In the eyes of these critics, cosmopolitan citizenship calls for innovative forms of organisation, ideology and mobilisation.

The decline of 'territoriality'

Chief among the alleged erosions of citizenship-as-belonging is the suggestion of an apparent declining significance of territoriality as a principal basis for belonging. This is associated with the fragmentation of once-dominant centres of authority and affiliation and increased migration of people and frequent movement of individuals, finance and information across borders as a normal part of contemporary life. Possible consequences include reductions in the different rights accorded to citizens and non-citizens in certain jurisdictions, and the growth of virtual communities.

Alongside such alleged weakening of attachments to a given state, the increased openness of borders, especially the opening up of migration within the European Union, has resulted in the arrival of large numbers of people in search of work in the UK. This has raised anxieties among some in the UK about possible increased demands on schools and social services, and the availability of housing, and downward pressure on wages for the occupations that migrants are willing to fill. There are calls for restricting the rights of migrants in the UK and not opening to them all of the rights that European Union membership usually entails. As Spellman (2008, p.211) observes, 'as long as poor migrants are viewed as taking more from the state than they contribute through taxes, native opposition to more generous admission policies, even where labour needs are acute, will remain strong'.

Concerns about national security or enhanced fears of 'foreign' hostile influences, especially in times of international terrorism, have also led to a narrowing and strengthening of the definition of citizenship, with people, especially 'newcomers', wanting to demonstrate that they are committed 'insiders' and not strangers inciting antipathy. In such circumstances, states and existing citizens are more likely to guard admission to citizenship with increased vigilance, requiring applicants to pass stringent tests with specified programmes of learning.

Benhabib notes with alarm that some of the apparent trajectories of an increasingly globalising world are at odds with democratic citizenship with its necessary concomitants of direct engagement, commitment, accountability and a deepening of attachments. In such circumstances, Benhabib believes that the hope for the emergence of a kind of global electronic citizenship operating through the Internet is illusory.

> *We are facing the genuine risk that the worldwide movement of people and commodities, news and information will create a permanent flow of individuals without commitments, industries without liabilities, news without a public conscience, and the dissemination of information without a sense of boundaries and discretion. In this 'global.com civilization', persons will shrink into e-mail addresses in space, and their political and cultural lives will proliferate extensively into the electronic universe, while their temporal attachments will be short-lived, shifting and superficial.*
> (Benhabib, 2002, p. 182)

Not all commentators share this pessimistic view. Croucher, for example, suggests that 'as a result of political globalization greater opportunities exist for people to participate in an emerging "global civil society" – a dense network of social movements and interest groups who organize and mobilize across and outside states' (Croucher, 2004, p.194). This sharing of concern and action in relation to issues that cut across traditional national boundaries and which require concerted action by engaged citizens in many parts of the world – in the name of a common 'humanity' and transcending narrower affiliations – is increasingly facilitated not just by a global mentality, but also by modern and often quite cheap and easily accessible technologies. (See also Mayo, 2005.)

Some challenges, argues Croucher (2004, p.59), emanate principally from 'below' or 'within', especially 'multiculturalism and the various related forms of identity-based social movements', some of them taking the form of local rather than regional or national responses to the perceived impact of global forces. Such initiatives Croucher calls 'sub-groupism', often linked specifically and deliberately to self-organised programmes of lifelong learning, in part aimed at strengthening the group's own sense of purpose and its members' sense of belonging.

> *The real and potential challenges of subgroupism to citizenship are multifold and affect not only its practice, but also our theoretical understandings of what it means. Localism entails demands for the devolution and decentralization of state power and control. In this regard, the state loses its privileged position as a primary site, referent or coordinator of belonging. (ibid., p.59)*

Against the traditional rights and affiliations of citizenship, based on the assertion of commonality, universality and formal equality, the State now faces a variety of claims for the recognition of distinctive cultural identities and practice which may clash with the established ways of life of the host or majority population. In such circumstances, not only is it difficult for the State to mobilise a singular sense of belonging – even with a determined education programme and the introduction of common rites and rituals – but also the traditional assumptions of citizenship, claiming to transcend inherently divisive matters of sex, race, ethnicity, creed, or culture, now need revision. Thus, 'the sacred bond between states and citizens has weakened as the former find their power and autonomy shrinking and the latter find their options for and capacity to pursue rights elsewhere are enhanced' (*ibid.*, p.61).

Although the so-called 'sacred bond' between individual states and citizenship may have been attenuated by the forces of globalisation and by options and the capacity for citizens to pursue their collective interests beyond the traditional confines of their home state, people still appear to need some sort of home base. Global citizenship, it seems, needs still to be rooted firmly in local and national opportunities for citizens' participation (Mayo, 2005). The prospect of global citizenship, extending a shared sense of identity, rights and duties beyond the limited boundaries of individual nation states, depends first upon 'strong' versions of citizenship and democracy (Barber, 1984 and 2004; Croucher, 2004). 'A global civilization that is to be shared by world citizens will need to be nourished by local attachments; rich cultural debates; contestations about the identity of the "we"; and a sense of democratic experimentation with institutional design and redesign' (Benhabib, 2002, p.184).

State, nation and identity

In line with the broad principles of the 'Westphalian' model of modern statehood, over the past two centuries or so, individual governments acted as if they took for granted that they had it in their power, through their control over the machinery of the State, to regulate the principal conditions pertaining to people's legal status, rights, loyalties, incomes and life chances. They assumed, too, that the main organisations and chief institutions in which people lived out their lives could similarly be shaped and protected according to the will of autonomous governments. These experiences were also expected to constitute a shared sense of history, place and culture – a common identity and sense of belonging.

What the new conditions appear to open up, to those with globalist perspective, is the possibility that people and organisations, cultures and identities, social relations and the centres of loyalty and belonging will no longer be determined principally by where people are born, earn their living or generally live out their lives. In a more heterogeneous world of movement, of increasing diversity and choice in lifestyle, affiliations and beliefs, not only can people as a whole manifest a similar heterogeneity of identity and of sense of belonging, but, as we have seen, individuals may also exist with a multiplicity of identities. To a greater or lesser degree, these different identities reflect the importance people attach to their various ethnicities, faiths, communities, sources of income, patterns of consumption, sites and sources of pleasure, sexual orientations, or the significance inscribed in their gender, religion, clan or provenance.

Where the UK is concerned, domestic constitutional change has added to, or maybe even reflected in to some extent, shifts in people's identity, sense of belonging and attachments. The two principal forms which these changes have taken are membership of the European Union, especially with some of its legal and administrative consequences, and the devolution of important elements of government to the constituent countries and territories of the UK.

It is scarcely surprising in these circumstances that governments and different groups of people look to learning to explain or reinforce their declarations and actions. Thus, for example in the UK, former Attorney General Lord Goldsmith published in 2008 a comprehensive review of British citizenship, *Citizenship: Our Common Bond,* which covers not just the various dimensions of the law and administration that regulate citizenship, but also a range of initiatives designed to construct what he calls 'a framework for belonging'. The aim, Goldsmith argued, should be the creation of a 'shared narrative about citizenship which threads through very many different aspects of our lives and our lives together', which recognises the importance of participation in civic activities. The review argued that a key part of that framework should continue to be provided by education. A revised schools' curriculum was introduced in September 2008 that focused on three broad subject areas: democracy and justice; rights and responsibilities: and diversity and identities (Goldsmith, 2008, p.89).

Research undertaken by MORI for the BBC and by Heath and Roberts for the Goldsmith (2008) review of citizenship demonstrates how citizens' sense of identification and of belonging both change over time and vary between different groups within the UK, and that some anxieties about the implications of population change are exaggerated. In contradiction to concerns that large numbers of people living in Britain – especially those either born in other countries, or with parents from other countries, or adhering to other religions such as Islam – currently demonstrate little or no attachment to this country, overall reported levels of belonging are high.

In the survey undertaken by MORI for the BBC in 2005, three-fifths of Muslims responding agreed that 'people who come to Britain should be free to live their lives by the values and traditions of their own culture'. There were no significant differences between their views and those of the national sample as a whole supporting immigrants who become British citizens being required to learn English (90 per cent Muslim, 82 per cent national), to pledge their primary loyalty to Britain (76 per cent Muslim, 73 per cent national) and swear allegiance to the national flag (55 per cent Muslim, 50 per cent national). There were similarities, too, between the two sets of respondents regarding requiring immigrants who become British citizens to accept the authority of British institutions (91 per cent Muslim, 93 per cent national) and integrate fully into British society (69 per cent Muslim, 73 per cent national). Similar proportions of the Muslim and national samples also believed, given the threat to Britain from terrorism, that either ethnic communities should be encouraged to integrate more with white British communities (43 per cent Muslim, 45 per cent national) or that greater tolerance should be encouraged between different ethnic communities (49 per cent Muslim, 50 per cent national) (BBC/Mori, 2005).

People in Britain also have changing images of themselves as far as being English, Welsh or Scottish is concerned, rather than British as such. For example, 61 per cent of those surveyed in Scotland in 1997 in research by Heath and Roberts saw themselves as entirely, or more inclined to be, Scottish, and by 2005 that had increased slightly to 64 per cent. The proportion in Scotland seeing themselves as both Scottish and British in 1997 was 27 per cent, and that had fallen to 22 per cent by 2005. In Wales, 42 per cent in 2005 described themselves as exclusively, or more inclined to regard themselves as, Welsh, and that rose to 44 per cent in 2005; those opting for joint Welsh/British identity rose from 26 per cent to 32 per cent, and those inclined to Britishness alone declined from 25 per cent to 18 per cent (Heath and Roberts, 2008, p.7).

When Heath and Roberts examined the attitudes of different age groups, especially when combined with ethnicity, some further striking differences were evident, with age appearing to be the 'strongest driver of belonging to Britain'. While about 40 per cent of those aged under 35 described themselves as feeling 'very strongly' that they belong to Britain, the proportion rose to 64 per cent in the 65- to 74-year-old age group and to 73 per cent among the over 75s. There were even more marked differences of attitude between young people from different ethnic backgrounds who expressed a weak sense of belonging to Britain. Whereas only 16 per cent of white and Indian 16- to 24-year-olds and 17 per cent of Pakistani or Bangladeshi ethnicity indicated a weak sense of belonging, among young people from Afro-Caribbean backgrounds the figure rose to 40 per cent.

Information and knowledge

An often associated feature of increasing globalisation is the claimed growing influence and apparent exponential expansion of the role of information and knowledge. Some observers and policy makers go so far as to declare that we are now witnessing the emergence of the 'information society' or even 'knowledge-driven' society.

The character, diffusion and uses of this knowledge, and of who has access to it or control over it, are the very stuff of citizenship and of politics more generally. Information and knowledge also matter in the ways in which people claim, defend or advance their various identities and interpret their different senses of belonging. Some observers see, in the widening opportunities offered by innovation in information and communications technology and the Internet, exciting possibilities for the 'democratisation' of information and knowledge. Others, more pessimistically, discern increasing tendencies for powerful individuals and organisations to shape and restrict information in ways intended only to advance their own interests. What is more, critics dismiss claims that social networking websites provide valuable opportunities for virtual interaction. Critics say that excessive use of the Web fragments collective life and isolates individuals from regular face-to-face encounters – precisely the human exchange that constitutes the lifeblood of participative citizenship and enables the rich expression of identity and belonging.

Information and knowledge, and the different functions they fulfil in contemporary society, are core concerns for those people devising strategies for lifelong learning and/or its delivery, and for professionals who are involved in its teaching, research and scholarship. If there is any validity in the claims that the production, distribution and application of knowledge and information are increasingly the defining features of the contemporary world, and that those who are able to exercise some control over their deployment can thereby increase their power and influence over events and over those lacking such resources, then debates about the information society go to the heart of citizenship and to considerations of the communicative sources of people's identities and their expressions of belonging (Castells, 1997). In particular, the threat of the monopolisation of information production and the potential narrowing of the meaning and focus given to information leads critics to doubt the inherent virtue of a future which is information saturated.

Not all commentators are convinced that the contemporary world can be distinguished from earlier eras by the salience of information, nor even that access to, and use of, information is the predominant source of power and either a threat to people's freedom or the key to unlocking its vast potential. Thus, for example, Webster suggests that a first task is to distinguish between five quite different usages of the notion of an 'information society': technological, economical, occupational, spatial and cultural. Confusion between these different perspectives on human society in the twenty-first century is likely to lead both to mistaken analyses of the implications and to the wrong strategies for dealing with them, including where education and learning and their effects on citizenship and belonging are concerned (Webster, 1995). Webster doubts the validity of a sharp division between, for example, work that is defined by the centrality of information and knowledge and that which is not. In any case, cautions the historian Peter Burke, observers should 'not be too quick to assume that our age is the first to take these issues seriously'.

> *The commodification of information is as old as capitalism. The use by governments of systematically collected information is, quite literally, ancient history (ancient Roman and Chinese history in particular). As for scepticism about claims to knowledge, it goes back at least as far as the ancient Greek philosopher Pyrrho of Elis. (Burke, 2000, pp. 1–2, cited in Welton, 2005, p. 62)*

In an enlightening, critical and cautiously optimistic review of some of the principal contemporary writers on the implications for citizenship of this explosion and increasing significance of information and knowledge, Michael Welton has indicated that the burning questions for adult educators are 'what do we mean by active citizenship in the information age' and 'what ought we be able to know and do to perform our citizen roles in the global, networked era?' (Welton, 2005, p.151). For Welton, although there is little doubt that we are living in a period that is information rich and 'media saturated in ways previously unknown to humankind', there is great danger in simply celebrating uncritically the dawning of an information age; above all, such a response tells us 'little about whether we as citizens are, in fact, becoming more knowledgeable and skilled in the managing of our personal affairs' (*ibid.*, p.65). This is crucial for Welton in his quest for a 'just learning society'.

Different kinds of knowledge

While Welton suspects that 'the actually existing information age, or information society, privileges resolutely a calculating, quantitative mentality amongst its participants and theorists' where 'to know is to have access to more bits of information' and hence power, the task for educators is first to distinguish between different kinds of knowledge, the use of knowledge and its relation to society's operations, including its structures of status and power (*ibid.*, p.69). In this, he commends Stephen Toulmin's analysis, after Aristotle, of the markedly differential value that

Western society has afforded to four distinct types of knowledge: *episteme* (embracing the intellectual and abstract 'high ground', such as pure mathematics)*, techne* (concerned more with the mastery of dealing with and solving practical problems; and the skill of making things), *phronesis* (the ability to consider and know how to put knowledge and techniques into action to achieve given ends, sometimes thought of as 'practical wisdom' of the sort gained best through experience) and *sophia* (the more philosophical and systematic search for, and love of, knowledge – often even for its own sake – resulting in a deeper kind of wisdom, or truth).

Welton concludes his stimulating review of the implications of the information age for citizenship by suggesting that, by applying this kind of Aristotelian clarification to different *kinds* of knowledge, we can begin to understand better how different societies 'actually function to increase our scientific literacy, enlarge the possibilities of technical mastery in all dimensions of our lives, nurture practical wisdom in our deliberations with each other, and increase our collective wisdom'. Increased wisdom, he argues, 'emerges from the considered interplay of the three primary modes of knowing'. Welton insists that 'it is inconceivable, for example, that our species could solve the problem of holes in the ozone layer without the products of scientific thought and technology' (*ibid.*, p.71), nor, one might add, without the development and application to such an urgent challenge for the whole of human kind of a thoughtful and critical 'moral economy'.

CHAPTER SIX

Social change, community and social solidarity

Changing Britain

Over the past 40 years or so, as an integral aspect of globalisation, but also sometimes independent of it, the UK has been experiencing widespread and profound changes in people's social, economic, political and cultural circumstances and experiences. These changes include often quite marked shifts in family forms and roles, in education and training, in the jobs that people do, in the industries they work in and where they live, in patterns of communication and consumption, in travel and leisure, in social and geographic mobility, and in the claims for and expressions of different identities, cultures and ways of life (Beck, 1992; Bauman, 2001 and 2007; Ferri *et al.*, 2003; Fryer, 2008).

One particularly salient feature of those social changes has been the decline or disappearance of some of the traditional foundations of community, and the erosion of some of the once-dominant primary roots and sources of sustenance of people's identities and their sense of belonging (Mason, 2000; Crow, 2002). The principal occasions and milieux of these trends include the demolition of long-established housing estates, the closure or collapse of traditional industries and their associated local communities and unions, the decline of deference, and the demise of the powers and popularity of local government.

Accounts of the decline of traditional attitudes and affiliations in the UK point to falling church attendance, to a retreat from collectivist into more individualistic mentalities, to the celebration of greed and acquisition, to increased geographical mobility, and to the emergence of new sorts of communities. Some of these newer communities manifest new kinds of culture and identity, some of which have resulted from migration and immigration, and others which exist more in cybernetic and virtual form on the Internet as social networking websites such as MySpace and Facebook.

Social solidarity

In much of the scholarly literature, as well as in more popular accounts and in people's everyday narratives, the idea of community forms the bedrock for people's sense of commonality and as the locale for the expression of mutuality and reciprocity in quite ordinary daily activities as well as at times of crisis (such as an explosion in a coal mine, the loss of fishing boats at sea, or the sudden announcement of mass redundancies).

The invocation of 'community' leads easily into considerations of social solidarity, community cohesion, a powerful sense of place and belonging, and an emphasis on self-organisation and self-direction. Expressions of social solidarity usually have their roots in strongly shared values, traditions, norms, cultures, ethnicities, languages, practices and institutions. They may manifest themselves in relation to a particular locale, territory, region or even nation state. Equally, social solidarity may spring from a common religious belief or faith, from shared political ideology or even from strongly held support for an organisation, sports team or social activity. More often than not, social solidarity is invoked in situations that stress 'us and them'.

The idea of social solidarity is central to classical sociological theory's attempt to understand the key foundations and dynamics of modern society. Crow provides contemporary examples of what are thought to be particularly 'solidaristic' communities. Social solidarity has often been deemed to be grounded in particular community-based industries, especially those characterised by relative isolation, homogeneity of employment, limited outward and inward mobility, male-only jobs, dangerous work, father-to-son employment in the same industry, high levels of trades unionism, a strong sense of 'us and them', and a history of industrial conflict. In traditional coal mining as well as in shipbuilding, deep-sea fishing and dock communities, 'the social ties of work, leisure, neighbourhood and friendship overlap to form close-knit and interlocking locally based collectivities' (Bulmer, 1975, cited in Crow, 2002, p.75). Less intense 'occupational communities' have also been identified in other jobs where the sense of similarity rests on a common culture, a common language or vocabulary, established rituals of introduction to the occupation (including education and training), a common gender, shared ideas of what constitutes 'appropriate behaviour' for fellow members of the community, and routine hostility to outsiders.

It is noticeable that the studies of industrial and occupational communities are largely concerned with the working lives of men and of the social, organisational and cultural institutions established in relation to men's working lives, as well as of the mores and social practices that reflect predominantly men's preoccupations, an often unspoken defence of their own sense of masculinity, and their domination of women (Cockburn, 1983). If these men experience a sense of their own subordination in work – counteracted by the solidarities of trades unionism and industrial conflict – the women and other family members in their lives are conventionally portrayed as secondary or as supporters, sometimes even in moments of historic struggle such as the great miners' strike in Britain in 1984–1985.

For some commentators, and especially for those framing social policy with regard to the sorts of industrial and occupational changes outlined above, the main challenge posed is the potential undermining of the traditional bonds of social cohesion and social solidarity. New ways of living, working and being – all central domains of the expression of citizenship and belonging – mean that the influences of older sorts of normative moral regulation and the subscription to core social values can no longer be taken for granted. The erosion of social cohesion is cited, too, as at least a partial cause for rises in crime and certain kinds of perceived disorder, and for increases in prejudice, hostility, the resort to violence to settle disputes, and community conflict. Some critics go so far as to indict education, especially schools, and the destruction of older forms of training, such as traditional apprenticeships and national military service for their alleged contribution to this loss of a sense of community and of belonging.

In one study, in the Canadian garment industry, of the relationship between solidarity at work and the development of learning, Fenwick (2008, p.110) observes that the workers (mostly immigrants) 'nested' negotiation of their work conditions in a range of learning practices: in their everyday lives, in small close-knit communities, in organising labour, and in English classes. Together, these practices, in which learning featured strongly, both generated and built on solidarity 'through learning about sociality, resistance and personal worth'. Fenwick's study rested on deliberately expansive conceptions of learning and solidarity that entailed 'an expansion of capacity, with focus on action that builds individual and collective agency, particularly to enhance workers' well-being and critical awareness of work structures, to foster more equitable structures, and to increase workers' control over their activity' (*ibid.*, p.112). In Fenwick's research, as in other analyses of social solidarity, the garment workers' shared and developing sense of community provided the basis for combining emancipatory and critical learning with collective action for transformation of both individuals' consciousness and their collective situations at work. At the same time, as Fenwick points out, not all solidaristic learning through work will necessarily entail such transformational consequences: it may lead to acceptance of the *status quo* and incorporation into the established order of things, irrespective of how inequitable and restrictive it may be.

Against mostly positive perspectives on solidarity, some commentators applaud what they see as the increased freedom of individuals in the contemporary world to shape their own lives and exercise a greater degree of choice, liberated from the impositions of traditional and restrictive communities. Others regard such pervasive individualism as a clear manifestation of growing selfishness, egoism and disregard for the common good – a palpable denial of the sense of mutuality, reciprocity and solidarity that should lie at the heart of citizenship and social cohesion. For such critics, an emphasis on 'self-regarding' behaviour is not only normatively undesirable, it is also a dangerous illusion and a snare, opening deracinated individuals to the predations of international capitalism and the meaningless obsessions of consumption.

All the same, in considering the potential virtues of solidarity, it is important to be wary of the oversimplifying myths of community which tend to stress its unifying, identity-enhancing and inherently progressive features. As Guijt and Shah summarise the argument, reflecting on the uses and experiences of participation and community in development studies, advocacy of participatory engagement in community, in which learning is deeply embedded, is intended to 'empower local people with the skills and confidence to analyse their situation, reach consensus, make decisions and take action, so as to improve their circumstances.' In practice, however, 'it is apparent that "community" has often been viewed naively, or in practice dealt with, as a harmonious and internally equitable collective'. What such a 'mythical notion of community cohesion' overlooks is complexity.

The complexity of community differences, including age, economic, reli-
gious, caste, ethnic, and in particular gender …a bias that favours the
opinions and priorities of those with the ability to voice themselves
publicly. (Guijt and Shah, 1998, p. 1)

In other words, just as a sense of belonging or of community can be a
source of strength, opportunity or joy, so it might also be the cause of
feelings of confinement, frustration and claustrophobia.

Feeling that one belongs to something larger and more permanent than
oneself is either a wonderful or a terrible thing. It is an inspiration for
heroism and the composition of sublime works of music and art. It is a
motivation for morality and a solace in the midst of suffering. Conversely,
it is sometimes the source of a claustrophobic sense of being trapped or a
crushing weight of responsibility. It makes some people quietly quell
doubts and support dangerous policies of nationalist leaders and makes
others feel an obligation to speak out. It is also the only way in which
many people are able to feel that they belong in the world.
(Calhoun, 2007, p. 290)

'Active' citizens: deliberation, discourse and action

From discussions of community and solidarity, including the need not to
overlook those who might be excluded, it is but a short step into the
vocabulary of *active* citizenship, another discourse replete with normative
and evaluative nuance. Of course, seen from the perspective of civic
republicans such as Oldfield, the use of 'active' in relation to 'citizenship'
serves no practical purpose. By definition, for them, citizenship necessarily entails active participation in public life – not only *should* it not be
passive, strictly speaking it *cannot* be. In practice, the phrase usually carries
other associated connotations, including especially the cultivation of an
independent and critical perspective, often through engagement in learning – whether formal, informal or non-formal – to be deployed in work
on behalf of a community. For Professor Sir Bernard Crick, distinguished
British political theorist and chair of three recent enquiries into citizenship in Britain, the notion of active citizenship is inherent in what he
terms as a 'revived' civic republicanism in which citizens can 'combine
together, to change things big or small; or to prevent undesired changes'
(Crick, 2002a, p.1).

In the formulation put forward by Evans, active citizenship is promoted by a form of 'education which develops critical and reflexive abilities and capacities for self-determination and autonomies' (Evans, 1995, p.17). In reflecting on the development of his pedagogy for 'critical consciousness' among Brazilian workers and peasants, Paulo Freire explained the importance of experience: 'people can only learn democracy by the experience of democracy'. Experience is not a matter of simply immersing yourself in activity, but doing so through critical debate. He called this 'an education of "I wonder", instead of merely "I do" '.

> *I was convinced that the Brazilian people could learn social and political responsibility only by experiencing that responsibility, through intervention in the destiny of their children's schools, in the destinies of their trade unions and places of employment through associations, clubs, and councils, and in the life of their neighbourhoods, churches and rural communities by actively participating in associations, clubs, and charitable societies. (Freire, 2007, p.32)*

One version of this latter perspective deserves special mention: the idea of community learning *in* 'social action', in which lifelong or adult learning and citizenship are bound up both in everyday living and in the course of particular struggles and campaigns. In the UK, learning in and through community-based social action was celebrated by Tom Lovett and his colleagues in Northern Ireland (Lovett, 1975; Lovett *et al.*, 1983). Similarly, Griff Foley, in introducing a series of case studies, draws attention to 'the widespread and powerful informal and incidental education and learning' that occurs 'naturally and socially in workplaces, families, community organisations and social action' (Foley, 1999, p.7). Foley is at pains to point out the quite different theoretical assumptions that underpin this approach to citizenship and learning to those which consist either of a traditional concern with 'de-contextualised individual learners, educational technique and course provision' or those of newer contributions that tend 'to the abstract, the epistemological, the psychological or the individualistic'. Such approaches, he argues, are 'overly concerned with debates among professionals, rather than working out ways of connecting adult education with struggles for social justice' (*ibid.*, pp.132 and 133).

During the 1980s and 1990s, the Northern College for Residential Adult Education ran a series of residential short courses for 'community activists' and 'community animateurs' (Grayson and Jackson, 2004), at a less intense level than those reported by Foley. People came to the college to enhance their skills in campaigning about, organising and understanding issues of particular importance to their communities. These people were usually working in local voluntary and community organisations, sometimes as unofficial leaders, and often unwaged or unemployed. The communities in question – frequently relatively impoverished in material terms – were based on geographical or topographical co-location (a neighbourhood, estate or village), shared interests (e.g. as housing tenants or women's support groups in the miners' strike of 1984–1985), or on a shared ethnicity (as in Asian women's health groups). In each case, the clear aim of the groups in question was, as active citizens, to mobilise knowledge and skills in support of the respective communities to which they belonged.

The role and functions of civil society

Concern with participation in electoral, representative or parliamentary politics by no means exhausts the ways in which people engage with the politics of social life, in part supported possibly by education or learning opportunities. There is also what, since first being systematically analysed by Hegel, is known as the realm of 'civil society' referred to by Holford and his colleagues (2003). There is much debate and there are many subtle variations in political philosophy about the precise meaning of 'civil society' and, hence, which elements of the social world are included (Cohen and Arato, 1992). There is, however, broad agreement that the notion embraces those associations, practices, organisations and networks that both stand between the individual and higher authority (typically the State) and also potentially link them.

One of the principal characteristics of civil society and the different types and sizes of civic organisation and association involved is that they have typically been organised on a largely private or voluntary basis outside the direct control of the State.

> *The realm of civic associations, thus, refers to the array of institutions and organisations in and through which individuals and groups can pursue their own projects. (Held, 1995, p. 181)*

The main domains of civil society in the UK include voluntary organisations, self-organised groups, social movements, networks, and associations such as special interest groups, professional associations, trades

111

unions, faith and religious groupings, charities, campaigning organisations and community-based bodies. Although such organisations are not
usually under the direct control of the State, they may be regulated by
governments, laws or specialist regulatory authorities; their defining
characteristics, however, are self-governance and independence.

Inevitably, too, these different sorts of organisation are implicated in,
and often involve themselves in, broader conceptions of power, politics
and identity than those circumscribed by the institutions of the State,
political parties and electoral politics. In that sense, the politics of civil
society is a politics of the 'small p', but no less influential upon the
everyday life of the citizen. Indeed, in certain historical examples,
involvement in civil society associations has either pre-dated or pre-
figured the legal, civil, political or social rights of citizenship.

New social movements: formation and identity

When new organisations or movements emerge in civil society, some of
their earliest activities may centre on rounding out a new and distinctive
identity. In these often-complex processes, the learning of the members
and would-be members and the development of their awareness of
themselves as a recognisable group – with its own identity, norms, values,
modes of operation and vocabulary – also often go alongside demands
that other elements of civil society accord the group recognition and
legitimacy.

> *These movements create new associations and new publics, try to render
> existing institutions more egalitarian, enrich and expand public discus-
> sion in civil society, and influence the existing public spaces of political
> society, potentially expanding these and supplementing them with addi-
> tional forms of citizen participation.* (Cohen and Arato, 1992, p.548)

Effective mobilisation of this kind requires that the emergent group
secure clarification of its identity, purposes, membership, methods of
organisation and the successful development of strategies for communication – the very stuff of learning. As a minimum, out of such endeavours
new groups expect their natural recruits and neophytes to develop a
strong sense of belonging to the group, defending its aims and integrity
and elaborating its own narrative ambitions.

Obvious examples of new social movements are the various instances of the women's and specifically the feminist movement, the campaigns by ethnic and racial groups for full citizenship rights, the claims for equality voiced by people with physical and learning difficulties and disabilities, and the successes achieved by lesbians and gay men (Rowbotham, 1973, 1989 and 1997; Okin, 1979; Jones, 1990; Tomlinson, 1996; Benhabib, 2002; Kenny, 2004; Benhabib *et al.*, 2007; Pateman and Mills, 2007; Benhabib, Shapiro and Petranovic, 2007). Similarly, the agenda of political discourse has been variously challenged and enlarged by the environmental and ecology movements, by peace and disarmament campaigns, and by protests against what are depicted as the damaging effects of increasing globalisation (Klein, 2001).

Such developments are aimed not only at securing innovative reconfigurations and differentiations of social life and the creation of recognisably new categories of social actor, they also often entail simultaneously both enlarging the overall domain of civil society and securing from the polity proper improvements in the status, rights and resources of the group. They may thus also shift issues from what is conventionally regarded as the personal sphere of private worries into the public domain, challenging and changing the established boundaries between individual psychology and the social life of collectivities. Cohen and Arato (1992) characterise these processes as linked spheres of politics and dynamic elements of social learning, centred on identity, influence and reform. All of these processes instantiate learning, which mostly finds its expression initially in informal or non-formal modes, but which may increasingly become expressed in formal terms and documentation and based on the conceptualisation and theorisation that is characteristic of academic analysis and scholarship.

These organisations and associations also all manifest opportunities for those involved in them to learn, practise and enjoy the benefits of active participation, including in many the chance of developing the capacities and skills of democratic engagement. They provide significant arenas in which people can learn, deploy and improve their capabilities for organisation, communication, deliberation, problem solving, reciprocity, mobilisation, campaigning, resource allocation, networking, bonding and securing change. They facilitate both trial and error, success and failure, assertion and compromise. Hence one of the most important contributions made to civil society and the continued vigour of democracy by voluntary organisations and social movements is the learning of citizenship through action and engagement. In common with much learning, too, they often develop increased autonomy along with a capacity to relate effectively to others in the system.

According to Andrew Parkin (1996), the different sorts of new social movement promise to perform four vital functions: strengthening civil society and social solidarity by establishing new sorts of independent association; offering arenas for public participation in deliberative and reflective learning outside the direct control of the State or the interest of private corporations; opening up the prospect of the development of a responsible global citizenry in the context of the increasing globalisation of capital, finance, communications and information; and manifesting a politics of inclusion where citizens are otherwise threatened with exclusion and marginalisation.

Needless to say, not all 'new' social movements are quite so new, and not all fulfil the admirable functions suggested by Parkin. Crucially, their chances of success depend upon a number of contingent circumstances, not least the availability of opportunities for sustained, critical lifelong learning – both formal and informal. Beginning with relatively banal lessons in developing the essential skills of organisation, finance, public speaking, communications and governance, active participation in such organisations can become 'schools of citizenship: places where people learn to respect and trust others, fulfil obligations and press their claims communicatively'. There are important responsibilities for organisations endeavouring to support such learning: 'the cluster of socialising agents have to create internal pedagogical environments characterised by a commitment to foster an inquiring, sceptical attitude to authority's beliefs and actions (indoctrination is not permitted)' (Welton, 2005, p.178; see also Fryer, 1990).

In his review of the implications of the arguments of Jurgen Habermas (1996) and Nancy Fraser (1992) concerning the implications of the new social movements in civil society for citizenship, Welton suggests that 'the achievement of a truly freewheeling, vibrant effusive civil society, as well as a parliament responsive to its dictates, demands that we radically challenges asymmetries of power'. This will only be possible if the 'crippling inequalities of capitalist society' and class domination are tackled – inequalities that currently mean that 'the idea of a freewheeling deliberative democracy' presently remains utopian (Welton, 2005, pp.169–170).

Trust and social capital

Not only does a varied associational life provide potentially valuable and critical experiences of practical citizenship and learning through action, but the different organisations of civil society also represent key centres for the development of high trust relations and of what has been termed 'social capital' (Bourdieu, 1986; Coleman, 1988 and 1990; Putnam, 1993 and 2000; Field, 2003). According to one authoritative account, social capital can best be understood as an interlocking of 'social networks, the reciprocities that arise from them, and the value of these for achieving mutual goals' (Baron, Field and Schuller, 2000, p.1).

The operations of these forms of social relations not only serve the needs and advance the interests of those who are engaged in them, but also act as wider mechanisms for binding society together, for the extension and deepening of democracy. Trust and the deployment of social capital has also been invoked for improving the performance of schools and pupils' educational attainment, for bridging otherwise potentially damaging social divides, for the expression of people's shared sense of identity and belonging, and for strengthening their feelings of inclusion. Just as high trust and resourceful deployment of social capital may be claimed to enhance individual and collective achievement, so too its absence or apparent decline is portrayed as a cause of concern.

There is plenty of evidence to suggest that people who possess higher-level educational qualifications or who remain longer in formal education are more likely than their less-schooled compatriots to engage with a wide range of institutions and activities that typify the workings of democratic society. That is, not only do the more qualified take greater part in electoral politics and the official machinery of governance, but also in the rich web of organisations and practices that make up 'civil society' and which often rest upon the application of their 'social capital'. The questions that this poses are whether less well qualified citizens are thereby disadvantaged, and what ought to be done about it (including possibly by learning), or whether people choose not to engage after weighing the pros and cons.

In a study of social capital and adult learning in Northern Ireland, Field reported that the findings broadly supported a positive association between attitudes towards civic engagement and participation in adult learning. However, the relationship between social networks and learning was complex, 'in which people actively develop learning identities and

115

strategies that enable them to tackle the circumstances in which they find themselves' (Field, 2005a, p.81).

While people in Northern Ireland used their social capital to encourage young people's formal achievement in education, adults were more likely to use 'information acquired informally through connections and skills picked up from workmates and family' than anything acquired through the formal institutions of education. Although social capital and adult learning may sometimes be linked in a kind of 'virtuous circle', they may equally substitute for or even cut across each other. Context and the 'specificities of time and place' matter, and care should always be taken in trying to read across findings from one social setting to another (*ibid.*).

Field's analysis (*ibid.*, pp.29–30) suggests that, at the most general level, learning and social capital may be associated in a 'process of dynamic inter-cognition', people may acquire skills in cooperation and through their connections, and social capital may create consensual pressures towards the value and benefits of learning. In some instances, learning or its relative lack may explain the presence and effectiveness of social capital. In others, it is the application of social capital, apparently, that opens up learning opportunities or leads to further learning and development. In still others, frankly, it is simply too complex to unravel the role and contribution of learning in the genesis, strength, application and consequences of social capital.

In England, there is evidence of considerable numbers of people reporting their involvement in 'civic activism', civic participation, civic consultation activities or events, and in volunteering. The principal forms of civil activism, reported by almost one in ten people overall in the Citizenship Survey in 2005, were: taking part in groups, making local decisions on local services, and acting as a school governor or local councillor. A fifth of respondents had been involved in a form of civic consultation over the past 12 months, and 38 per cent had taken part in civic participation by contacting a political representative or government official, by attending a public meeting, rally or demonstration, or by signing a petition.

Most of these forms of community involvement or action also show recent signs of a modest increase, although the proportions trusting their local council or parliament were lower than those who trusted the police, and these figures showed only modest improvement between 2001 and 2005. Levels of trust in the police and courts were lower among white people and those of black Caribbean ethnicity than among the Asian respondents (Department of Communities and Local Government, 2006).

Bowling alone?

Alongside anxieties about an apparent contemporary retreat from formal politics, analysts of social capital have also drawn attention to a recent decline in civil society. Because the organisations and voluntary behaviour of people in civil society are thought to have played a key role in focusing and mobilising people's interests and helping to define their identities and aspirations, their alleged decline is bound to attract comment.

In one of the most celebrated analyses of civil society, Robert Putnam, who has been partly responsible for popularisation of the concept of social capital in large-scale empirical inquiry, suggested that, increasingly, America now 'bowls alone'. In a wide-ranging study of participation in politics and public affairs, of involvement in clubs, societies and a variety of voluntary associations, of membership of trades unions and professional bodies, of leisure pursuits, volunteering and philanthropy, Putnam reaches pessimistic conclusions. Despite variations and the evidence of some cross-currents and counter-indications, Putnam claims to have discovered 'common, powerful tidal movements that have swept across American society in the twentieth century' (Putnam, 2000, p.27). At first, those tides carried people into deep involvement in their communities, but latterly what Putnam refers to as a 'treacherous current' has swept that involvement into retreat.

As an emblematic indicator of American communal sociability, the once-popular leisure pursuit of bowling is now in apparent decline, alongside active and face-to-face involvement in a range of clubs and associations, religious organisations and politics. One brief extract from Putnam's extensive analysis offers an example of his wider thesis.

> *Organizational records suggest that for the first two-thirds of the twenti-*
> *eth century American involvement in civic associations of all sorts rose*
> *steadily, except for the parenthesis of the Great Depression. In the last*
> *third of the century, by contrast, only mailing list membership has*
> *continued to expand, with the creation of an entirely new species of*
> *'tertiary' association whose members never meet. At the same time, active*
> *involvement in face-to-face organizations has plummeted, whether we*

consider organizational records, survey reports, time diaries or consumer expenditure. We could surely find individual exceptions – specific organizations that successfully sailed against the prevailing winds and tides – but the broad picture is one of declining membership in community organizations. (ibid., p.63)

Some reservations

Alternative accounts need to be contrasted with Putnam's pessimistic conclusion. First there are those observers who contend that Putnam and those of like mind have mistaken an accurate account of the *changed* forms and locales of civic involvement and community participation for their *decline.* They argue that analysts of contemporary activism should examine the new ways and means of participating and communicating and the different focuses of concern, especially among younger people. Here, they suggest looser forms of association and new kinds of campaign – for peace, in respect of sustainable ecology and against environmental degradation, and protests at the dangers of reckless globalisation – and provide a more balanced perspective on the nature and health of contemporary civil society.

Although the insights of social capital analyses have been potent and suggestive, the use of the concept has also been beset by reservations and criticisms. Scepticism about the analytic value of the concept and its deployment has included allegations of conceptual confusion and of stretching its meaning to a point of such generality and flexibility as to render it virtually worthless. Some researchers employing the concept are accused of working from flawed research designs, collecting inadequate data or using invalid indicators of social capital. Some critics dispute the very applicability of the notion of 'capital' to the aspects of human interaction being studied (Portes, 1998; Baron, Field and Schuller, 2000; Field, 2003 and 2005a and 2005b). More cynical commentators suggest that social capital amounts in practice to little more than what we already know from our everyday experience, namely that well connected, well informed, well resourced, articulate and mostly middle class people are able to get their way more often, take advantage of situations better and succeed more frequently than those lacking such attributes. In other words, social capital may just be another label for, and way of, understanding power, influence and advantage.

This monograph is not the place fully to evaluate the fairness or appropriateness of all of these various challenges. However, in fields of study already marked by fierce conceptual and interpretative debate, awareness of the challenges and the extent and provenance of the support for the various authors at least points to caution in embracing the concept. The implications of social capital analysis for lifelong learning are often far from self-evident.

The 'dark sides' of activism and social capital

Assessments of the role and functions of social capital also need to include an analysis of its potential for creating perverse effects, and an understanding of what Putnam (2000) and Field (2003), among others, have termed its 'dark' sides. These aspects can range from the scope that certain sorts of social capital may afford for excluding, stereotyping and scapegoating those outside the inner circle, to its use in promoting cronyism and corruption. Certain forms of social capital may thus also support criminality or help promote extreme forms separatism and violent nationalism, or even underpin the promulgation of racist attitudes and behaviour, and the formation and mobilisation of fascist political movements. Each of these instances may also claim to be a feature of contemporary civil society, albeit with what are generally regarded as dystopic implications.

Despite these reservations, it may still be reasonable to assume that life is bleaker for those people not active in, or who are excluded from, the various beneficent locales, practices and institutions of civil society, or who lack the resources and opportunities to participate. This assumption may be reasonable unless, of course, such people's personal circumstances of power, autonomy, control over resources, or mere preference to live their lives largely separate from the rest of society, render the busy worlds of association and voluntary organisation unnecessary, irrelevant, inconsequential or uninteresting.

CHAPTER SEVEN

Work and consumption in an era of digitisation and corporate responsibility

Citizens as workers and producers

A new economic order

Many governments and much recent public policy have deliberately represented globalisation as requiring workers' rapid up-skilling, their frequent re-skilling, and an increased 'flexibility' of both labour and labour markets – all in the names of improved industrial competitiveness and the defence of established living standards and prosperity (Leitch, 2006). It is not the concern of this monograph either to analyse or to evaluate such perspectives, except to note that even within unashamedly economistic depictions of globalisation there are still competing conceptions of the implications for lifelong learning.

On the one hand, there are those commentators who emphasise lifelong learning's potential contribution to what may be termed 'adaptability', framing workers' learning to develop new competences, to increase productivity and to foster their capacity to accept continuous change in the so-called knowledge economy. On the other, there are the advocates of stronger independent representation of workers' interests in the face of multiple shifts in the world of work. Workers' lifelong learning and that of their (union) learning representatives offers some hope of resisting and maybe even shaping such changes in order to better reflect workers' interests and meet their needs.

For some critics of recent political and economic change in the UK, the claims of both liberal and republican theories of democracy need to be

120

set against the ways in which the increasing domination of markets and international capital has weakened the protections previously afforded by the gradual strengthening and extension of citizenship, especially in matters concerning liberty.

> *Consider, for example, the current predicament of the British people, who have for so long prided themselves on the enjoyment of their liberties. They now find themselves living more and more under asymmetric relations of power and powerless. The triumph of free markets, with the concomitant collapse of trade union movements, has left successive governments subject to blackmail by multinational corporations while leaving the workforce increasingly dependent on the arbitrary power of employers. (Skinner, 2003, p.25)*

A renewal of 'industrial citizenship'?[13]

'Industrial citizenship', historically, has been proposed under different headings (and usually with quite markedly different implications) such as guild socialism, industrial democracy, workers' self-management, and workers' control. Today, it takes its lead from well documented accounts of widespread and profound shifts in traditional industrial and occupational structures, especially in the 'older' industrial capitalist democracies, and from equally radical changes in the ownership, finance, organisation, management and marketing strategies of companies, especially those operating trans-nationally or globally. In all cases, the argument for a renewal of industrial democracy begins in the workplace – the site of most workers' experiences of the subordinations and uncertainties of everyday working life, as well as presenting the best opportunities for achieving improvements in the immediate circumstances of their work, not least through the contribution of learning.

In a pioneering study of the genesis of active citizenship in the learning society, Roseanne Benn compared the views of 75 adult education students, 71 per cent of them female, on the contribution of six different sites of learning, including the workplace, to ten aspects of active citizenship. Her conclusion was that 'the workplace is the social setting

---

13 T. H. Marshall drew attention to the growth and development of trades unionism in nineteenth-century Britain as giving rise to a 'sort of secondary industrial citizenship'. It did so by 'enabling workers to use their civil rights collectively'. (Marshall and Bottomore, 1992, p.40)

where most people gain their skills of citizenship' (Benn, 2000a and 2000b, p.25). In the workplace, Benn adds, although citizenship needs to be learned like any other skill, the most effective learning will not occur through a formal curriculum but through positive experiences of citizenship in practice.

Trades unionism in the UK

Trades unions and, especially, their shop-floor volunteers who operate as 'learning representatives', have a vital role to play in promoting learning of all kinds among their members. As some of the most important and long-established institutions of UK civil society, trades unions that were once strong are now also undergoing a marked reverse in their fortunes. Along with the radical shift in the structure of paid employment over the past 30 years or so – the decline of 'heavy' manufacturing industry, the disappearance of many traditional occupations and skills, the growth of white-collar work and the private services sector – trades unionism has declined. Trades unions and union membership have seen substantial reductions in membership numbers and density, in popularity and in influence.

Once associated with the growth of factory-based skilled and semi-skilled work in manufacturing, and with such occupational communities as textiles, deep-sea fishing, ship-building, car manufacture and mining, trades unionism in the UK is now more typically located in the public sector. Whole swathes of paid employment are characterised by either an absence of unions or by low levels of membership, and by the trades unions' inability to exert much influence over the terms and conditions of their members' working lives. Even where unions continue to operate, it is said that there has been a marked decline in members' involvement in their internal governance – trades unions were claimed to be schools of both solidarity and practical democracy for working people – and in their emphasis on the advantages of collectivity. Increasingly, it is said, trades unions have to attend more to their members' individual needs and interests, and to manifest such a shift in their organisational structures and the skills and provenance of their officials.

Despite their recent loss of membership, their virtual disappearance from large swathes of manufacturing industry and the private sector in the UK, and some loss of influence, unions nevertheless remain important locales for membership and for day-to-day participation for 7 million adults at work. For many workers, the union remains their major channel for expressing a collective voice at work and for seeking to influence the decisions of senior management, employers and government. Trades unions still constitute one of the major forms of voluntary organisation in the UK – ones in which formal opportunities for members to share in governance and decision-making are enshrined in their rulebooks and constitutions, in part reinforced by the law of the land. Unions' achievements – through both collective bargaining and by securing changes in the law – include advancing members' rights at work, for example in relation to health and safety, equal pay, minimum wages and employment recruitment strategies. Trades unions have also demonstrated great inventiveness and resourcefulness where the lifelong learning of their members is concerned.

In addition to providing members with opportunities both to learn and to practise participation in decision-making and organisation, how to present argument, debate and persuade others – practical, work-based citizenship – unions have also always shown great interest in more formal education. On the one hand, unions have concerned themselves with the provision of public education, both for their own members and the wider public – from elementary schooling and the appropriate organisation of secondary education, and for increasing opportunities to achieve formal qualifications, right through to opening up access to higher education and the professions. On the other hand, unions – sometimes in collaboration with educational bodies such as the Workers' Educational Association or the extra-mural departments of universities, and sometimes quite independently – directly provided education to their officials, elected representatives and members. This has included education for trades union officers, the training of large numbers of lay officials, especially shop stewards and workplace health and safety representatives, and more latterly the development of a cadre of union learning representatives to advocate and support increased opportunities for lifelong learning through, at, or for work (Payne, 2001).

For all their known weaknesses and current setbacks, trades unions in the UK still constitute significant arenas for the expression of what a Conservative party research paper over 60 years ago referred to as 'industrial citizenship'.[14] Moreover, without too much exaggeration, it

---

14 Anticipating one of the arguments of this monograph, Schuller and Bengtsson (1977) refer to industrial democracy as a 'chameleon concept'.

could be claimed that the investment in skills and work-related qualifications advocated by Leitch (2006) and being energetically pursued by the
government constitutes a version of industrial citizenship, albeit one of a
limited and diminished kind according to critics (Coffield, 2007).

Citizens as consumers

In a world increasingly dominated by an abundance of markets and the
ready availability of a plethora of goods and services not even known to
earlier generations, some commentators argue that consumption now
constitutes a principal arena for the expression of both citizenship and
belonging. Consumption and working to acquire funds to use in shopping occupy a large part of the contemporary lives of citizens, and for
most people the standard processes of behaving as a consumer become
normal parts of their everyday lives from quite a young age.

The argument runs that it is by their daily acts of consumption in a
variety of markets that people are able to exercise choice, give voice to
priority, make rational decisions affecting their own well-being, move
with ease between different domains, mix with like-minded others,
manifest agency, and realise their various and increasingly multiple identities. Aggregated together, it is this array of choices and decisions that
really constitutes 'society', rather than some abstract or, at best, formal
conception of citizenship (Clarke *et al.*, 2007).

> *The rise in prominence of consumption in everyday life is also mirrored in
> language. In the public services, specific references to passengers (rail),
> patients (NHS), and service users (social care), are now often replaced by
> 'customers' (Vidler and Clarke, 2005). Recent research shows how it is
> 'customers' or 'consumers' who now frequently figure instead of 'the
> public' or citizens. Whilst the new approach embraced by government is
> predicated on the well-informed, individual consumer exercising personal
> choice and preference, the situation in practice is more complex. Although
> people seeking to use, say, the NHS, welcome greater choice, they still
> want more control and safety-nets to protect the public and 'also want to be
> sure the rights of citizens are maintained'. (Livingstone et al., 2007)*

If identity and belonging – in what Bauman has called the 'late' modern
world of increasingly 'liquid' society – resides in the shared and progressively universalising experiences of consumption and the marketplace, it

is but a short step to reconfigure the citizen-as-political-and-social-being as the citizen-as-consumer[15] (Clarke *et al.*, 2007). As Welton (2005, p.153) summarises this argument, the role of 'consumer has elbowed out that of citizen'. If it is relevant at all in such circumstances, the particular (if rather atrophied) contribution of citizenship may be to afford the opportunity for choice and lifelong learning, either to describe what is 'on offer' or to provide the understanding to put choice into effect, including of course the choice of identity.

Needham (2003) points to a stark difference between the ethic of citizenship and that of consumerism. Where the first rests upon a concern for the common interest, collective deliberation and determination, and loyalty to a shared political community, the second centres on individuals who are primarily self-regarding and who state preferences without reference to others (other than to follow fashion), and act through a series of purely instrumental bi-lateral relationships. The effect, Needham argues, is 'to turn democracy into a marketplace, downgrading those elements of citizenship that presume a more collectivist and political linkage between individual and state'. In short, not only does a model of the citizen as consumer prioritise the interests of the individual over those of the community, it also 'encourages passivity, downgrades public spaces, weakens accountability, and privatises citizenship' (*ibid.*).

David Marquand (2004) suggests that the rise and eventual triumph of a revived neo-liberal philosophy, achieved through what he characterises as a '*kulturkampf*', accounts for the 'decline of the public' in the social, economic and cultural life of the UK in the last quarter of the twentieth century. Marquand emphasises that the idea of the 'public' is neither synonymous with nor should be confused with the 'public sector', although there are some overlaps between the two. At the heart of this neo-liberal vision is 'the central notion of the rational, self-interested individual utility maximiser'. The champion of this vision was the 'freely choosing consumer, making her own decisions, standing on her own feet and spending her own money in her own way, without having to pay heed to externally imposed constraints' (*ibid.*, pp.91 and 93).

The weapons in this war were not only ideas. Few established public institutions 'escaped the cultural revolution unscathed', as the notion of

---

15 Clarke and his colleagues, in drawing attention to no fewer than nine variants of the concept of 'consumer' advanced by Gabriel and Lang (1995), argue that the concept is no less contested and complex than that of 'citizen'. (Clarke *et al.*, 2007, p.5).

citizenship was gradually hollowed out to be replaced wherever possible by the logic of the marketplace. This was not always an assault on otherwise inviolable institutions and traditions cherished by the citizenry at large. Indeed, Marquand is of the view that many of these public institutions and organisations contributed to the successes of neo-liberalism through their own failure to maintain their distinctive and legitimating virtues, and through their distortion by producer interests.

The targets in this war included weakening and restricting the powers of local authorities, a systematic dismantling of the publicly owned utilities and industries, privatisation of public services or subjection of them to the pressures of quasi or proxy markets, the imposition of targets, an emphasis on 'performance management', and a huge expansion of the audit culture.

> *In virtually every institution, eighteen years of neo-liberalism exalted managers, often recruited from the corporate sector, at the expense of the professionals who formed the backbone of the institution concerned. (ibid., p.110)*

In asserting the centrality of market mechanisms not merely for the allocation of goods and services, but also as the only effective form of accountability, the neo-liberal onslaught included attacks on previously self-regulating professions and independent 'intermediate' institutions such as universities, and the undermining of the traditionally neutral role of the civil service and other public servants. In all of this, citizenship consisted principally of acting alone, exercising choice and, effectively, 'playing the market' purely for individual benefit. Marketisation, privatisation, and denigration of all things 'public' chimed well with the accompanying cult of individualism.

Ideology rarely enjoys implementation in pure, unadulterated form. So it is with neo-liberalism. First, its application in different institutional settings was influenced by the histories, cultures and balance of professional and other interests of each context. Secondly, other ideological forces also came into play when incorporated into the political programme of New Labour, with its declared intention of reversing the social inequalities, the increase of which was highlighted before Labour's success in the 1997 general election. Thus, for example, the introduction of choice into the NHS has been mediated in practice, both by the continuing need to apportion resources between competing demands and by an increasing policy focus on health inequalities (Clarke *et al.*, 2007).

126

Digital citizenship

Over the past 40 years or so, but increasingly in the past two decades, remarkable advances in electronic communication and information technologies (and their progressive financial cheapening) have suggested the possibilities of a revolution in the ways in which people keep in touch with each other, can store, analyse, retrieve and share large amounts of data, can access hitherto unreachable information, and can create virtual communities of interest and action with others usually separated by geographical, social and political distance.

Enthusiasts for this kind of increasingly networked society (Castells, 1996, 1997 and 1998) have suggested that such developments open up new avenues for the practice of citizenship, for the construction of identities, and for the expression of people's various senses of belonging. According to Manuel Castells, the prolific writer and deeply influential sociological analyst in this field, the most innovative and potentially liberating feature of networks is the scope they offer for challenging traditional hierarchical structures of social action, such as bureaucracies and highly centralised state formations. Thus, in place of societies and social relations predicated on predominantly *vertical* structures, networks enable *horizontal* forms of social organisation. It is not just a question of the new technologies enabling dramatic *quantitative* increases in the *volume* and the *rapidity* of transmission of information, but also of a decidedly *qualitative* shift, especially in the ability of contemporary information and communication technologies to 'self-expand their processing power' and their capacity 'to derive new, unforeseen processes of innovation by their endless reconfiguration' (Castells, 2004).

Recent advances in information technologies have particularly enhanced the flexibility, scalability and survivability of networks.

> *Flexibility: they can reconfigurate according to changing environments, keeping their goals while changing their components. They go around blocking points of communication channels to find new connections. Scalability: they can expand or shrink in size with little disruption. Survivability: because they have no center, and can operate in a wide range of configurations, they can resist attacks to their nodes and codes, because the codes of the network are contained in multiple nodes, that can reproduce the instructions and find new ways to perform. (ibid.)*

Castells describes what he sees as the radical potential of information technology to combine and re-form previously quite disparate forms of knowledge, production and communication: 'from shared art creation to the political agora of the anti-globalization movement, and to joint engineering of networked corporate labs, the Internet is quickly becoming a medium of interactive communication beyond the cute, but scarcely relevant practice of chat rooms (increasingly made obsolete by SMSs and other wireless, instant communication systems)'.

> *The added value of the Internet over other communication media is its capacity to recombine in chosen time information products and information processes to generate a new output, that is immediately processed in the net, in an endless process of production of information, communication, and feedback in real time or chosen time. (ibid.)*

Thus rapid growth in the use and ownership of information technology figures in popular contemporary conceptions of its application to citizenship and belonging, and also in governmental uses of new technology for administrative and consultative purposes and, on occasions, to enable political and citizenly participation. In the context of citizenship and belonging, through their increasing use of the Internet and World Wide Web and facilities such as MySpace, YouTube and Second Life, people can access a great diversity of information, communicate with like-minded individuals and groups, demonstrate their preferences and easily cross the conventional boundaries of experience determined by locality, region, nation, gender, ethnicity, or age. The UK Government increasingly makes use of the Internet to provide certain kinds of public service. The principal digital government portal, www.direct.gov.uk, gives online access to people who, for example, want to: obtain advice and guidance on welfare benefits; register motor vehicles; apply for driving licences or passports; submit tax returns; be consulted on government policy proposals; explore all matters of local government; and find information on education and training, and guidance on welfare arrangements. People can reserve library books online, find out all about British nationality and citizenship, make job applications for work in the public sector, order a birth, death or marriage certificate, learn about the latest police initiatives on crime and disorder, or apply for local planning permission to modify buildings. People can also now create, sign or view petitions to the government online: in the first ten months of its operation, the

10 Downing Street website for petitions registered nearly 5.5 million signatures from almost 3.7 different email addresses (Ufi, 2008).

For some observers, widespread daily use of the World Wide Web and the Internet, especially by young people, constitutes an (as-yet-unfulfilled) promise of new ways in which citizens can communicate with each other, join in virtual communities, mobilise support and give instant publicity to events and discoveries in the pursuit of their common goals. As well as representing valuable resources of information, enthusiasts say that new electronic media, the Internet and its various offshoots open up opportunities for citizens to engage in critical scrutiny of the decisions and operations of public authorities. Moreover, cyberspace provides scope for citizens' creativity and inventiveness, as well as for their sense of play and for benefiting from membership of a range of virtual self-help organisations that centre on their self-defined needs.

Thus, for example, the recent publication *Digital Britain*, sponsored by the two London-based government departments responsible for culture, media and sport and for business and enterprise, notes that over the last decade the UK has experienced a 'quiet revolution' at work, at home, in the commercial marketplace and in leisure, thanks to the increased application of digital and, especially, broadband technologies. In addition to emphasising the importance of digital technology for Britain's business competitiveness and its improved productivity, the report stresses the key role that these technologies can play in securing greater social inclusion and fairness, better provision of public services, and giving citizens more opportunities to gain 'access to information, participation and influence, not least in the democratic process'. The aim is to make sure that arrangements are in place for 'the necessary education, skills and media literacy programmes to allow everyone in society to benefit from the digital revolution' (DCMS/BERR, 2009, p.5).

In this connection, the UK Government was responsible for the launch in 2000 and funding of one of the world's first nationwide e-learning initiatives, Ufi/learndirect, and has established a national network of neighbourhood UK Online centres. In the five years up to 2007–2008, Ufi/learndirect received just under £1 billion of public expenditure. Ufi/learndirect and UK Online are especially valuable for those individuals or groups who are unable to access information technology at home or through work, and who thus risk being disadvantaged by the digital divide (a recent estimate published by UK Online put this at 39 per cent of the adult population). Thus Ufi/learndirect currently supports 690 local learning centres in England and Wales, and UK Online provides 6,000 local centres. In these, people can gain free or low cost access to the Internet, develop basic skills in information technology and access online learning materials.

Ufi/learndirect now provides more than 600 different programmes of study and, since opening, more than 2.5 million people have followed almost 7 million courses with the service. An evaluation of Ufi/learndirect published in 2003 concluded that the service was especially valuable in recruiting new and less-qualified learners, retired people and those who were economically inactive, and was generally strong in widening adult participation in learning (IES, 2003). Almost three-quarters of Ufi/learndirect learners are qualified below Level 2, almost half of them have done no other learning in the three years prior to enrolling, and two-thirds have progressed to other programmes of study provided by Ufi/learndirect.

Ufi/learndirect is not alone in the UK in extending the use of e-learning to enable people to access new ways of learning, a wider range of content, a variety of venues and a new diversity of sources of information and argument, and to join virtual communities of learning and practice distributed over broad geographical areas and sometimes separated by different time zones and cultures. Schools, colleges, universities, business corporations, voluntary organisations, community groups and campaigning bodies now employ their own combinations of email, websites, chat rooms, wikis, blogs, electronic gaming and digital social networks in a variety of communicative and educational activities. These innovations are made available by evolving information and communication technologies and their constantly reducing financial costs to users.

Not such a rosy picture

Against such essentially optimistic and potentially enabling initiatives, critics and doubters point to the downsides of the electronic information revolution. Critics point first to the already marked digital divide in the UK, in which people and communities, often those already suffering multiple deprivations and social exclusion, have little or no access to the new media. Secondly, critics highlight how digital electronic technologies provide the scope for the development of a 'surveillance society' in which the lives, movements, transactions, work activities, patterns of consumption and social networks of citizens can be captured, monitored, analysed, stored and used against them not only by governments, police and other public authorities, but by business corporations, advertisers and even by criminal and terrorist organisations.

Thirdly, observers who are not convinced of the entirely beneficial effects of a world increasingly circumscribed, defined, conducted and framed by digitisation, indict the new media for their allegedly corrosive impact upon the face-to-face interaction among people to explore, enjoy and gain, both emotionally and cognitively, from real-life social experience. In this everyday reality, they indicate, actions, gestures and feelings have concrete consequences, affecting real people in ways that never occur in virtual life.

Fourthly, say the critics, a mere explosion of information on the Internet is of little value if much of it is rubbish or if its would-be users have no skills or reliable criteria by which to differentiate the good from the bad, the authentic from the deceiving, the useful from the useless. In any case, as the saying goes, one risk of the increasing digitisation of information and knowledge is 'rubbish in, rubbish out'.

Fifthly, critics have argued that there are few examples of use of the new information and communications successfully challenging established structures and domains of power. Rather, they suggest, the reverse is more frequently true: it is the already powerful who are best placed to appropriate the new resources to boost their scope for domination, exploitation, accumulation, control and exclusion. To take just one example, the so-called information society could, with equal validity, be designated as what Wernik (1991) terms a 'promotional culture', in which powerful and innovative forms of persuasion are deployed to 'train us for our main roles as consumers and customers. Emptying civil society of dialogical interactions, promotional culture scarcely frets for a moment about the degradation of everything public, from broadcasting, libraries, parks, information to education' (Welton, 2005, pp.159 and 160).

Finally, say the critics (arguing that this applies as much to the negativity of the pessimists as it does to the excessive and ultimately naive optimism of the enthusiasts), there is too much of an assumption of technological determinism in the simple belief that it is the new communication and information technologies that will shape societies in the future, rather than human agency, perhaps in ways and forms as yet still inchoate.

Digital futures

In one of the earliest and most intellectually balanced reviews of the 'issues and illusions' of the information society, David Lyon (1988) spelled out the rival ideological, utopian and practical possibilities of the new digital technologies. Although there is clearly a risk that new digital technologies may threaten human freedom, not least by implying that issues that entail fundamental questions of ethics, politics and informed human choice can be reduced to technical considerations, and that, by placing new tools of obfuscation, propaganda and subordination in the hands of unscrupulous authorities, alternative futures are also possible.

As Lyon suggested, 'anyone worried about the encroaching tyranny of technocratic power embodied in IT should not ignore countervailing movements also present in contemporary societies'. In addition to modern versions of Luddism that reject not so much the technologies themselves as the oppressive social relations inscribed within them, a variety of social movements can reinvigorate ethical and political debates about the future ownership, use, transparency and accountability of information and communication technologies. There is still scope for citizens to support effective legislative and other regulation, and for them to seek to re-channel technological developments or to re-configure people's participation in them.

> *Some such strategies have an egalitarian impulse, in which access and control are key issues, whereas others go beyond this to inquire as to whether in certain contexts proposed or established new technologies are appropriate at all. (ibid., p. 154)*

At local level, too, 'the twin concerns of justice and appropriateness may be confronted again'. To instance this, Lyon referred to successful moves to decentralise communications systems, in which public access is guaranteed, such as experiments in local broadcasting and reversals of conventional patterns of technological development that start from 'research on social and personal "needs". These relate in particular to disadvantaged groups, such as the disabled, single-parent families, isolated elderly people, and so on' (*ibid.*, p.154). Lastly, insists Lyon, echoing the argument advanced by Castells, and in an assertion with profound implications for human and activist conceptions of citizenship, belonging and lifelong learning, 'in all "information society" discourses, it must be remembered that technological potential is not social destiny'. Rather than technological development having pre-set social effects that are either predictable and universal, or necessarily either wholly benign or inescapably malignant, they are 'the outcome of social shaping itself, including certain deliberate political, economic and cultural choices' (*ibid.*, p.157). As Castells puts it, 'nothing predetermined the trajectory taken by the information and communication technology revolution … Historical evolution is an open ended, conflictive process, enacted by subjects and actors that try to make society according to their interests and values, or more often, produce social forms of organization by resisting the domination of those who identify social life with their personal appetites enforced through violence.'

> *What we observe throughout history is that different forms of society came and went by accident, internal self-destruction, serendipitous creation, or, more often, as the outcome of largely undetermined social struggles. True, there has been a long term trend towards technological development that has increased the mental power of humankind over its environment. But the jury is still out to judge the outcome of such process measured in terms of progress, unless we consider minor issues the highly rational process of mass murder that led to the holocaust, the management of large scale incarceration that created gulag out of the hopes of workers' liberation, the nuclear destruction of Hiroshima and Nagasaki to finish off an already vanquished nation, or the spread of AIDS in Africa while pharmaceutical corporate labs and their parent governments were discussing the payment of their intellectual property rights.* (Castells, 2004)

The corporation as 'collective citizen'

There is a long paternalist tradition in the UK, now largely in decline, of employers demonstrating a deeper commitment to the care of their workers and of the communities in which they live than the minimum necessary for people to acquire the skills needed to undertake the work allocated to them, and for employers to secure people's basic health and safety at work and remunerate them at least at an acceptable level. Such employers have seen it as not only in their direct business interests, but also as their moral duty, to extend the benefits afforded to employees, their families, and often other local inhabitants, to include affordable housing, sports and leisure facilities, schooling, libraries and adult education. Such practices were typical of the Quaker traditions of responsible employment associated with firms such as the chocolate manufacturers Cadbury's, Terry's, Fry's and Rowntree's – all of them now incorporated into foreign-owned international companies – and the schemes initiated by Lever Brothers in Port Sunlight, and the extensive sporting facilities provided by toolmakers Alfred Herbert in Coventry.

Of course, there was always another side to this paternalism and commitment to workers' welfare. This was manifest in the employers' desire to supervise and control the social, moral and family lives of the workers, as well as being devices to head off what they saw as the divisive workplace politics of conflictual industrial relations (Bendix, 1956; Child, 1964; Martin and Fryer, 1973; Newby *et al.*, 1978; Gilchrist, 2007). At its core, paternalism was always a clear enough relationship of power and domination, and of the legitimation of capitalist hierarchy and class control. As such, it was replete with contradictions, and its benign image usually disguised as much as it revealed. Moreover, it was equally clear that the various additional benefits were always at the behest and discretion of the owners and employers, and always susceptible to unilateral withdrawal by them: they were in no sense 'workers' rights', not even of the ancillary kind secured through negotiation and collective bargaining and through trades union representation. Even so, paternalism inscribed in the routine life of the business corporation a wider set of social responsibilities and duties to the community than those laid down in company and commercial law.

In the contemporary world, such old paternalism finds its modern echoes in the variety of schemes operated by employers that commit a portion of their profits or resources to charitable activity, or that encourage staff to engage in (mostly local) voluntary work – often in company time – or open up facilities such as information technology out of hours to community use. In addition, there exists now an extensive literature on 'corporate social responsibility' (CSR), sometimes even referred to as 'corporate citizenship'. According to the current Wikipedia entry, where a company voluntarily commits to its CSR, as well as doing so for the consequential business benefits, it would also 'embrace responsibility for the impact of its activities on the environment, consumers, employees, communities, stakeholders and all other members of the public sphere'.

Furthermore, CSR-focused businesses would proactively promote the public interest by encouraging community growth and development, and voluntarily eliminating practices that harm the public sphere, regardless of legality ... An approach for CSR that is becoming more widely accepted is community-based development approach. In this approach, corporations work with local communities to better themselves. For example, the Shell Foundation's involvement in the Flower Valley, South Africa. In Flower Valley they set up an Early Learning Centre to help educate the community's children as well as develop new skills for the adults. Marks and Spencer is also active in this community through the building of a trade network with the community – guaranteeing regular fair trade purchases. Often activities companies participate in are establishing education facilities for adults and HIV/AIDS education programmes. (Wikipedia, 2010)

There are many variants of CSR in the modern business world, especially that occupied by companies at the top of the FTSE 100 in the UK and the Fortune 500 in the USA, or which are distinguished by their national or multi-national prominence. Mostly, CSR is a dimension of corporate governance that is embraced by larger publicly quoted firms. Prominent among current approaches is that entitled 'creating shared value', promoted in the prestigious *Harvard Business Review* by the celebrated business guru Michael Porter and his colleague Mark Kramer in their article entitled 'Strategy & society: The link between competitive advantage and corporate social responsibility'. In reviewing many CSR policies, Porter and Kramer focus on the value of seeing business success and company commitment to social responsibility as 'interdependent' features of the modern corporation, and not locked in a 'zero-sum' game in which corporations move beyond what is too often a 'cosmetic' approach. From the business point of view, Porter and Kramer argue, CSR needs to be regarded as 'much more than a cost, a constraint or a charitable deed – it can be a source of opportunity, innovation and competitive advantage'. What is more, Porter and Kramer add, when looked at strategically, 'CSR can become a source of tremendous social progress, as the business applies its considerable resources, expertise, and insights to activities that benefit society' (Porter and Kramer, 2006, p.1). According to the two authors, 'broadly speaking, proponents of CSR have used four arguments to make their case: moral obligation, sustainability, license to operate, and reputation'. The problem that they discern, is that:

All four schools of thought share the same weakness: they focus on the tension between business and society rather than on their interdependence. Each creates a generic rationale that is not tied to the strategy and operations of any specific company or the places in which it operates. Consequently, none of them is sufficient to help a company identify, prioritize, and address the social issues that matter most or the ones on which it can make the biggest impact. The result is oftentimes a hodgepodge of uncoordinated CSR and philanthropic activities disconnected from the company's strategy that neither make any meaningful social impact nor strengthen the firm's long-term competitiveness. Internally, CSR practices and initiatives are often isolated from operating units – and even separated from corporate philanthropy. Externally, the company's social impact becomes diffused among numerous unrelated efforts, each responding to a different stakeholder group or corporate pressure point. (ibid., p. 4)

In an even more critical review of the strategy of CSR, based on wide-ranging historical and empirical enquiry and focused on the *latent* purposes of companies' involvement in CSR rather than just its *manifest* claims, and on the hopes that activists in civil society pin on its implementation, James Rowe argues that the primary value to business of supporting such voluntary codes 'is the forestallment of precisely what global civil society hopes to gain through them: the binding regulation of transnational corporations ... The primary reason for business's trenchant interest in corporate codes is that they are an effective means of quelling popular discontent with corporate power and the political change that discontent might impel' (Rowe, 2005, pp.4 and 5). Although having its origins in business responses to the expression of public concerns such as consumer protection, product safety, environmental degradation, the squeeze put on suppliers and small local competitors, threats to staff employment security, and, more recently, in the context of large 'anti-globalisation' demonstrations, CSR has thus played a largely defensive and deflective role. In regarding the flourishing of CSR as a cause more of concern than optimism, Rowe concludes that 'my research has convinced me to approach corporate codes of conduct less as exemplars of business ethics and more as effective business strategy'.

Some possibilities

Despite these critical and disappointing findings, it does not follow that cynicism and despair are the only possible responses to CSR and to the prospect of engendering some genuine commitment to, and collective benefits from, companies' potential contribution to citizenship in today's world.

First, it would be premature to write off the pressure that can successfully be brought to bear by consumers, the general public, politicians, shareholders, trades unions and protestors – even on celebrated corporate household names, as was demonstrated by the embattled plight of BP in the wake of the oil spillage in the Gulf of Mexico at the time of writing (mid 2010), and by successful local UK campaigns to deny the expansion of Tesco supermarkets.

Secondly, there is always scope for CSR to be moved from the realms of voluntary and elective initiative onto a more publicly regulated basis, if necessary backed by amendments to company law.

Thirdly, leading companies could set the trend, enforce among their respective supply chains and give due publicity to the business policy that they accept that the privilege granted by the community to business to make and sell products, employ staff, trade and make profits, and often to benefit from an array of other planning, financial and fiscal benefits should be seen as one side of a social compact, in classic liberal style. On the other side, in addition to all the potential benefits to the community of jobs, taxes and consumer choice, would be an acknowledgement of the requirement of business to engage in, and report on, a clutch of corresponding social responsibilities – for example in respect of their carbon footprint, promotion of equal opportunities (including progress towards equal pay), contribution to environmental sustainability, and investment in the learning and development of their staff. All of this could be supported by the development and promotion of appropriate national accountancy standards, and could be institutionalised in the UK as strict entry criteria for membership of prestigious trade and other business associations such as the CBI, British Chambers of Commerce, and Association of Small Businesses.

Finally, if such trend-setting, leadership-by-example initiatives and their emulation remained the exception rather than the rule, they could be given statutory force, extending the individual and collective social rights and obligations of citizens. There could easily be introduced an imaginative combination of a framework statute with a host of voluntary joint collective regulation (backed by statutory rights), such as enabled marked progress to be made in health and safety at work following the enactment of the 1974 Health and Safety at Work Act and its associated regulations (Fryer et al., 1998).

137

CHAPTER EIGHT

Inclusion, pluralism and social cohesion

Social exclusion and inclusion

The contemporary expression of social rights for citizens is often couched in terms of ensuring that particular social groups, categories of people, or localities do not risk or suffer from 'social exclusion'. The language of exclusion, and its opposite social inclusion, and instances of public policies invoking the notions, have become more common in the UK over the last quarter of a century or so. This has partly reflected an increasingly European inflection and has partly stemmed from a reluctance to resort to diagnosis based on class analysis or on a commitment to social equality as a core political principle, or to think of disadvantage as residing mostly in one particular dimension such as poverty. As social structures have changed, it is said that other social differences and cleavages now matter that cannot be adequately explained by those frameworks, once so influential in the social democratic tradition (Byrne, 2005).

Social exclusion draws attention to the various structural, organisational, experiential or relational aspects of 'society' that need to be challenged for individuals to be able to operate as modern, responsible and independent citizens, not least by obtaining paid work, or at least by demonstrating their employability and by no longer depending on welfare benefits. The targets thus have included achieving reductions in poverty, chronic unemployment, long-term ill-health, homelessness and poor housing, and general disconnectedness from the rest of society. In addition to getting people into work, social inclusion entails overcoming limited access to public services, eliminating systematic and hostile

138

discrimination, tackling social isolation, or reversing low levels of educational attainment and a lack of key skills. Very often, such strategies explicitly invoke a key contribution to be made in this by education, training, qualifications and employment skills development (Leitch, 2006).

With the rise of 'New Labour' in politics and government, the emphasis on social inclusion has also fitted well with its advocacy of 'third way' politics (Miliband, 1994; Giddens, 1994). An emphasis on social inclusion and its opposite, exclusion, changes the politics in a number of ways. First, it insists that excluded people suffer from multiple and often mutually reinforcing disadvantages and deprivations. Secondly, it denies that there is any single overriding cause of these, especially their social class location. Thirdly, it allows that one element of the exclusion might be normative, and that people – maybe even generations – suffering exclusion may be embedded in a system of norms and values that offer no promise of escape or aspiration, and possibly incline them to dependency. The shift moves attention from vertical relationships between different levels of social stratification or exploitation to one more concerned with the horizontal relations between the mainstream of society and those individuals, groups or neighbourhoods that stand outside or are systematically disconnected.

In a critical review of the different discourses around social exclusion and inclusion, Levitas (1998) discerns three different contemporary perspectives. The first, more traditionally socialistic, is redistributionist; the second, more moralistically, emphasises the problems of dependency and the alleged emergence of an underclass; and the third centres more on social integration, especially via employment. Levitas argues that New Labour's policy discourse favoured a combination of the second and third approaches, thus allowing it 'to differentiate itself from uncaring and unsocial Thatcherism whilst remaining committed to the neo-liberal, anti-collectivist and globalizing agendas which Thatcherism made central to UK governance' (Byrne, 2005, p.56).

Debates about social exclusion and inclusion frequently focus on their implications for 'social cohesion'. Social cohesion is a concept with many different meanings, affording plenty of scope for debate and conflict, especially where its imputed links with education are concerned. In one of the most systematic empirical studies of the relationship between education, equality and social cohesion (Green, Preston and Janmaat, 2006), it is suggested that, according to context, one or more of

139

six elements of social cohesion may be emphasised. They are: shared norms and values; a sense of shared identity or belonging to a common community; a sense of continuity and stability; a society with institutions for sharing risks and providing collective welfare; equitable distribution of rights, opportunities, wealth and income; and a strong civil society and active citizenry.

Whatever other merits or drawbacks it may have, the idea of social inclusion, when figuring as an element of either citizenship or belonging, implies that there should be some notion of a 'totality' – a whole, a broad unity, a communality – in which all should be included or 'integrated' as full members. That commonality may be defined by place or geographical or national boundaries, by legal status, by social or legal category, by shared aspirations, or by common interests, cultures, values and traditions.

Societies characterised by commitment to social cohesion usually seek its achievement through one of two ways. On the one hand, broadly echoing the 'negative freedom' liberal approach to citizenship, social cohesion is made possible by the extension of individual freedom where the role of the State is to open up such opportunities to all. On the other hand, reflecting more the European Social or Christian Democratic traditions, the State and public sector promote social solidarity and equality among all citizens. In either case, education may play a role: in the first as an avenue of opportunity through which individuals can advance into their appropriate place in society; in the second, as a key mechanism for the promotion of social solidarity and mutuality. In general terms, the first typifies the 'Anglo-Saxon' approach emphasising economic competitiveness, flexible labour markets, employability' and high levels of labour market participation. The second is characterised by the countries of continental Europe and, especially, by Nordic societies with their 'social' model based on labour market regulation, widely diffused workforce skills and investment in technology.

In their rigorous cross-national statistical analysis of the relationship between education, inequality and social inclusion, Green and his colleagues found strong correlations between educational inequality and income inequality, and between income equality and social cohesion. The statistical modelling techniques they used indicated an association between educational inequality in those societies with 'weak comprehensivisation and strong marketisation', and a range of measures indicating a lack of social cohesion, including limited civil and political rights and crimes against the person (Green, Preston and Janmat, 2006, p.15). The research also suggested that the ways in which education has an impact on social trust and tolerance are complex and highly context-bound, but that greater ethnic homogeneity within nations appears not to make them more trusting than those manifesting heterogeneity. In the UK, Green and colleagues suggest, the current emphasis on skills for employability does 'promote a form of social cohesion which is positive but partial since it fails to address the sharp divisions that arise with increasing income inequality amongst those in work' (*ibid.*, p.17).

Migration, race and ethnicity: conflict and cohesion

It is in the fields of migration, race and ethnic relations – often especially in relation to the possible impact of Islam on national and community social cohesion in the UK – that debate has raged most furiously. At its heart, the argument that certain racial, ethnic or 'coloured' groups of people should be denied the full rights of citizenship or refused the opportunity fully to belong rests on an assumption not just of their difference, but also of their inherent inferiority. The whole history of slavery, of racial oppression and exploitation, and of racist hostility to black people enshrines such toxic beliefs. Women, too, have shared a similar history, and race and gender have often been a dual basis of exclusion from full citizenship and of being denied equality.

The political theorist Carole Pateman and the philosopher Charles Mills – who have challenged theories of social contract for their inherent biases against, and neglect of, respectively, the positions of women and black people – recently explored the implications of the intersection of race and sex in political analysis, philosophy and social practice (Pateman and Mills, 2007). The work of Pateman and Mills underscores the limitations of previous political theorisation and practice. As they comment in their joint introduction, they each in their own way 'excavated the role of the classic theorists in justifying the patriarchal, racial and imperial structures that have shaped the modern world, and examined the legacy of these structures in societies whose self-conception is so thoroughly, and misleadingly, informed by notions of individual freedom and equality'. In the realms of both political theory and political practice, 'for three centuries there was no doubt that white women and non-whites were deemed inferior to white men, were second-class citizens or outside citizenship altogether' (Pateman and Mills, 2007, p.2). As Pateman and Mills observe, the continuing challenge in addressing these issues, particularly in the rich industrial democracies of the West, is the deep paradox that matters of race and gender are embedded 'in a context of formal equality, codified civil freedoms, and antidiscrimination legislation', where multiple examples of racism and sexism are regarded either as unfortunate hangovers from a less civilised past or as instances of minority prejudice. In other words, even where it occurs, the granting of *formal* rights of citizenship may coexist with a powerful ideological commitment on the part of ruling, host or majority populations to their own *substantive* superiority, thereby serving as a potent barrier to any shared sense of belonging or common desire for social cohesion.

Historically, the position of ethnic, cultural, religious and linguistic 'minorities', whether in their own countries of origin or in the 'host' society, have reflected powerfully the relationships of hierarchy and domination that forged the circumstances of their lives. These were the stark binary relationships of conqueror and conquered, of coloniser and colonised, of settler and 'native', of master and slave, of 'civilised' and 'barbarian', and of 'normal' and 'deviant'. In those countries where access to full citizenship was from the outset deliberately and systematically denied, there have been 'whole categories of people':

> ...who can be described as 'denizens', people who are foreign citizens enjoying permanent legal resident status, or as 'margizens', long-term immigrants who lack secure resident status: illegal workers, unauthorised family entrants, asylum seekers, refused asylum seekers who have not (yet) been deported and temporary workers who are in fact permanently integrated into the workforce. (Keane, 2003, p. 20)

In the UK, as in other European countries with a history of empire and colonial rule, the arrival of immigrants resulted in decades of experience of systematic exclusion from housing and jobs, of racial violence, jibes and hostility, of harassment at the hands of the police. Even in countries such as the UK where 'new Commonwealth' migrants initially enjoyed most of the formal rights of full citizenship (until limited by legislation in the early 1980s), their real experiences were often of exclusion, prejudice, discrimination, racism, and of a feeling of not really belonging in 'Babylon' (Rex and Moore, 1967; Solomos, 1989).

Public anxieties expressed by governments and community representatives – claiming to speak on behalf both of native, mostly white, British people and minority ethnic and black communities – have centred

142

on racial tension and what they fear is the prospect of increasing communal violence and mutual hostility. This has already been variously manifested in riots in London, Oldham, Blackburn and Bradford, in increased racial violence against ethnic minorities, and in the rise in popularity of the British National Party. There has been concern, too, that children from minority ethnic groups, especially boys from Afro-Caribbean backgrounds, underperform at school, are more likely to be excluded from school and, post school, suffer higher rates of unemployment than their white compatriots.

Multiculturalism again, but with a difference

Patterns of behaviour and relationships grounded in racist attitudes and ideology were first challenged by liberation movements or by minorities and migrants opposed to inequalities and unfairness, and by adherents of the liberal approach to citizenship. The next phase of responses from states and governments to claims for recognition of legitimate difference by minority or oppressed groups, where they were no longer met with direct denial or even suppression, usually took the form of insisting on the 'assimilation' of the claimant group into the assumed common 'mainstream' ways of life of the majority population, and of their integration into an undifferentiated, shared national unity. The aim was to transcend differences in the interests of constructing homogeneity – of identity, loyalty, outlook and sense of belonging. All of this was to be achieved by the combined effects of schooling, the adoption of a common language, by adherence to a common set of cultural norms and values, by the promotion of shared symbols, and by intermarriage.

Over time, and especially since the adoption of the Universal Declaration of Human Rights in 1948, and in the wake of major campaigns and struggles – such as the civil rights movement in the USA – these integrationist and assimilationist responses to claims for the recognition of difference have gradually been replaced by the development of various versions of what became known as 'multiculturalism' (Kymlicka, 2007). Multiculturalism – the public acknowledgement of the legitimacy of claims for difference and its recognition in law, in the granting of particular statutory rights, in showing respect for distinctive cultural practices, and in the provision of education (especially for children) – has usually been manifest with regard to three kinds of minority group. First, there are rights granted to *indigenous* peoples, often accompanied by an acknowledgement of past state actions that deprived such peoples of their traditional rights, land, language and ways of life. Secondly, there are what Kymlicka (*ibid.*) terms 'substate/minority nationalisms', where groups with claims to a distinctive and often historically based statehood are granted some degree of autonomy in respect of governance, economy, taxation, administration and culture. Thirdly, and most controversially, is the recognition (sometimes supported by special funding or separate provision) afforded to immigrant groups in respect of their ethnicity, language, cultural and religious practices, modes of dress and representation. In all three versions of multiculturalism, there are significant implications for both citizenship and belonging, as well as for education, especially where the schooling of children is concerned.

The systematic extension of formal rights and the simultaneous according of increasing honour and respect to groups that were formerly excluded have all contributed to what Kymlicka (*ibid.*) described as 'citizenization'. This is the process of 'replacing uncivil relations of enmity and exclusion with more equitable relations of liberal–democratic citizenship' (*ibid.*, p.261). Citizenization is rarely a matter of a simple legal transaction conferring the new status upon individuals or groups. Most recently in the UK, this process has involved special 'citizenship ceremonies' to mark people's transition to full British citizenship. It has also included the requirement for candidate citizens to demonstrate competence in English and to pass a 'citizenship test' in which they must show knowledge of, and familiarity with, aspects of British history, the workings of British institutions, the make-up of the population of the UK, and the nature of British culture.

The adoption of multiculturalist policies and strategies in the UK owed much, first, to the continuation by migrants and their descendents of patterns of behaviour which they valued and which enabled them to demonstrate their shared identity. Secondly, public authorities responded positively to the various campaigns and claims of immigrants and their supporters that important and cherished aspects of their lives and identities, deserving of recognition and respect, were being scorned or denied. Thirdly, public policy in favour of multiculturalism was increasingly shaped by experts in race relations, community development, equality and diversity, and, most recently, human rights. As Fahrmeir observed of the UK (and the same went for a number of other European states), 'debate on immigration, naturalization and refugee policy in the late 1980s and early 1990s gave the question of citizenship and immigration an unprecedented degree of contemporary relevance' (Fahrmeir, 2007, p.5).

Islam and fear

What has stalled and in some cases reversed progress in the UK towards multiculturalism is an increase in fear and anxiety about some of its possible consequences, especially as regards migrant communities adhering to and preaching the Islamic faith. Fear of the local and national impact of large-scale population migration upon UK communities – especially the immigration of people actively professing to Islam – has provoked anxious and often alarmist discussion, intensified in the wake of 9/11 and the July 2005 bombings in London.

Central to the argument has been the expression of doubt about the extent to which newly migrated individuals and groups are at one with the norms, values and cultures of the UK. This anxiety seems only to have been exacerbated when the religious beliefs and practices of whole communities were evidently quite different from the 'official' Christian religion of the UK as the 'receiving' country. There is also now a popular perception in the UK that the faith most in question, Islam, denies equality to women and even, in some versions, sanctions 'genital mutilation' of girls and young women, as well as violent punishment of those deemed to have transgressed its customs or rules. The publicity given to militant Islamic leaders and their open hostility to Western values, denunciation of American and British invasions of Iraq and Afghanistan, coupled with the association portrayed between Islam and the leadership and actions of Al Qaida, have all stoked up anxiety. Thus, in the most outspoken criticisms in the UK, newly arrived migrants have been portrayed as constituting a threat to traditional community cohesion and even to public safety. In June 2010, the online attitudes survey research firm YouGov, in a poll of 2,152 adults, commissioned by the Exploring Islam Foundation, found that 58 per cent of those questioned linked Islam with extremism, and 69 per cent believed Islam encouraged the repression of women.

Further concerns have arisen about the establishment of separate educational provision for the children of migrants, such as the opening of 'Madrassa' faith schools by Muslim groups. Sometimes the fear extends to a suspicion that such separate organisation of education fosters inter-communal suspicion and hostility, and can even recruit young people into

145

terrorism. In such circumstances, suspicion can all too easily be escalated up to that most corrosive fear of all fears, the insidious fear of the dangerous 'stranger' in our midst.[16]

Strangeness and difference, overlaid with stereotypes of Muslim fundamentalism and fears of *jihad*, have translated into an embattled discourse over identity and belonging, focusing on restricting access to equal rights and denying Muslims admission to citizenship. Accentuating the conflictual and irreconcilable character of difference centres on strategies for containment and control and, if need be, even expulsion. Will Kymilcka, in an analysis of an apparent 'retreat' in some Western democracies from that aspect of multiculturalism that concerns immigration, and noting the increased 'securitisation' of state–Muslim relations, confirms that it is particularly since the attacks of 9/11 and the terrorist bombings in Madrid and London that fears have mounted that 'locally settled Muslims might collaborate with enemies of the West, serving as a fifth column. As a result, a number of issues that used to be in the "normal democratic politics box" have been put back in the "state security" box' (Kymlicka, 2007, p.125).

It is easy to see how a potentially dangerous and deeply divisive tangle has resulted from an injudicious, sometimes deliberately fostered, intermingling of the issues of immigration, race and ethnicity, Islamism, separation of populations into neo-local concentrations of housing (ghettos) and into special schools, different dress codes and persistent adherence to foreign languages, and the claims of Al Qaida. With anxieties thus heightened and even mobilised by political activists, rather than diversity and difference being tolerated for the social richness they promise for national culture, the outcomes have ranged from confusion to outright hostility and even community conflict and violence.

Doubts about multiculturalism

It is in respect of state policy and public support regarding the third dimension of multiculturalism – that which is directed particularly to immigrants and to their children and grandchildren – that Will Kymlicka

---

16 In a parallel example, Ulrich Beck, seeking an answer to the problem of 'how neighbours become Jews', has noted that 'in reflexive modernity, the construction of strangeness is doubly politicized. First, the politicization of the question of security mobilizes the control instruments of civil society and the strong state. Second, the figure of the bureaucratically constructed stranger replaces the cultural stranger' (Beck, 1998, p.139).

has discerned something of a recent palpable retreat in most Western democracies, although, as he stresses, the picture varies substantially between different nation states. Even one-time supporters of multiculturalism have begun to suggest that the scope that it opens up of people living 'parallel lives' in separate communities might mean that the UK is 'sleepwalking into segregation' (Phillips, 2005). In a related argument, Cantle argues that separate parallel communities – in terms of ethnicity, faith, language, culture, housing, employment, leisure, lifestyle and educational experience – threaten the mutual respect, tolerance and the valuing of diversity which lie at the centre of genuine multiculturalism.

Some critics of the idea of multiculturalism allege that the notion is not merely muddled, it is also tokenistic and risks merely emphasising the exoticism of difference. Others argue that it does no more than legitimate or even reinforce the worse established differences, standing against any real prospect of building cohesive citizenship, shared values and a genuinely common culture. In any case, say critics, discourse that rests principally on a binary division between 'majorities' and 'minorities' not only polarises difference, but often rests on an assumption that any difficulties between people with different identities can be resolved either by integration or assimilation of the minorities, or by the majority simply demonstrating tolerance, possibly promoted by education.

Immigration and citizenship

The citizenship perspective on migration has two variants. On the one hand , it is argued that such new arrivals cannot be granted full citizenship until they demonstrate an agreed level of understanding and integration. This is the approach that informs the current UK Government's policy on citizenship for non-European-Union migrants into the UK, whereby the Home Office becomes the prime government department concerned with the learning involved, rather than the one usually responsible for education.

The second perspective argues in favour of combining recognition of difference with admission into full citizenship, where necessary supported by immigrants' learning.

Empirical evidence on the issue of immigration into the UK is mixed, and research on attitudes to immigration usually demonstrates quite widely divided opinions on the subject. In the 2004 European Union survey of attitudes on values and belonging, overall, 38 per cent of respondents agreed with the statement that 'immigrants contribute a lot in our country', as against 52 per cent who disagreed (32 per cent and 59 per cent respectively in the UK). On the question of whether 'immigrants threaten our way of life', overall 42 per cent of respondents agreed and 48 per cent disagreed; of UK respondents, 54 per cent agreed with the statement against 37 per cent who disagreed. (All data from European Union, 2004.) Some of these findings appear to have been echoed in a recent survey on UK attitudes to immigration conducted by the public opinion polling firm IPSOS/MORI on behalf of the BBC in April 2008. In this survey, 59 per cent said that the UK had 'too many immigrants', 76 per cent agreed that there was racial tension in the UK, and 64 per cent believed that this tension was likely to result in violence. Overall, almost half (49 per cent) believed that the government should encourage immigrants to leave the UK. In voicing these opinions, almost four out of every five respondents (79 per cent) rated themselves as not racially prejudiced (BBC/IPSOS MORI, 2008).

In addressing these concerns, Kymlicka has suggested that the fears of mutual mistrust and social conflict arising out of 'differentiated citizenship' based on the legitimation and emphasis of difference are overstated.

> *The demands of immigrants and other disadvantaged groups for polytechnic rights and representation rights are primarily demands for inclusion, for full membership in the larger society. To view this as a threat to stability or solidarity is implausible, and often reflects an underlying ignorance or intolerance of these groups.* (Kymlicka, 1995a, p. 192)

One relevant example of this ignorance is the fact that new settlers in the UK often risk discrimination, or at least miss out on the full advantages of residence, until they are granted full citizenship. As Quentin Skinner (2003, p.25) has observed, in contemporary Britain, 'ethnic minorities remain under continuing pressure to conform to a normative account of what it means to be British, an account that devalues much of their culture while undermining their freedom to criticise.'

Pluralism or fragmentation?

For some commentators, claims of difference and for differential rights immediately suggest the 'irreconcilable tension' (Hall and Held, 1989) that seems to arise 'between the ideals of equality and universality

148

embodied in the very idea of the citizen on the one hand and the 'postmodern' emphasis on difference and diversity on the other ... [However], one does not have to be a signed-up postmodernist to accept that it is no longer good enough to accept gender analysis based on an understanding of women and men as unitary categories' (Lister, 2000, p.35), or any simplistic binary categories of ethnicity.

An acceptance of difference does not, of necessity, entail a commitment to separate development, mutual hostility and the inevitable impossibility of developing cohesive relationships between different faith and ethnic communities, or even of creating or willingly submitting to a wider overarching unity or sense of cohesion. Thus, for example, Cantle (2008) has charted what he calls 'the journey to community cohesion' in the UK, in the promotion of which he has played a leading part. Drawing a contrast between 'social' and 'community' cohesion, Cantle suggests that community cohesion was adopted in Britain as a counter to fears of social unrest; the search for cohesion focused on the development of shared values across ethnic divisions. For Cantle, the essence of policies aimed at promoting greater community cohesion is not so much to promote increased interaction between groups with different ethnic or religious identities, but rather 'to break down some of the prejudice and intolerance of others that allows discriminatory behaviour to continue and fester' (Cantle, 2008).

According to Isin and Wood (1999, pp.153 and 154), giving full and proper recognition to groups claiming a particular identity comes down to reconciling the two related questions of genuine pluralisation, on the one hand, and of fragmentation, on the other.

> To recognize only one logic at the expense of the other is to misrecognise the variety of experiences and subjectivities that arise under advanced capitalism ... While academic and non-academic populism emphasizes fragmented identities, the new social movements can be seen as efforts to redefine and reconstitute identities through political and discursive struggles over group rights and values.

The task for 'radical democrats' is then 'to harness the contradictory but democratizing tendencies of advanced capitalism towards new political arrangements and recognition of group rights' (Isin and Wood, 1999, p.155). What Isin and Wood envisage as their ideal is the 'possibility of a richer and multi-layered conception of citizenship understood as an ensemble of different forms of belonging rather than a universal or unitary conception' (*ibid.*, p.21).

As Isin and Wood express this challenge, 'the question facing us today, therefore, is not *whether* to recognize ethnic identities or protect 'nature' or to enable access to cultural capital or to eliminate discrimination against women and gays or to democratize computer-mediated communications, but *how* do you do all and at the same time?' (*ibid.*, p.154, emphasis in original). In response to their own question, the two authors conclude that the framework for modern citizenship first adumbrated by Marshall is no longer adequate. What they term the 'new cultural politics' requires that the constitutions of modern nation states now need to recognise diverse group rights. Cautioning against too early an assumption that the nation state is ineluctably on the wane under the joint impact of postmodernism and globalisation, Isin and Wood point to the twin effects of the 'late modern condition': 'severe *upward* and *downward* limits on modern citizenship, not only as a form of political and national identity, but also as a legal status capable of mobilizing and accommodating the fragmented identities of the late modern condition' (*ibid.*, p.155, emphasis in original).

In Isin and Wood's simple metaphor of 'harnessing', there are problems in ensuring that the creatures harnessed together do not work in conflict and end up damaging each other and, in the process, possibly even destroying the 'vehicle' they have been brought together to help move forward. For example, insofar as a particular claim rests, at least partially, on a group's sense of disadvantage, should this mean that members of such a group are granted additional or special rights over and above those of the citizenry at large, once recognition of the group's difference is achieved? In response to this question, some protagonists argue that, if political authorities want to address the problems of disadvantaged groups, then the relatively privileged – heterosexual men, white people, younger people, the able bodied – will need to 'recognise the justice of the group based claims of the oppressed to specific needs and compensatory benefits' (Young, 1998, p.283).

The limits and possibilities of constructing a shared narrative

All of this underlines the point that the central difficulty, as we saw in the earlier discussion of particularity, is that, at its heart, common citizenship entails powerful connotations of equality, at least formally speaking, and any institutionalisation or formal recognition of cultural differences may be challenged precisely as undermining the overriding commonality of shared citizenship. The question is to determine how to assert commonality and equality in circumstances of not just difference, but of palpable inequality, especially where some groups of citizens or would-be citizens allocate some or all of the responsibility for the persistence of that inequality, or some key elements of it, to the behaviour or even the culture of other groups, especially ones seen as relatively privileged. Phillips captures well the dilemmas involved in this, especially for democratic governments or other authorities:

> *Institutionalising group representation seems to conflict with what has moved away from group privilege and group representation and towards an ideal of citizenship in which each individual counts as one.* (*Phillips, 1995, p.290*)

The source of opposition to multiculturalism in the UK now rests in claims – and perceived concessions to the demands accorded to migrant, and especially Muslim, communities – not just for recognition and respect, but for: the use of other languages in official documents and proceedings; for separate education; for wearing distinctive dress; for the application of different rules and standards regarding animal slaughter; for independent political representation; for acceptance of women's subordinate status; for the right (claimed by some) to continue to practise female circumcision; for tolerance of the use of physical violence in so-called 'honour' retribution; and for the application of sharia law to resolve certain sorts of dispute in Muslim communities.

Those who are wary of or, increasingly, outspokenly opposed to continuing or celebrating multiculturalism in Britain perceive its long-term effects as not so much instantiating civilised practices to be expected of politicians and citizens in a mature pluralistic society, but rather as a dangerous and destabilising separatism, boosted by an encompassing separatist morality, religion and ideology, and threatening inter-community strife. Seen in this way, practising multiculturalism will not, in the view of those opposed to multiculturalism, deliver the benefits of increasing mutual respect, the gradual forging of a new commonality enriched by diversity, or the development of an attractive, sophisticated, welcoming and modern example of mutual respect that, for example, twenty-first-century global cities such as London might offer, particularly to young professionals. They regard all of this either as wishful thinking, or, worse, as the experience of a privileged elite rather than of benighted, poor and socially excluded white working class communities, who lay some of the blame for their plight on the adoption of multiculturalism and on migrants – for their loss of employment opportunities, inadequate housing, unsuccessful schooling, and perceived abandonment by conventional political parties. Not surprisingly, this is fertile ground for extremist, including racist, politics. So, how can it be tackled if mere insistence on pressing on with multiculturalism, regardless of the response from such evidently disgruntled communities, probably has little prospect of success?

Some authors bluntly deny liberalism's capacity to provide an adequate response to the different identities and claims for civil rights of migrant and ethnic groups. Thus, for example, Van Dyke (1995, p.33) has asserted that 'liberalism cannot be trusted to deal adequately with the questions of status and the rights for ethnic communities, most of which are minorities within the state.' This brings us back to the central question facing the construction of Goldsmith's elusive objective of achieving a 'shared national narrative' in the UK: how to accord recognition and legitimacy to a rich variety of cultural, ethnic and religious identities and yet simultaneously forge them into some kind of overall consensus, or sense of unity. This is especially challenging where one source of difference consists of historical memories of colonial oppression and continuing experiences of racial hostility and even violence, whilst another group fears that recognition will only add up to separation and rejection of any kind of integration into a common narrative and shared citizenship based on the values of freedom, justice, equality and mutual respect. Put another way, how is it possible to acknowledge a demand that some may express not only to be *seen* as being different in significant ways, but also to be *treated* differently, and yet still uphold the notions of common standards, equity and universal rights and obligations that sit at the heart of the liberal tradition of citizenship? How should we conceive of and respond to people's feelings of being somehow 'different' and yet enable them to feel genuinely 'included' in some wider grouping with others (who also might well have their own particular feelings of legitimate difference)?

Relational differences

In an echo of the arguments made by Walzer and Kymlicka, Iris Marion Young suggested, first, that recognition of what she called a 'relational conception' of difference rests upon an understanding that 'group identity is not a set of objective facts, but is the product of experienced meanings'. Secondly, and most importantly, in regard to this question of reconciling difference and commonality, Young asserts that acknowledgement of the legitimacy of difference is not at all incompatible with 'political togetherness' (Young, 1998, p.272). At the same time, expecting people to adopt abstracted, impartial and generalised attitudes to citizenship and democracy is both politically unrealistic and sociologically unlikely.

People necessarily and properly consider public issues in terms influenced by their situated experience and perception of social relations. Different social groups have different needs, cultures, histories, experiences and perceptions of social relations, which influence their interpretation of the meaning and consequence of policy proposals and influence the form of their political reasoning. (ibid., p.270)

As far as Young is concerned, the public policy objective should be neither to negate the centrality of equality and universalism to a full version of citizenship, nor to argue for complete interest group separatism. However, the danger, Young perceives, is that 'the attempt to realise an ideal of universal citizenship that finds the public embodying generality as opposed to particularity, commonness versus difference, will tend to exclude or put at a disadvantage some groups, even when they have formally equal citizenship status' (ibid., p.269). Where some groups are systematically oppressed or disadvantaged, a democratic public 'should provide mechanisms for the effective representation and recognition of (their) distinct voices and perspectives' (ibid., p.275). In Young's view, undue emphasis on universality and commonness – whether in respect of citizenship or identity – does not simply overlook difference and particularity, it effectively excludes and disadvantages certain groups, even when *formally* they enjoy shared citizenship rights and identities.

Yet other approaches suggest that the quest for common conditions of citizenship and the full acceptance of diversity are not necessarily incompatible features of late-modern 'inclusive' democracies. Ruth Lister (1998), for example, believes that the way forward is to accept what she calls 'differentiated universalism'. In avoiding a retreat into essentialism and particularism, this could provide the grounds for accepting that both individuals and the polity at large are 'made up of manifold, fluid, identities that mirror the multiple differentiation of groups', facilitated by the sort of open dialogue envisaged in Habermas's theory of communicative democracy (*ibid.*, p.77, cited in Delanty, 2000, p.45).

Such a point of view accords well with the argument strongly emphasised by Amartya Sen (2006) that it is absurd and dangerous to seek to limit anyone or any community to a single all-defining identity. People commonly live their daily lives through a host of identities, giving salience to one or other according to circumstances at any given time.

> *In our normal lives, we see ourselves as members of a variety of groups – we belong to all of them. A person's citizenship, residence, geographic origin, gender, class, politics, profession, employment, food habits, sports interests, taste in music, social commitments, etc., make us members of a variety of groups. Each of these collectivities, to all of which this person simultaneously belongs, gives her a particular identity. None of them can be taken to be the person's only identity or single membership category.* (*ibid., p. 5*)

For third parties to attempt to confine people to just one of their multiple identities not only distorts the complexity of their lives, it also denies them the freedom to determine what aspect of their identity to emphasise. Nor, adds Sen, is it sufficient for such attempts to point to the shaping influence of culture on people's identity. Despite culture's undoubted importance, it is neither overwhelmingly *determining* nor does it necessarily 'involve any *uniquely* defined set of attitudes and beliefs that can shape our reasoning' (Sen, 2006, p.35, emphasis in original)

Against the oversimplifying, negative view that multiculturalism implies an ever-increasing pluralisation and, worse, fracturing of the social order into separate and potentially conflicting social groups, Bhikhu Parekh (Bhabha and Parekh, 1989, p.4) provides a definition that centres on multiculturalism's two simultaneous, essentially dynamic and positive, functions. They are, first, that multiculturalism envisages 'a community which is creating, guaranteeing, encouraging spaces within which different communities are able to grow at their own pace'. Secondly, multiculturalism is concerned with 'creating a public space in which these cultures are able to interact, enrich the existing culture and create a new culture in which they recognize reflections of their own identity'.

Similarly, Walzer (1995, p.146) argued that particular versions of political pluralism can combine the idea of a shared culture with full recognition and acceptance of ethnic difference: 'in addition to common culture, overlaying it, radically diversifying its impact, there is a world of ethnic multiplicity'. What needs to be understood, Walzer argues, is that the forging of any such ethnic identity functions almost as the equivalent of a kind of national liberation as members of the group defend their cultural differences against easy or enforced 'cultural naturalisation', but this need not amount to a repudiation of wider unification. Such communities need appropriate opportunities within the unified republic not just to celebrate their identity as they learn and adopt the ways of the wider community, but also to sustain their 'reborn' sense of distinct culture and community with some control over resources, including educational and welfare services.

Walzer's view suggests the need for patient, active, gradual and possibly painful processes of achieving a new kind of shared narrative based neither on forced integration, whereby ethnic minorities are obliged to abandon cherished elements of their identities or their expression, or by submitting to what Mason calls 'radical assimilation'. What Mason favours, in contrast, is 'moderate assimilation' where the aim is 'to create a polity in which everyone is able to speak the same language (viz., the language of the dominant group) even if they have different first languages, and in which minority cultural communities abandon those customs and practices which are either unjust or in conflict with some of the central customs and practices of the dominant group'. Mason's approach requires, first, acceptance that there exists both dominant and minority cultures.

In Mason's view, it would not be implausible to suppose that 'moderate assimilation would be enough to provide the conditions needed for citizens to come to the belief that they belong together' (Mason, 2000, p.122). As described by Mason, it would be perfectly acceptable, under conditions of moderate assimilation, for tolerance and even respect to be given to group differences and, for example, to other religions, where their central practices do not conflict with the central practices of the dominant group (or the core principles and values underpinning all citizenly behaviour). Moderate assimilation would eschew measures such as the imposition of draconian laws banning certain minority practices, but would include:

Giving the customs and symbols of the dominant culture public status and respect (giving public holidays for festivals recognized by the dominant culture but not others); employing the language of the dominant culture in public affairs; requiring that state schools teach in that language, and educate the children in the history, geography and literature of the dominant culture; subsidizing the dominant culture in various ways or giving tax cuts to those who participate in it. (ibid., p.123)

In Mason's view, following such a pathway, whilst establishing a shared sense of belonging to a common polity, does not entail the development of a shared national identity, even if this may be regarded by some as preferable in shoring up people's sense of belonging and of sharing a common national fate. However, Mason accepts that even achieving a shared sense of belonging to a common political community – what he describes as an 'inclusive political community' – will be hard work: citizens would not need to share a common view on how, when or why the core institutions and values of a given polity emerged, or believe in the chief myths and stories that sustain it, but only believe that their current form and operations are valuable and worthy of endorsement. Such beliefs can be fostered and reinforced by 'ensuring that members of different cultural groups are effectively represented within the polity's major decision making bodies' and by 'granting "cultural communities" as much self-determination as they want and can be feasibly given' (*ibid.*, p.143).

Mason also allows that more radical observers such as Iris Marion Young and Will Kymlicka will object that moderate assimilation still requires that minorities accept both the idea of a dominant group and that they either gradually abandon or accept as secondary their own cultural practices in favour of those developed by the dominant group. In other words, minorities would have willingly to engage in processes and institutions whose original construction owed nothing to their own contribution. What radical pluralism would suggest, instead, would be a shared construction of new institutions and procedures, still with a firm foundation in the defining characteristics of liberal democracy, and upholding its core values of liberty, equality and justice, and respecting and, as appropriate, reflecting the customs and cultures of the majority.

All of this will require open and vigorous debate about what overarching values, rules and authorities need to apply, in pluralistic politics, in assessing the legitimacy of claims to difference, and its manifestations, and in any attempt to bind together distinctive identities and communities into a common citizenship with a shared sense of belonging. It will also require that demands from all citizens for fairness, including from those who blame immigration and multiculturalism for their loss and suffering, need to be taken equally seriously, not simply dismissed as ignorance or unthinking prejudice, and, crucially, be subject to the same open, rigorous standards of assessment. Ethnic, religious and cultural differences – and conflict – create precisely the sorts of difficult issues that need to be addressed through a critical, reflective education grounded in genuine dialogue.

Ethnic and religious diversity: issues for a plural and inclusive education

Multicultural education has at least four dimensions: in its aims and purposes, both manifest and latent; in the way in which it is organised for delivery; in its curriculum or content; and in its pedagogy. Some opponents of multicultural education in any form argue that it is more likely, at best, to promote separatism or, at worst, to encourage an undifferentiated relativism in which no perspective is preferred and which has little prospect of securing both respect for difference and commitment to a wider unity. Against this, supporters of multiculturist education declare both the realism of their approach in recognising the empirical circumstances of life in the contemporary world, and its value in endorsing tolerance, mutual respect and the common framework of values emphasising equality, justice and freedom that underpins the practice of such reciprocity.

For Mason, the implication of his advocacy of 'moderate assimilation' for multicultural education in the creation of a sense of shared belonging to a polity, especially through schooling and public education, is the promotion of what he terms a 'constrained pluralist' model. Constrained pluralism consists of children being taught 'in such a way as they become aware of themselves and of each other as future citizens of a particular liberal democratic state, and (in so far as possible) acquire the capacities, virtues and knowledge necessary to be good citizens of that state' (ibid., p.154). Mason favours this approach to multicultural schooling against, first, the suggestion that state education should adopt a strictly neutral stance, in which, when making pupils aware of a diversity of cultures, 'teachers should not take a stand on which culture's ideas, values or practices are the best, or which culture's practices embody the correct values', but introduce each culture 'in its own terms' (ibid., p.150).

Secondly, Mason differentiates constrained from unrestrained pluralism in which, for example, separate schools would be free simply to promote their own favoured cultures. The risk here would be that such pluralism would 'reinforce separate cultural identities in such a way as that a widespread sense of belonging becomes impossible' and, consequently, 'many citizens will not be able to identify with society's major institutions and practices because these institutions and practices will be suffused with cultural commitments they do not share' (*ibid.*, p.154).

The growth of 'multiculturalism' in Britain has been the focus of much controversy recently (Laden and Owen, 2007). In a survey conducted by MORI for the BBC in 2005, one-third of those questioned thought that 'multiculturalism threatens the British way of life'. Almost three-fifths also thought that 'people who come to live in Britain should adopt the values and traditions of British culture'. By contrast, only 13 per cent of Muslims living in Britain who were questioned saw multiculturalism as a threat to the British way of life, and over four-fifths thought that 'multiculturalism makes Britain a better place to live in'. The same poll reported that a large majority of respondents (68 per cent overall and 74 per cent of Muslims) opposed the view that 'the policy of multiculturalism in Britain has been a mistake and should be abandoned' (BBC/ MORI, 2005).

The issue of ethnic and religious diversity is one of the issues that recent UK initiatives in 'education for inclusive citizenship' envisage as a major challenge. The Crick report on teaching democracy and citizenship in schools referred to 'worries' about the increasing complexity and greater cultural diversity of the UK. In response, the report urged that 'a main aim for the whole community should be to find or restore a sense of common citizenship, including a national identity that is secure enough to find a place for the plurality of nations, cultures, ethnic identities and religions long found in the United Kingdom' (Crick, 1998, p.17). In the view of the Crick advisory group – reflecting its view that tolerance and understanding under conditions of social, ethnic and religious diversity is largely an even-handed, two-way process on the journey to common citizenship – the aim should be to create a society in which:

Majorities must respect, understand and tolerate minorities and minorities must learn and respect the laws, codes and conventions as much as the majority – not merely because it is useful to do so, but because this helps foster common citizenship. (ibid., pp. 17 and 18)

Subsequently, Sir Bernard Crick, who chaired the advisory group, conceded that 'the original advisory group put too little emphasis on learning for diversity, on questions of identity and on explicit anti-racism', although he did not accept that 'civic republicanism necessarily relegates ethnic and religious diversity to the private sphere' (Kiwan, 2008, p.xiii). One response was to advocate the teaching of multiculturalism in schools. In her review of the debate about multiculturalism, Kiwan (*ibid.*), who was a member of a further Crick advisory group on immigration and citizenship education (the 'Life in the UK' advisory group), observes that recently there has been growing discontent with both the term and the practices it supports, especially in education.

One particularly relevant outcome of the Labour Government's revised approach to the achievement of British citizenship by migrants into the UK has been the requirement for applicants to pass the UK citizenship test. To help applicants succeed in this, a whole panoply of 'self-help', books, courses and classes has been developed. This might be thought of as 'learning to be a British citizen'.

Many of the traditional virtues and pedagogic assumptions of adult education and lifelong learning can also make positive contributions here: building people's confidence in their ability to express views and have them taken seriously, promoting involvement through genuine dialogue, subjecting ideas to critical and informed discussion, and commitment to the deliberative and patient working through together of issues, towards agreed outcomes and, perhaps, common goals. In other words, lifelong learning can offer a method, a process and some protocols regarding the use of evidence, and some rules of debate. It can give weight to the validity of people's experiences – not necessarily as 'truth', but as worthy of respect and fair consideration. It can open up the possibility of considering how things might not only be different, but might even be improved.

As we shall see, in some approaches, and certainly in the one favoured in this monograph, adult education and lifelong learning provides the chance of adopting a more critical and radical perspective than those advocated by either Mason or Crick. It is in that sense that lifelong learning might offer what Raymond Williams referred to as a 'resource of hope' (Williams, 1989). What lifelong learning cannot provide, of course, is a set of pre-prepared 'answers' to the tricky, substantive problems engendered by acknowledging the legitimacy of divergences of identity and expressions of difference where matters of citizenship and belonging are at issue.

CHAPTER NINE

Education for citizenship and civil renewal

History and context

In common with the various ideas of what should constitute the key features of citizenship and the central notions of belonging, the world of education is a deeply and often fiercely contested territory. Arguments rage as to what should be its core purposes, its principal content, its pedagogy, how it should be funded and where responsibility chiefly lies for designing and overseeing its various practices, especially as regards the role of the State. This is perhaps especially true in respect of the formal education and general formation of young people, and the role and functions of schools and colleges. As Carr and Hartnett seek to demonstrate in their analysis of schooling's development in England in the nineteenth and twentieth centuries, and in their close critique of the educational reforms in what they term 'the neo-liberal offensive of the New Right' in the 1980s and early 1990s, 'conceptions of education are always constituted by diverse intellectual and political traditions that speak to different visions of the good life and the good society'. According to this account of the politics of educational reform under the Thatcher and Major governments, 'the New Right looked back to nineteenth century liberal and conservative traditions' with their own perspectives on what constitutes and promotes freedom.

> *Thus, the New Right's educational reforms were not only about the neo-liberal aim of 'rolling back the frontiers of the state'. They were also an attempt to re-impose on the educational system the neo-conservative cultural goal of reproducing a traditional, pre-democratic and hierarchical*

system of social roles and relationships. (*Carr and Hartnett, 1996, p.181*)

Rather than upholding a philosophy and practice of education aimed principally at a 'gentling of the masses' and their preparation for work and life in a world shaped by market forces, Carr and Hartnett wanted to construct a 'democratic theory' of education in which the primary aim would be 'to impart those democratic virtues such as tolerance, integrity, truth telling, impartiality, fraternity and the use of critical reason' (*ibid.*, p.188). In their view, this would require the promotion of what, following Held (1987), they call 'double democratisation' – 'a process aimed at the simultaneous democratic development of both education and society'.

A democratic vision of education would need to be founded on acceptance of four core principles: first, the fostering of a 'wide public debate in which "educational" policies and proposals can be tested through critical dialogue' and 'in which all can participate irrespective of occupational status or technical expertise'. Secondly, a rejection of 'the language and values of market forces' that treat education simply as 'a commodity to be bought and consumed', endorsement of the idea that 'education is a public good rather than a private utility', and an acceptance that, in a democracy, 'education has to be constantly re-formed as part of a wider process of social change aimed at empowering more and more people consciously to participate in the life of their society'. Thirdly, for the complex policy issues that will arise in pursuing such an educational philosophy 'to be addressed and resolved in a way that takes account of the diverse values, needs and interests of the different social groups and communities that constitute a society' rather than being largely the 'outcome of a competitive struggle for superiority between conflicting political ideologies'. Fourthly, would be a presumption that 'the need to educate all its future members to participate collectively in shaping the future of their society is a moral obligation quite independent of instrumental considerations or utilitarian concerns'. This, Carr and Hartnett argue, would sustain the view that 'the primary aim of education is to ensure that all future citizens are equipped with the knowledge, values and skills of deliberative reasoning minimally necessary for their participation in the democratic life of their society' and the teaching and learning 'of those civic virtues – such as fairness, tolerance, empathy and respect for others – which democratic deliberation requires' (Carr and Hartnett, 1996, pp.191 and 192).

Learning citizens

In practice, education and learning *for*, *through* and *in* citizenship features in all schemes and visions for preparing people to handle the responsibilities and multiple challenges of living in a world of turbulence, risk, diversity and ubiquitous change. This is true irrespective of which model or ideal of citizenship is being elaborated and, indeed, whether or not those charged with formulating or implementing educational policies are aware of the philosophical foundations and principal assumptions underpinning those policies and their practice. For citizenship to count, however, and to make a difference, it thus entails a special mix of competence, knowledge, confidence, know-how, attitude, determination, respect for others, and an ability to combine understanding and commitment with action.

> *Being a citizen is a role that, somehow or other, has to be learned. Citizens need knowledge and understanding of the social, legal and political system(s) in which they live and operate. They need skills and aptitudes to make use of that knowledge and understanding. And they need to be endowed with values and dispositions to put their knowledge and skills to beneficial use.* (Heater, 1999, p.164)

Learning to become a UK citizen means studying to pass the new 'Life in the UK' test, alongside being able to demonstrate competence in the English language. There are many guides for sale on how to pass this test. Six categories of knowledge have to be successfully negotiated; these are set out in the Home Office publication *Life in the UK: A Journey to Citizenship*. The categories are, first, 'a changing society' (migration; the changing role of women; and children, the family and young people, including education, work and health). Second comes 'a profile of the UK today' (population, including ethnic diversity; the nations and regions of the UK; religion, including Christianity and patron saints; customs and traditions, including festivals and sport). Third is 'how the United Kingdom is governed' (including the British constitution; the monarchy; government and elections; the European Union and the 'UK in the world'; the main political offices of state; political parties; the civil

162

services; the devolved administrations; local government; the system of justice and police; the media and quangos). Fourth comes 'everyday needs' (housing, including rental and purchase; services and utilities – gas, electricity, water, telephones, refuse collection; money and credit, health; education; leisure; and identity documents). Fifth, is 'employment' (looking for work, including qualifications and making applications; equal rights and discrimination, including sexual harassment; contractual and other matters at work, including national insurance, pensions, health and safety and the role of trades unions; dismissal, redundancy and unemployment; working for yourself; and childcare at work). Last comes 'knowing the law' (the rights and duties of a citizen; crimes, the law and police duties, including search, arrest and complaints; the workings of criminal and civil courts; legal aid; human rights, including equal opportunities, marriage, divorce, same-sex partnerships and domestic violence; children, including parental responsibility and child protection; and consumer protection).

This is a formidable range and depth of knowledge, especially for someone who has not acquired it through childhood and early adult life, and through experience, listening to the radio and watching television. It is not clear what is intended to be the relationship between a migrant demonstrating this kind of detailed knowledge and feeling able to act as a full citizen, express their own identity and feel a sense of belonging in the UK. Also, those teaching in this area will be under pressure principally to help students pass the test rather than become citizens.

Teaching and learning citizenship in schools and colleges

The theories and conceptualisations of citizenship have exerted most influence in the realms of public policy concerning the education of children and young adults in the UK. Beginning in 1998, the late Professor Sir Bernard Crick produced the report *Education for Citizenship and the Teaching of Democracy in Schools*. The report centred on three main themes for educating school pupils in citizenship and democracy: self-confidence and social and moral responsibility; learning about and involvement in the life of the community; and political literacy – becoming effective in public life through knowledge skills and values. Crick and the members of his advisory group set their ambitions high.

163

> *We aim at no less than a change in the political culture of this country both nationally and locally: for people to think of themselves as active citizens, willing, able and equipped to have an influence in public life and with the critical capacities to weigh evidence before speaking and acting. (Crick, 1998, p. 7, emphasis added)*

Crick's proposals were subsequently implemented in extensive curriculum reforms in English schools from September 2002, by way of a non-statutory framework for Key Stages 1 and 2 and in statutory form for Key Stages 3 and 4 (QCA/DfEE, 1999). The order introducing the new citizenship curriculum in 1999 was wide-ranging and carefully worded, and is worth quoting.

> *Citizenship gives pupils the knowledge, skills and understanding to play an effective role in society at local, national and international levels. It helps them to become informed, thoughtful and responsible citizens who are aware of their duties and rights. It promotes their spiritual, moral, social and cultural development, making them self-confident and responsible both in and beyond the classroom. It encourages pupils to play a helpful part in the life of their schools, neighbourhoods, communities and the wide world. It also teaches them about our economy and democratic institutions and values; encourages respect for different national, religious and ethnic identities and develops pupils' ability to reflect on issues and take part in discussions. (QCA/DfEE, 1999)*

It is impossible to do justice to the sheer volume and diversity of curriculum development that followed the government's endorsement of the Crick report, and to the investment in staff training and other developments preparatory to the introduction of the new citizenship educational programmes for schools. In addition, wide-ranging schemes of research, monitoring and inspection have been instituted, and educational scholars have pored over the rationale, implementation and operation of the Crick proposals. Although the Crick recommendations were not starting from scratch, and were able to build on earlier initiatives and existing good practice, it is fair to say that the Crick recommendations and their introduction represented a notable shift in citizenship education in England.

The second Crick report on education for citizenship, aimed at the education and development of young adults, followed two years later, and was entitled *Citizenship for 16–19 Year Olds in Education and Training* (Crick, 2000). In Chapter 4 of that second report, Crick and his colleagues set out what they described as the 'importance of citizenship' in the development of all young adults. In addition to training for jobs, young people, they argued, also required 'training and education for life and the challenges which it brings … Whether in school, college or the workplace, young people should have opportunities to learn about their rights and responsibilities, to understand how society works, and to enhance the skills they need to be active citizens' (*ibid.*, p.12).

The sort of activism Crick had in mind would be 'as effective members of society at large, and of all kinds of public and voluntary bodies' in a complex, changing world marked by the decline of manufacturing, the growth of services, technological advance, and globalisation. The changes acknowledged by Crick and his colleagues included shifts in the political and social culture of the country; 'despite worrying indices of alienation and apathy, we were encouraged by the many examples of voluntary involvement of young adults working with the community that demonstrate what can be done'. Whether in political parties and pressure groups or not, it was important that young people, 'through the skills and knowledge which they have developed, take some control over their own lives and influence decisions which affect them' (*ibid.*, p.13).

As an appendix to this second report on young people's education and development in citizenship, Crick and his colleagues presented a matrix, with 70 cells, of the seven principal roles that young people should be prepared for in life and the ten sets of key skills they need to fulfil those roles. The template was provided to evaluate existing citizenship programmes, as a model specification for designing new programmes, as the basis for ensuring skill development, and as a starting point for the development of an appropriate framework of qualifications.

Independently of the English educational initiatives, the devolved government in Scotland endorsed a discussion and development paper from its Advisory Council of Teaching and Learning Scotland, aimed at 'developing children and young people's capability for thoughtful and responsible participation in political, economic, social and cultural life'. The strategy, based on the four key aspects – knowledge and understanding, skills and competence, values and dispositions, and creativity and enterprise – was concerned with providing capable citizens with political literacy, the ability to be active, make decisions, and 'take action where appropriate' (Advisory Council of Teaching and Learning in Scotland, 2001).

Similarly, in Wales in 2006, the Welsh Assembly Government's Department for Education, Lifelong Learning and Skills produced a strategy for action concerning education for sustainable development and global citizenship. The document, aimed at all sectors involved with education and training, higher education, and adult and continuing education, constituted an action plan to underpin the acquisition by students at all levels of 'the necessary skills, knowledge base, values and attitudes to be active global citizens in creating a sustainable society'. This would be achieved through the development of appropriate 'curricula, pedagogy and experience' and the provision of a 'comprehensive programme of continuing professional development for practitioners at all levels' (Welsh Assembly Government, 2006).

Reflecting on these findings and on other issues raised by his review, Lord Goldsmith proposed a key role for schools and education more generally in constructing a framework through which the common bonds of active and participative citizenship could be advocated and practised alongside a proper recognition and celebration of British diversity. Goldsmith's approach to citizenship education envisaged a combination of both classroom- and community-based activities: 'this focus on action is critical … active participation is needed to … engage young people at an early age in making a positive difference to British society and understanding that this is the potential that they have' (Goldsmith, 2008, p.90). The curriculum would embrace a wide range of 'citizenship-enhancing' skills and activities, designed to link schools to their communities. These skills would include: presenting a case to others about a concern; conducting a consultation, vote or election; organising a meeting or event to debate an issue; representing the views of others; creating or reviewing a policy; lobbying; setting up an action group; and training others in democratic skills.

Amy Gutmann argues that any democratic government will have a special interest in preparing its children for future citizenship, and therefore particular responsibility for their education. Children must not only understand and embrace the core values of democracy, they must also learn tolerance and respect for others and must develop their capacity to make informed choices. To that extent, insists Gutmann, such a task cannot be left entirely to the preferences or whims of parents and families. Only the State has the authority, mandate, resources and independence to carry out, or at least regulate and oversee, such a key undertaking. Further, she suggests, governments must be in a position to enforce this sort of education, exposing future citizens to the ideas of difference, comparison and change in their judicious exercise of choice.

For Gutmann, choice is not meaningful unless those exercising it have also developed 'the intellectual skills necessary to evaluate ways of life different from that of their parents'. Without the teaching of such skills as a central component of education, children will not be taught 'mutual respect among persons'.

> *Teaching mutual respect is instrumental to assuring all children the freedom to choose in the future ... Social diversity enriches our lives by expanding our understanding of differing ways of life. To reap the benefits of social diversity, children must be exposed to ways of life different from their parents and – in the course of their exposure – must embrace certain values, such as mutual respect among persons ... (Gutmann, 1994, pp.30–33)*

Assessing the implementation of citizenship education and development

Not surprisingly, interest quickly turned to examining how effectively, with what assurances of good quality, and with what sorts of results the new school programmes were proceeding. The early results were mixed.

To some extent, some of the early problems encountered might have been anticipated. A valuable analysis of the development of citizenship education in 16 countries, carried out by David Kerr for the influential INCA study (he subsequently played a central role in the research programme associated with the implementation of Crick), outlined the principal challenges, which were (Kerr, 1999, p.26):

- clarity of definition and approach;
- secured position and status in the overall curriculum;
- teacher preparedness and training;
- an appropriate range of teaching and learning approaches;
- the quality and range of resources;
- the development and wide dissemination of good practice; and
- influencing the attitudes and behaviour of young people.

The report also outlined two 'modal' strategies for citizenship education based on either 'minimalist' or 'maximalist' approaches, echoing the notions of 'thick' and 'thin' democracy in the writing of Barber and others. The first is typified by a narrow, formal, content-led, knowledge-based perspective, which is delivered principally in a didactic fashion. The second emphasises activism and participation, and is process-led and values-based. Where the first is relatively easy to measure, the second presents many more difficulties. Reflecting on the challenges, Kerr observed that practice normally lags behind policy and, in any case, 'There needs to be much deeper thinking about what is meant by "effective citizenship education". It is quick and easy to define as an aim of education, but difficult, messy and time consuming to achieve and sustain in practice' (*ibid.*, p.26).

In 2005, the Department of Constitutional Affairs published an extensive 'mapping' review, prepared by the National Foundation for Educational Research, of the links established between citizenship education and the department's priorities as set out in its five-year strategy. David Kerr and his colleagues observed that 'despite the frantic policy activity concerning citizenship in the curriculum and in other education and training sectors, there is common acceptance that citizenship education in England is still in its infancy in terms of the development of effective practices in schools and colleges' (Kerr *et al.*, 2005, p.15).

In commissioning the research, the department wanted to discover how far the new citizenship curricula 'could help young people to become more fully informed about the areas covered by the DCA policies and resources' and its five key priorities, namely: reducing crime and anti-social behaviour; speeding up the asylum and immigration appeals system; protecting the vulnerable, especially children at risk; promoting and delivering faster, effective and proportionate dispute resolution; and strengthening democracy and rights. The study revealed 'ample resource provision in the priority area strengthening democracy and rights where there is a surplus of material but little that engages students and captures their enthusiasm and interest'. Elsewhere, the materials surveyed showed either large gaps in resource provision, uneven resource provision or a lack of resources (*ibid.*, p.4).

In a lecture given in 2005, quoted in the Russell report on volunteering among young people, the then Chief Inspector of Schools in England drew attention to the generally poor standard of teaching of citizenship in schools at that time.

> *The overall quality of citizenship provision is unsatisfactory in 26 per cent of schools ... Some schools made a late start introducing the subject; in others, key management decisions were based on a misunderstanding or scepticism. Unsatisfactory teaching of the subject is most often found where it is taught through other subjects rather than distinctively. (Russell, 2005, p.35)*

In similar fashion, a wide-ranging review of the published literature, produced by Neil Selwyn in 2007 for FutureLab, focused on the experience of providing learning for citizenship in schools and further education, and of the application of digital technologies to support learning for citizenship, and reached equally gloomy conclusions. Although acknowledging that the two programmes were in their infancy and would need time to bed down fully, research and inspection already suggested that they faced serious challenges in being implemented in line with Crick's vision.

Ofsted's annual report for 2004–2005 reported that the teaching of citizenship was only a qualified success, with the subject less well taught and less well established in the curriculum than other subjects. In September 2006, however, Ofsted reported that significant progress had been made in implementing National Curriculum citizenship in secondary and post-16 education and training. Despite progress, the 2006 report indicated that 'there is not yet a strong consensus about the aims of citizenship education or about how to incorporate it into the curriculum. In a quarter of schools surveyed, provision is still inadequate, reflecting weak leadership and a lack of specialist teaching' (Ofsted, 2006, p.1). The report indicated that a minority of schools had embraced citizenship education with enthusiasm; however, the post-16 citizenship programme was showing signs of success in schools, colleges, youth centres and work-based training. The report noted that the intentions for citizenship 'remain contested and are sometimes misunderstood', 'aspects of knowledge and understanding were treated lightly' and in some schools there is 'insufficient reference to local national and international questions of the day'.

Despite these early difficulties, the ambition evident in the two Crick reports stimulated enthusiasm for citizenship at school and college level and in the associated research community. In January 2008, Ofsted produced a report *Leading Citizenship in Schools*, based on a conference held the previous May for 'secondary schools in which citizenship was

169

judged to be good'. In addition, an annual research survey has been established in conjunction with the National Foundation for Educational Research to monitor progress, provide relevant information, and publish relevant studies of citizenship education. A specialist association was launched for teachers engaged in delivering the citizenship curriculum, with Crick as its first president and with its own specialist journal to which Crick also contributed.

The 'democratic school'

This enthusiasm for citizenship education is evident in the advocacy by some practitioners and organisations of the 'democratic school', in an echo of John Dewey's (1916) ideas on the key role of the school in promoting democracy. For these advocates, some of whom submitted evidence to the Inquiry into the Future for Lifelong Learning, it is because schools play such a central role in the formation of a society's future citizens that it is essential for them to provide young people not simply with the arguments for active citizenship, but also to afford them plenty of opportunities to learn some of its key practices, including democracy. Thus, for example, in the UK, the Institute for Citizenship has developed and made available curriculum materials, practical guides and examples that enable school pupils not simply to understand better the challenges and implications of such issues as 'representation', 'accountability' and 'constituency', but also to take some practical part in their own schools' decision-making and formulation of policy.

Similarly, the Citizenship Foundation has issued a brief guide *Citizenship in Schools*. In reminding readers that the Crick report urged that school pupils be provided with 'structured opportunities' to engage actively with issues that will affect their lives, the Foundation observes that 'effective understanding and participation of the kind envisaged has a particular significance when we consider the possibilities for pupils learning through democratic involvement both within the school and in the life of the local community'. At the same time, the guide recognises that, although schools are not in any real sense 'mini-democracies', and that pupils in the UK do not have the right to vote before they are 18 years of age, nevertheless the school exists within 'a framework of democratic governance both at local and national level and that Article 18 of the United Nations Convention on the Rights of the Child affirms the right of children to express views freely and have them given due weight according to their maturity'.

Many schools in the UK already have a school council, and others have developed a variety of ways of consulting and engaging with their pupils about some of the policies and decisions that regulate school life, including such matters as school codes of behaviour, bullying and discipline. University researchers on democracy and citizenship in Scottish schools found that effective school management was 'associated with a genuinely consultative style that employs and promotes inclusive practices' and thereby 'models democracy so that pupils can learn about political processes first hand in their day-to-day life in schools' (Brown *et al.*, 2008).

The CBBC Newsround website also carries information on what school councils do, what roles they embrace, what makes a good one, whether they manage to get anything done, whether representatives on school councils can get out of lessons, and what is the history of the councils. In another example, Kent County Council has issued guidance in *Local Democracy in Schools – your contribution counts,* together with a teaching pack and resources aimed at increasing young people's awareness about local democracy, increasing participation in the longer term, and helping teachers to encourage awareness of democracy 'in an innovative way' and 'to engage pupils by making the information relevant to their daily lives and informing them how they can become involved at a school, district and county level through schools councils, youth forums and the Kent County Youth Council.'[17]

In an echo of Dewey's earlier proposals, part of the Council of Europe's recent study of 'Education for Democratic Citizenship 2001–2004' centred on the potential role and contribution of the school as a 'democratic learning community'. The report's author begins by observing that although there was no question but that the school should be involved in the 'democratic socialising of its students', the real issues were 'whether the school in its present form is able, empowered and willing to fulfill this role' (Dürr, 2005, p.9). Alongside the family, the report notes, school is the most important locale for the creation of informed, responsible and participative citizens, and as such should have four objectives: to empower students for their future role as citizens; to provide opportunities for 'democratic learning'; to open up areas for active participation and co-responsibility in the school environment; and to encourage pupils to participate actively in the social life of the community.

---

17 See also, the Wikipedia entry on 'Student Voice' at http://en.wikipedia.org/wiki/Student_voice

Among the problems discussed in the report is the apparent reluctance of schools and political authorities to involve school pupils in some kind of 'co-production'. 'There still seem to be strong reservations about the actual and co-responsibility of pupils in the decision-making process. On a very fundamental level, there are widespread concerns that the school – with its comprehensive mandate for education and even "creating" the competent, informed and responsible citizen – cannot possibly allow far-reaching co-responsibility or co-determination by its pupils' (*ibid.*, p.11). However, although there is respectable and long-standing pedagogical advocacy for making schools spaces of 'democratic living, learning and experience', in practice developments of a more radical kind in UK and the rest of Europe have been limited.

Thus, according to Dürr, in those programmes that have been introduced, the very notions of what constitutes democracy and the democratic process have been excessively narrow and the practice of organising the school in accordance with democratic principles has been almost entirely neglected. The report's author sees this as regrettable, not only because school potentially offers many opportunities for democratic experiment, but also because threats to democracy – 'extremist movements, violence, racism, xenophobia and social exclusion' – are 'just as virulent in the classroom' and require 'a new understanding of the rights and responsibilities of future citizens'. 'Intercultural learning is just one of the subjects which must be given more weight', in a pragmatic fashion rather than 'overburdening lesson plans with theoretical knowledge about democracy and the civil society' (*ibid.*, p.10).

Civil renewal and active learning for active citizenship

Public policy on citizenship development in the UK has not been limited to departments of state concerned with education and training: other departments have built on the work initiated in education and elsewhere in government to advance their own policies. As already indicated, the Department for Constitutional Affairs, with support from senior experts at the National Foundation for Educational Research, produced a comprehensive mapping study that connected the department's five-year strategic priorities with the provisions for citizenship education; only one of the department's priorities centred on strengthening democracy and citizens' relationships with the State.

Other recent policy initiatives have focused on questions of citizenship and belonging and have concerned ways of promoting civil engagement, strengthening social cohesion, renewing or regenerating communities, developing a common narrative of nationhood and belonging, and defining the conditions and requirements for admission to full citizenship of the UK. In addition to their articulation with the twin themes of citizenship and belonging, all these policy initiatives appear to ascribe a central role to learning for their successful implementation.

In particular, over the past decade, there have been numerous public policy initiatives in the UK focused on civil and neighbourhood renewal and economic and community regeneration, most of them stressing 'active' learning for 'active' citizenship. Hence in 2006, the Department of Communities and Local Government for England and Wales produced a 'national framework for active learning for active citizenship' entitled *Take Part*. Funded initially by the Home Office's Civil Renewal Unit, the national framework was the government's response to research findings in the 2005 Citizenship Survey that 61 per cent of people felt that they could not influence public bodies. In addition, the government declared its desire to empower citizens to be able to help improve provision of public services. The national framework comprised a report of pilot projects, a practical resource and a guide aimed at supporting adults to 'acquire the knowledge, skills and confidence to make a difference in their communities'. The document defined active learning for active citizenship as 'a flexible approach to personal and community development through experiential learning' that promotes 'personal effectiveness, social enterprise and lifelong learning' based on the values of 'participation, cooperation, social justice and equality with diversity'.

While he was Secretary of State at the Home Office in 2003, David Blunkett also pursued the commitment to citizenship demonstrated when he was Secretary of State for Education, with the publication of two major papers: *Building Civil Renewal* and *Active Citizens: Progressing Civil Renewal*. The first of these, a consultation document, built on Blunkett's Edith Kahn Memorial Lecture and set out its vision for civil renewal.

> *Civil renewal depends on people having the skills, confidence and opportunities to contribute actively in their communities, to engage with civic institutions and democratic processes, to be able to influence the policies and services that affect their lives, and to make the most of their*

communities' human, financial and physical assets. (Blunkett, 2003b, p.5)

Building Civil Renewal explained the government's views that, although individuals play important roles in civil renewal, 'the development of sustainable activity in the end depends on people acting together – in groups, organisations and networks', and so a key objective was to build 'community capacity'. This would be founded on six key values: social justice, participation, equality, learning, co-operation and environmental justice. In turn, implementing civil renewal and capacity building would embody the following principles: flexibility, democracy, empowerment, inclusion, self-reliance, sustainability, partnership working, and recognition of existing skills, talents, knowledge and awareness.

In *Politics and Progress*, Blunkett set out the case for a wholesale renewal of politics – what he called the 'social democratic imperative' – that 'requires us to articulate, defend and practice a new form of democratic politics, based on individual empowerment and active citizenship within strengthened communities' (Blunkett, 2001, p.15). Blunkett's challenging project embraced the strengthening of community through formal participation and practical engagement in the renewal of democracy and the promotion of lifelong learning, stimulating an increase in people's autonomy and their involvement in an active citizenship that 'offers a greater sense of belonging and identity in the future to reinforce our sense of history, culture and nation' (*ibid.*, p.29). For Blunkett, forging a common political citizenship did not mean an insistence on cultural uniformity, but rather the promotion of common bonds between different communities, the practice of respect for diversity and pluralism, and a determination 'to tackle discrimination and disadvantage wherever it exists, so that genuine opportunity can be achieved within and between communities' (*ibid.*). All of this would entail the 'rebuilding of democratic dialogue and discourse' that would include: a 'revitalisation of public political culture' through all sorts of media of communication; a spread of asset ownership among currently impoverished and excluded individuals and deprived communities; an improvement in 'political literacy and social and moral responsibility'; an extension of deliberative democracy through the likes of neighbourhood meetings, resident consultations, citizens' juries, town hall debates and other forums; compulsory registration of voters; the expansion of 'mutual and community associations in which people come together to discuss and debate social and political issues'; ensuring 'better representation of women and ethnic minorities in democratic decision-making at all levels'; an expansion of volunteering; and the renewal of democratic engagement, by facilitating people's participation in voting and by politicians enabling them 'to do things for themselves that would otherwise not be possible'. All of this would also depend on bridging the existential gap between citizens' aspirations and the capacity of governments to act on them (Blunkett, 2001, pp.136–140).

In *Active Citizens*, Blunkett argued that civil renewal meant 'supporting interdependence and mutuality, not simply leaving individuals or communities to fend for themselves' (Blunkett, 2003a). Overseeing all of this work was the Home Office's Civil Renewal Unit, whose brief was the active engagement of people in their communities, the ability of people to define the problems they faced, and their capacity to tackle them together in partnership with the government and other public bodies. Civil renewal was seen as being at the heart of the government's vision for communities, and believed to be an effective way of bringing about sustainable change and improving the quality of people's lives.

Until responsibility passed to the Department of Communities and Local Government in May 2006, the Home Office was also responsible for conducting a citizenship survey in 2001, 2003 and 2005. The main topics covered included: social networks, feelings about communities (including cohesion), trust and influence, volunteering, civic renewal, race and religious prejudice and discrimination, rights and responsibilities, and demographic and geo-demographic information. Since 2007, these data have been collected continuously on a quarterly basis.

Towards a 'citizens' curriculum'

The report of the independent Inquiry into the Future for Lifelong Learning, *Learning Through Life* (Schuller and Watson, 2009, Chapter 8), proposed that support for citizenship and people's sense of belonging in the UK should be provided by the development of a citizens' curriculum built around four main areas of capability or 'capacities to achieve well-being': digital capability, health capability, financial capability and civic capability. The Inquiry's focus on these four capabilities reflected its consideration that all citizens, in every one of the four stages of the life course identified in its report, would need to develop and deploy these capabilities in order not merely to survive but also to thrive, make the most of themselves and of the opportunities presented to them, develop a strong sense of themselves, and enjoy as much well-being as possible in every dimension of their lives. The Inquiry had in mind not so much the development of a series of formal educational programmes oriented towards these four capabilities but, rather, the provision for all people in the UK – both those enjoying full citizenship status and those living here as residents – of a wide range of opportunities, experiences and interventions through which they could acquire and enhance their well-being. Naturally, that would include ensuring that all domains of formal education organise their teaching and learning in ways that embrace the four capabilities and that combat conventional inequalities and barriers to learning. It would also mean that, where informal or non-formal learning is possible, authorities should encourage the participation of all citizens in practical learning with opportunities for interaction, reflection, skills development and innovation.

As has often been remarked, the connection between developing an active, participative citizenry and learning – in particular adult education – has a long tradition in radical education circles, owing much in the UK to R H Tawney, the so-called 'patron saint' of adult education.

> *R H Tawney believed that engagement in adult education was a necessary pre-requisite to and continuing part of participation in the institutions of democracy. Ensuring for all future citizens their liberation from ignorance and potential servitude and exploitation is secured by guaranteeing them access to all forms and fields of human knowledge, understanding and communication in a high quality, wide-ranging and dynamic curriculum in a wide range of institutions devoted to the education of the present and future electorate. Such a curriculum provides people with one of the principal means of personal empowerment, emancipated understanding and informed choice in exercising the duties and responsibilities of a citizen in a participative or representative democracy. (Aspin and Chapman, 2001)*

A modern citizens' curriculum would not simply enhance the capabilities and capacities of individuals. It would also provide structured opportunities for people to share their learning and development with fellow citizens, understand their common interests and identities, and respect and value each other's legitimate claims for difference. A citizens'

176

curriculum would strive simultaneously to add to the strength of collectivities and widen individuals' opportunities to express choice and
independence.

Volunteering

In many public policy and government initiatives, as in education, there is
evidence of renewed enthusiasm in the UK for volunteering and for
engaging in unpaid work to support good causes.[18] SENSE, the national
charity for deaf and blind people, refers to volunteering as a hot topic
currently, especially among politicians and policy makers, commenting
that this is a 'hugely exciting time for volunteering'. Not only does
volunteering feature in educational programmes promoting citizenship,
there is also evidence that people volunteer in a wide variety of ways and
settings.

Data from the 2005 UK Citizenship Survey indicated that 50 per
cent of people in England had undertaken volunteering at least once a
month in the previous 12 months, which the survey estimated could add
up to just over 20 million people. Over two-thirds of the respondents to
the survey reported participating in informal volunteering, defined as
giving unpaid help to someone who was not a relative, and 37 per cent
had done so at least once per month. Over three-quarters (78 per cent)
reported having given to charity in the four weeks before the survey was
conducted, with those who volunteered being more likely to have done
so.

The 2005 survey found that the proportion participating in voluntary activities at least once per month was greater among people with
formal educational qualifications. Those with no formal educational
qualifications, suffering from an illness or disability, and respondents from
minority ethnic groups were less likely to report that they had volunteered. The most common forms of what the survey called 'informal'
volunteering were giving advice (52 per cent), transporting or escorting
someone (38 per cent), keeping in touch with someone (38 per cent),
looking after someone's property or pet (38 per cent), babysitting or
caring for children (37 per cent), doing shopping or collecting a pension
(34 per cent), writing letters or filling in forms (32 per cent), and doing

---

18 A Google search on volunteering produced 1.62 million results from the UK alone and over 15
million worldwide.

cooking, cleaning or laundry (29 per cent). People involved in 'formal' volunteering had either raised or handled money by taking part in a sponsored event (51 per cent) or organising or helping to run an activity or event (47 per cent) (Department of Communities and Local Government, 2006).

The charitable body Volunteering England has a website providing everything from research and an index of opportunities to volunteer through to guides to good practice. Volunteering England supports the Institute for Volunteering Research. There are equivalent bodies in the constituent governments and administrations of the UK: The Volunteer Centre Network Scotland, Volunteering Wales, and the Volunteer Development Agency in Northern Ireland. The mission statement of the Northern Ireland agency is to create a 'caring, inclusive and participative society', and the agency is driven by the values of inclusiveness, participation, quality and openness. Its strap line is 'promoting and developing volunteering to build stronger communities'.

Reporting in 2005, the Russell Commission was established jointly by the Home Secretary and Chancellor of the Exchequer in 2004 to develop a 'national framework for youth action and engagement' for the whole of the UK, taking into account the devolved nature of volunteering programmes for young people in the different administrations of the UK. The Commission's report adopted the broad definition of volunteering used by the United Nations which explicitly 'encompasses ideas of participation and active citizenship' (Russell, 2005, p.13).

The Commission's proposals were presented to help realise a vision 'in which young people feel connected to their communities, seek to exercise influence over what is done and the way it is done, and are able to make a difference by having meaningful and exciting opportunities to volunteer' (*ibid.*, p.5). A key theme of the report was for the framework to be youth led, involving 'young people themselves in the design and implementation of volunteering activity'. The report refers to young people campaigning on particular issues, reviewing local community services and formulating proposals for change, getting involved in schools councils and youth parliaments, taking on governance roles, and initiating projects designed to tackle needs identified by young people.

One of the Russell Report's specific recommendations was that all UK education institutions should have a volunteering ethos, so that it could become 'commonplace for young people to volunteer whilst they are at school, college or university', with the possibility of such activity attracting academic accreditation and other awards. Volunteering would provide opportunities for young people to 'enhance their personal social skills, including communication, planning, problem-solving and effective team work'; knowledge and skills, the report observes, should be directly transferable to employment (*ibid.*, pp.39 and 91).

The Institute for Volunteering Research, as part of Volunteering England, exists 'to develop knowledge and understanding of volunteering in a way that is relevant to practitioners and policy makers' and publishes its own journal, *Voluntary Action*. As part of the evidence for the Russell Commission, Angela Ellis (2004) from the institute conducted research into the attitudes to volunteering of young people, *Generation V*, and Katherine Gaskin (2004) reported on the relationship between young people's volunteering activities and the idea of volunteering as 'civil service'.

The 2005 Citizenship Survey was followed by a further study, *Helping Out*, focused on volunteering among groups deemed to be at risk of social exclusion. This study was carried out by NatCen and the Institute for Volunteering Research on behalf of the Office of the Third Sector within the Cabinet Office. Whereas 42 per cent of those adults responding who were not at risk reported regular formal volunteering, the proportion of those 'at risk' doing so was 32 per cent, with the lowest level (28 per cent) being among adults with long-term illness. Volunteers 'at risk' were also less involved than those not at risk in the organisation and management of volunteering (Low *et al.*, 2007). The main reasons given for volunteering were: 'to improve things, help people' (53 per cent); because the 'cause was important to me' and they 'had time to spare' (both 41 per cent); 'to meet people, make friends' (30 per cent); because it was 'connected to the interests of family or friends'; or to 'meet a need in the community' (both 29 per cent).

Without wanting to dismiss entirely the potential value of volunteering in the context of citizenship programmes, or of what in the USA is usually called 'service learning', Bernard Crick (2002) voiced some telling reservations about current, largely governmental, enthusiasm for its promotion. The dangers are that volunteering may be offered as a poor alternative to professionally provided and properly funded public services, and that the (usually young) people so involved are instructed by those who are older and/or more powerful, and accept this uncritically. In any case, there is a central paradox in the idea of people being required to 'volunteer'.

CHAPTER TEN

Some problems and concerns

Vastness and complexity

Looking at the implications of the analysis of citizenship, belonging and lifelong learning outlined in this monograph, the most immediate concern is the sheer scale and complexity of the issues covered. The Inquiry faced the challenge, on the one hand, to do justice to the main ideas and arguments concerning citizenship, belonging and lifelong learning, and on the other to do so in ways that did not overbalance the Inquiry. Part of the problem resides in seeking to explore not only the three substantive topics in their own right (each of which could easily be the focus of a separate monograph), but also to try to understand the existing or possible future relations between them. As a consequence, this monograph proposes that the debate continues within the overall framework, priorities and policy focus proposed by the final report of the Inquiry, *Learning Through Life* (Schuller and Watson, 2009).

Clarity and validity of concepts

A second, closely related difficulty arises from the contested nature of most of the concepts and theories that are either articulated in debates about the three themes under review, or that underpin particular arguments or propositions. It is one thing to note some of these differences of meaning and interpretation, but utilising them to present a coherent and achievable way forward will require not only further debate but also great efforts at clarification and differentiation.

Even the very language in which argument is presented needs to be handled with care. As Giroux (1989, 1992 and 1997b), Williams (1990) and others have demonstrated, language in the areas of policy around citizenship, belonging and lifelong learning often either carries value implications or serves (deliberately or unintentionally) as a smokescreen for the underlying assumptions or models being advanced.

Norms and values

The difficulties are only multiplied by acknowledging that not only are the debates about citizenship and belonging most often couched in normative terms, but that teaching and learning about either often centres on issues of values, ideals, standards or preferences. This is clear in not just the formulation and implementation of educational policies for the teaching and learning of democracy in schools and colleges, but equally in the strategies adopted for social inclusion, social cohesion, renewal and regeneration. These are all heavily value-laden notions, and some engagement with deconstructing their meaning and purpose cannot be avoided. At the same time, it is not realistic to seek to escape these difficulties simply by not engaging with them at all. The challenges of eschewing both ideological preference and disingenuous neutrality are clear in the literature.

For those charged with organising or delivering learning in relation to either citizenship or belonging, there are particularly difficult challenges in dealing so centrally with values. The risk always will be that one group or party will level the charge that the teaching is biased or unfair, or that it amounts to indoctrination.

Recognising and assessing progress

Citizenship in particular, but belonging and identity increasingly, have attracted much public debate and been the cause of a great deal of public policy in the UK over the past 20 years or so, even before Labour's general election victory in 1997. There is no pretence in this monograph that the brief consideration here has done all initiatives full justice, and, in any case, some are of only recent origin.

The more long-established schemes are increasingly subject to comment, scrutiny and independent research. Thus it has become essential to provide a balanced view of their objectives and of the political drive

181

behind them, as well as giving some account of the progress of their implementation. The dangers to avoid are becoming uncritically enthusiastic because the issues appear to have been given some recognition, often in public policy, or lapsing into dismissal and condemnation of initiatives.

Regulation and restriction?

Chief among the criticisms directed at contemporary invocations of citizenship by governments and other authorities are those that focus on the alleged tendency for the UK government increasingly to use the rules and processes associated with citizenship and belonging for purposes of social regulation and restriction. Not only have the rules been successively tightened for people seeking British citizenship, the procedures and regulatory processes involved are said to be restrictive, and there is evidence of unacceptable state incursion into the lives, human rights and even beliefs of people (Delanty, 2003). Criticism of this kind is sometimes expressed somewhat differently. The argument runs that there are some notable contradictions between the liberal rhetoric with which initiatives are announced or launched and their implementation, subsequent operation and eventual effects.

Unsavoury manifestations

Much of the discussion so far has explored claims made for the more positive aspects of citizenship, lifelong learning and belonging. However, each can be highly exclusive, promoting the interests of the privileged insiders at the expense of those excluded.

As Osler and Starkey said, in writing of citizenship, 'citizenship from its beginnings, has been experienced as exclusive and has involved female, racial and class subordination' (Osler and Starkey, 2005, p.14). In his wide-ranging historical and comparative analysis *The Dark Side of Democracy*, Michael Mann (2005, p.55) points out that there tend to be two sharply contrasting versions in conceptions of 'the people'. The first is 'stratified', in which differences and conflicts between groups or classes, cultures, languages, ethnicities, faiths or identities are mediated and regulated by the State within a broader framework of democratic functioning. The second version is 'organic', in which the purity of 'the people' is secured and maintained by exclusion, suppression and, if necessary, by violent 'cleansing'.

Exclusions can follow from formal or legal rules governing entitlement, from wider inequalities or lack of opportunities, or, most invidiously, from the very practices and purposes inherent in the version of citizenship or lifelong learning in question. Exclusions may be intentional or unintended. Whatever the cause, the consequences of exclusion can be much less edifying than those associated with either the promise of citizenship or the enlightening potential of learning.

Nor are the various purposes to which learning, participation or association put always virtuous. 'Voluntary associations are not everywhere and always good. They can reinforce anti-liberal tendencies; and they can be abused by antidemocratic forces' (Putnam, 2000, p.341). Social capital can easily be put to evil use and for the fostering of intolerance of others and other ways of life, especially when it is a source of tight bonding within socially, politically or ideologically homogeneous groups that operate under strict and rigid internal codes of discipline. As Amy Gutmann (1998, p.19) has observed, some kinds of associational activity in the USA are 'downright hostile to, and potentially destructive of, democracy'.

Against this, voluntary associations that are more open, diverse in membership, and given to deploying what Putnam calls 'bridging' social capital in their external links with other social groups are less likely to manifest anti-democratic tendencies. 'Other things being equal, the more economically, ethnically, and religiously heterogeneous the membership of an association is, the greater its capacity to cultivate the kind of public discourse and deliberation that is conducive to democratic citizenship' (*ibid.*, p.25).

Just as learning can promote good things and change for the better, so evil skills and antisocial capabilities can be acquired through learning. Only the supremely confident educational rationalist believes that learning will always overcome narrow self-interest or wickedness. Powerful groups or (especially) governments can subvert the noble purposes of lifelong learning and twist the learning better to meet their own objectives (Martin, 2003).

Similarly, only the greatest optimist will assert that the processes of citizen involvement and engaged debate will necessarily lead to the good society. Some instances of citizenship have sat perfectly comfortably with gross inequality, social exclusion, exploitation and even repression. Moreover, freedom can facilitate the schemes of 'ugly citizens' (Ulrich Beck, 1998) just as much as those of the conventionally virtuous. Nor is it a satisfactory response to such counter-examples to claim that they are distortions of the true path of either learning or citizenship: as pointed out earlier, both operate in the realm of norms and values.

Lastly, as has been observed already, belonging in itself may not always connote virtue, at least when one of the consequences of belonging is taking actions that disadvantage or harm other people who do not belong or who belong to another group. Of course, such behaviour is at odds with the core tenets of liberalism. The State is justified in restricting such behaviour, provided always that the people threatened with damage do not also reject liberalism's insistence that, in exchange for enjoying the rights of non-interference, they too must accept their duties to others and to the community at large. In this case, even those offended against cannot insist on their rights as citizens to defend their own identities in whatever manner they see fit.

CHAPTER ELEVEN

The challenges and promise of lifelong learning

Aims

I have three aims in this penultimate section of the monograph. First, briefly to examine the current state of play with lifelong learning and to consider those challenges to it that have been made in the light of its apparent subordination to a narrowing British government agenda of preparing learners for work skills and the labour market. Secondly, I ask what kind of lifelong learning policies and practices are likely to respond adequately to the issues and challenges raised in the earlier sections of the book, and maybe take them forward. Thirdly, and closely connected to the first two objectives, I conclude by setting out some core principles that might underpin a progressive, humanistic and deliberately optimistic approach to lifelong learning, aimed at enhancing the prospects for a participative and autonomous citizenship and acceptance of a diversity of identities and belonging.

The educational and pedagogic traditions that I am seeking to invoke in this section of the monograph and to bring to bear upon the issues of citizenship, identity and belonging do not currently constitute the educational 'mainstream' in the UK – and certainly not in lifelong learning or even in adult education. That is so whether viewed from a level of activity perspective, or in terms of the provision of public funding, especially where post-school education is concerned. Where they exist at all, the traditions and orientations that I am seeking to build upon have been increasingly challenged and displaced by a growing emphasis on learning centred on skills, jobs, markets and competitiveness. Moreover, it is fair to say that, even within adult education circles themselves, only a minority of practitioners have focused attention directly on the issues of citizenship, identity and belonging. Where such matters have engaged adult learning, they have usually emerged somewhat tangentially or adventitiously from a principal concern with separate and important but related issues such as community development, social and economic regeneration, social inclusion, anti-poverty strategies, community campaigns, and so on. What I advocate in this last section is not so much a 'renewing' of a once-vibrant movement in lifelong learning that was concerned to engage with the burning issues of citizenship and belonging. It is rather a call for a determined and urgent effort to push these matters centre stage in lifelong learning, perhaps for the first time in nearly a century, since the famous '1919 Report' on adult education declared that:

> *Adult education must not be regarded as a luxury for a few exceptional persons here and there, nor as a thing which concerns only a short span of early manhood, but that adult education is a permanent national necessity, an inseparable aspect of citizenship, and therefore should be both universal and lifelong. (Ministry of Reconstruction 1919, p.5)*

Too vague to be useful?

A first challenge that needs to be addressed is that the idea of lifelong learning is too vague and deserves to be dismissed as trying to be all things to all people in its generalities and, hence, is more or less worthless for purposes of serious, rigorous enquiry or to serve as the basis for a focused strategy or policy framework (Smith, 1996 and 2001). This alleged tendency for lifelong learning to have so many different meanings and beneficial purposes means, paradoxically, that it 'risks losing its richness and precision as a concept. It becomes too useful for too many purposes. The meaning of the term is often either obcure or meagre' (Larsson, 1997, p.251). For Burke and Jackson, similarly, the problem with lifelong learning is that 'its meanings are shifting and far from clear, although the term is used politically in ways which suggest hegemonic understandings' (Burke and Jackson, 2007, p.9).

These charges have also been levelled at the many different uses of both citizenship and identity. However, lifelong learning, at least when expressed as a philosophy or theory, as against an everyday practice, is the poor relation here. Its intellectual roots and political endorsement are both much more recent than are those, especially, of citizenship, and it has received much less systematic attention from thinkers and scholars and been much less subjected to rigorous conceptual debate and practical tests. However, its relatively recent arrival on educational, political and policy scenes does not provide any consequential protection against the dismissive accusation of, at worst, analytical vacuity or, at best, empty idealism devoid of specific practicality. As has been aptly remarked, 'the problem with lifelong learning is that it is used as a vision but is rather empty of content. It therefore tends to be idealistic because it does not say how it can be transformed into practice' (Gustavsson, 1997, p.239).

While fully recognising the risk of this disabling weakness at the heart of the notion of lifelong learning, John Field, in a wide ranging review of its various meanings and uses, offers four reasons for keeping it. First, the notion that lifelong learning is valuable because of the engaging 'aspirations that it embodies'. Secondly, despite the evident weaknesses and confusions in current usage, 'something new is under way'. Thirdly, lifelong learning is now also 'a mechanism for exclusion and control'; as well as empowering people, it also creates new and powerful inequalities, and deserves attention for this reason alone, if for no other. Fourthly, the idea of lifelong learning 'is worth keeping because its linguistic reach can help provide a kind of intellectual forum' (Field, 2006, pp.3–6). Similarly, in a consideration of the links between democracy, lifelong learning and the idea of a 'learning society', Peter Jarvis has made a compelling case for lifelong learning's potential contribution to the creation and sustenance of a humane, open, democratic, just and caring society'. This would be a 'society in which we need to have citizens who love the world, love living, love relating and love learning and we need a society in which the love of learning is fostered' (Jarvis, 2008, p.225).

To these arguments, the retort may be made that, to the extent that 'lifelong learning' lacks precision regarding both its conceptualisation and the formulation and implementation of policy, this is why it deserves (or even demands) critical attention. Indeed, it would be most valuable to be provided with analysis of its various meanings and usages by different social actors, in different locales and milieux, in different historical moments, and with a variety of consequences, such as might be provided by experts in socio-linguistic, phenomenological or 'discourse' analysis. Such insights are the kinds of serious intellectual work that C. Wright Mills expected of a responsible 'sociological imagination' that would throw light on the relationship between people's 'private problems' and the shaping of 'public issues' in the contemporary world (Mills, 1959).

A narrowing of the lifelong learning agenda?

My second task in this section of the monograph is to address the arguments made by some prominent adult educators that the political embracing of lifelong learning in the UK and elsewhere has entailed a systematic narrowing and distortion of the role and purposes of learning in a democratic society.

Sceptical, disappointed and hostile commentators draw attention to what they claim constitute the current intellectual narrowing and practical distortions inscribed in the current uses, and especially public policy uses, of lifelong learning in the UK. For example, Ian Martin (2000, p.1) urged caution when governments become interested in lifelong learning, but 'when they add active citizenship and social inclusion to the list, it may be time to be positively sceptical – not to say suspicious'. The current dominant discourse about lifelong learning and citizenship, argues Martin, is highly political and its core perspective, is 'narrowly individualistic, instrumental and reductionist'.

There are, says Martin, two principal versions of this powerful discourse. In the first, people are depicted as mere 'creatures of the cash nexus' – workers or producers – and education is 'the engine of economic competitiveness in the global market'. In this variant, lifelong learning becomes a mere supply-side contributor to economic rationality and the official skills agenda, mostly led by governments and employers. Learning is driven to an increasingly narrow and exclusive focus, where the subjectivity of learners appears to feature only in so far as they are forever exhorted to make themselves flexible and 'employable' in a rapidly changing labour market. The second 'constructs the adult learner as consumer or customer', and adult education is reduced to a commodity that may be bought and sold in the marketplace, just like any other commodity (*ibid.* p.2). According to this point of view, learning is to be determined largely by the demands made upon it by governments, employers or by individuals seeking principally to enhance their skills for work.

In a similar vein, Frank Coffield (2007, p.16) has criticised the 'fundamentalism' of British governments in continually basing their educational policy on three 'underlying and damaging assumptions'.

These are, first that 'our future depends on our skills'; secondly that in all matters concerning vocational skills strategy it is appropriate 'to put employers in the driving seat'; and thirdly that 'market competition is essential to make (educational) providers efficient and responsive'. Ove Korsgaard (1997) earlier drew attention to the comparative analysis of educational systems in the 1980s undertaken by Alfred Telhaug that indicated 'when new school planning is formulated, ideals about social justice and personal development are exchanged for concepts from management discourse such as competition, quality and productivity'.

Korsgaard noted that this shift of vocabulary has also become increasingly evident in much adult education. 'In most countries during the last 15 years there has been a marked change from language and objectives relating to the quality of life and of the community to the language of the marketplace' (ibid., p.18). If there is any place for any other sorts of learning – such as learning for its own sake, for purely aesthetic purposes, for spiritual enlightenment, for sheer pleasure, to enhance citizenship, or for no immediately specific purpose at all – it constitutes a residual category. It would certainly not be one whose main costs would normally be met by the State or by employers.

In addition, John Field has questioned whether the relatively new language of lifelong learning has become attractive to politicians and policy makers because of its role as a stalking horse for purposes that are more sinister. Thus, because contemporary use of the term 'lifelong learning' 'embraces learning everywhere and at all times and in every corner of life, governments can use the rhetoric of lifelong learning to conceal the process of dismantling adult education and replacing it with work-related training' (Field, 2004, p.199).

In a critique of the tendency for knowledge and curricula to become increasingly indistinguishable from corporate priorities and concerns and the application of market rationality, Denis Gleeson argues that 'economic rationalism treats people as objects, as if the economy is an end in itself. The effect of this "master discourse" obscures an active view of citizenship and learning which in democracy is the end point for which all systems of society exist ... [It] suppresses diversity and pluralism including alternative views of knowledge, learning and citizenship ... Notions of the good society and public good give way to individualism and self-determination in which education is reduced to the production of ideal individuals who are separated from the *social relations* which sustain them' (Gleeson, 1994, p.68; cited in Heath, 1999; emphasis in original).

Even more critically, but with a main focus on public policies for higher education in Australia and the UK, Janice Dudley has observed that 'it is no coincidence that the titles of both the UK's Dearing Report ... and Australia's West Review ... are based on the notion of life-long learning'.

> *This organising principle – variously 'lifelong learning', 'learning for life' and 'the learning society' – is a recasting of the privileging of the economic that has been characteristic of the OECD countries since the late 1970s ... In the 1990s it has been reconfigured as 'globalisation' – a grand narrative of incorporation into a global capitalist economy ... a form of economic fundamentalism, an absolutist closed discourse which privileges 'the market'.... Education policy in particular, has been directed towards constructing citizens whose subjectivities – that is their sense of identity, their understandings and orientations to the world – are in accord with these imperatives, and who will therefore contribute to enhancing the nation's economy in the international capitalist market place. (Dudley, 1999, pp. 65 and 66)*

Martin's point of view, Coffield's critique and Field's speculation are not intended to imply that work, skills, employment or training are unimportant (although it is not clear that the same could fairly be said of Dudley's comments). The problem they identify, rather, is that an almost *exclusive* focus on these issues narrows and distorts both adult education and lifelong learning in which, as Martin observes, 'as educators we are not just servicers of the economy or traders in the educational marketplace'.

> *On the contrary, our real interest lies in enabling people to develop to their full potential as 'whole persons' or rounded human beings. This suggests that adult education should help people to engage in a wide range of political roles and social relationships which occur outside both the workplace and the marketplace. (Martin, 2000, p.2)*

Linking adult learning and citizenship, Martin argues, should be about *learning for living* and not be limited just to learning *for a living*. He thus invokes for adult learning a reconstitution of the 'Agora' – the ancient Greek assembly place in which citizens debated the key issues of the day.

The aim should be reviving a conception of learning and citizenship that, in figuring as more human, holistic and civically oriented than its contemporary narrow and distorted versions, treats the learner 'as a political agent and social actor'. In this context Martin invokes the tradition of 'social purpose' learning that engages critically with matters of active citizenship and lifelong learning with both 'clarity and conviction'. In this tradition, with its distinctive pedagogy and particular manner of generating the curriculum, 'learning is essentially about *making knowledge which makes sense of [people's] world* and helps them to act upon it, collectively, in order to change it for the better' (*ibid.*, p.3, emphasis in original).

Rennie Johnston (1999, p.175), too, has argued for a 'reconstruction of the social purpose tradition' in adult learning 'as a necessary challenge and counter-focus to the dominant discourse of lifelong learning shaped by the economic imperative and framed very much in terms of human capital'. Johnston's proposals are apposite for the focus of this book, in his suggestion of four overlapping dimensions to social purpose in adult education: learning for *inclusive* citizenship, for *pluralistic* citizenship, for *reflexive* citizenship and for *active* citizenship. Together they provide, he concludes, a way forward for adult educators to 'continue to "stand for something" and avoid "falling for anything"' (*ibid.*, p.188).

Other criticisms of 'narrowness'

Other critics and groups who claim to have suffered from the exclusions and limitations of the current concept and practice of citizenship have been equally vocal in pointing out its inherent narrowness and distorted representation of humanity. Thus, recent writing on feminism and life-long learning has criticised lifelong learning for its alleged limiting and exclusionary perspective where women are concerned. This time, the argument is that the field of lifelong learning, in both policy documents and academic literature, pays insufficient attention to:

> *Adult and continuing education, community based learning and the personal and political learning that takes place in, for example, trades unions, women's groups, or groups from marginalised people, such as gay and lesbian groups, black and minority ethnic groups and so forth. (Burke and Jackson, 2007, p.9)*

In a quest to 'reclaim conceptual frameworks', the authors 'draw on feminist and post-structuralist analyses to examine the different and

191

competing conceptual frameworks that are currently available, and to consider the ways that these constrain or open up opportunities for lifelong learning' (*ibid.*, p.9). Other feminist critics of traditional and current conceptions of citizenship have pointed out that, despite the centrality of equality and of universality to virtually all versions of citizenship, in practice – both in purely *formal* terms and in everyday *substantive* experience – the provisions of citizenship have deliberately excluded all women or certain categories of women (married, for example). Alternatively, women's interests have been deemed to lie principally in the *private* domain rather than the *public* sphere of politics and civic life. In Iris Marion Young's epigram, 'the discourse that links the civic public with fraternity is not merely metaphorical' (Young, 1998, p.266).

In like fashion, when critically examining adult education's perspective on the experiences of African Americans, and in response to arguments made by African-American intellectuals, Stephen Brookfield (2003) proposed the need for a 'distinctive Africentric epistemology'. Brookfield argued that adult education theory is *racialised*. 'When a phenomenon is racialised, it is viewed through the distinctive lens of a racial group's experience of the world.' Sensitivity to such racialisation leads to a 'positive recognition of how one's lifeworld, positionality, and sense of cultural identity compose a set of preconscious filters and assumptions that frame how one's life is felt and lived.' The challenge, then, is to develop a critical theoretical perspective in adult learning that transcends 'the dominant conceptualizations and mechanisms ... for the production and dissemination of knowledge (that) are grounded in one particular racial group's experiences (in the case of adult education, White European Americans) and the forms of thought that flow from these' (*ibid.*, p.154).

In all of this, and despite the problems necessarily involved, it seems unavoidable that the range of issues raised in this monograph in connection with citizenship, identity and belonging point to an unequivocally values-driven approach to lifelong learning. Such an approach would be decidedly humanistic, life-wide, relevant to the whole life course, developmental and emergent, inclusive, egalitarian, participative, both formal and non-formal, dialogic, deliberative, critical, reflexive, democratic and emancipatory. In truth, such an orientation may be best regarded as being utopian, constituting an ideal against which to measure existing practice or proposals for change, rather than representing any prospect of being achieved in the foreseeable future. However, that would be to limit unnecessarily such a perspective. It could also be used to inform the drive for, and even the design of, what Welton (2005) has termed 'the *just* learning society' (emphasis added).

The perspective that I advocate has much in common with Welton's ambition, as it does with the approach to adult and lifelong learning that has progressively emerged in the writing of Peter Jarvis (1987, 1997, 2004, 2007 and [especially] 2008). The approach preferred here also echoes the argument put forward by Ranson (1994) in his insistence on the need for the creation of a genuine 'learning society' that can become 'a constitutive condition of a new moral order'.

> *It is only when the values and processes of learning are placed at the centre of polity that the conditions can be established for all individuals to develop their capacities, and that institutions can respond imaginatively to a period of change. (ibid., p. 106)*

Having looked at different approaches to lifelong learning currently on offer, the problem is not simply that no single approach can capture or throw light on all of the matters touched upon in this monograph, but rather that it is clear which perspectives are most likely to be disqualified by virtue of their self-imposed narrowness. For example, lifelong learning strategies, policies and practices that deliberately privilege the realm of the economic above all others, even to the virtual exclusion of other issues shown in this monograph to be significant for either citizenship or belonging, will not meet the diversity requirements involved. However important matters of economy, competition, or skills for employment may be, an approach to lifelong learning that seeks to concern itself *only* with the economy and skills for work is bound to be limited and ignorant of the dynamic interplay of markets with other aspects of citizens' lives.

Equally, any suggested approach to learning that concentrates exclusively on advancing only the sectional interests of a particular group, however worthy and pressing, will not fit the bill of looking at the wider fields involved – of wider citizenship, the role of the State, or individual identity. Again, lifelong learning that insists only on a particular form or mode of engagement or method of learning is likely to limit the chances of some people's involvement or their chances of success. This might be because of people's lack of opportunity or resources, because their preferred styles of learning are different, or because their original motivations for becoming engaged make them better suited to other ways of learning.

If life*long* learning is intended to be life-*wide* as well, it is unlikely that a framework for its application that works well only in one setting will be as appropriate in different circumstances. For example, an approach to lifelong learning that is especially effective in the workplace or in regeneration initiatives may work much less well when dealing with matters of ethnicity or cultural politics, or the State's desire for a more disciplinary orientation to citizenship. Finally, a suggested approach to lifelong learning that completely ignores context – historical, political, geographical, cultural, linguistic or biographical – may have all the qualities of abstract intellectual rigour and pristine design, but simply not work in the specific context of its intended application. Or else, it may simply miss the point.

For all of these reasons, an excellent starting point for any consideration of the potential contribution of lifelong learning to questions of citizenship, belonging and identity remains the 1998 'Delors report' for UNESCO, *Learning: The Treasure Within* (Delors, 1998). In a still unsurpassed and truly visionary perspective, and building on the seminal work of Edgar Fauré a quarter of a century earlier, Delors and his colleagues proposed that lifelong learning should constitute a ' broad, encompassing view' enabling 'each individual to discover, unearth and enrich his or her creative potential, to reveal the treasure within each of us. This means going beyond an instrumental view of education, as a process one submits to in order to achieve specific aims (in terms of skills, capacities or economic potential), to one that emphasizes the development of the complete person, in short, *learning to be*' (Delors, 1998, p.86, emphasis in original). Lifelong learning should, therefore, be founded on four main pillars: learning to know, learning to do, learning to live together, and learning to be.

For Delors and his colleagues, lifelong learning policies and practices constructed on these four pillars would not be content with bringing people together to understand or even to subscribe to the norms and values shaped by the past. It would also seek to 'answer the question as *what for and why we live together* and give everyone, throughout life, the ability to play an active part in envisioning the future of society' (*ibid.*, p.61, emphasis in original). To this end, Delors and his colleagues argued 'the education of each citizen must continue throughout his or her life and become part of the basic framework of civil society and living democracy. It even becomes indistinguishable from democracy when everyone plays a part in constructing a responsible and mutually support-ive society that upholds the fundamental rights of all.' They regarded education for citizenship and democracy as '*par excellence* an education that is not restricted to the space and time of formal education' (*ibid.*, p.63 and 62).

In like fashion, the Sixth World Assembly of the International Council for Adult Education at its Ocho Rios meeting in 2001 not only affirmed 'the right to education and the right to learn throughout life for women and men'. It also declared an unswerving commitment to 'the central role of adult education in support of creative and democratic citizenship', acting as a key counter-influence to discrimination, social exclusion, degradation and fragmentation in contemporary society (International Council for Adult Education, 2001).

Couching its concerns in rather dramatic and starkly challenging terms, the International Council drew attention to the dilemma in which it found itself, caught 'between the possibilities of a genuinely democratic and sustainable learning society, and the passivity, poverty, vulnerability and chaos that economic globalisation is creating everywhere'. Against such bleak prospects, the authors of the famous Ocho Rios Declaration shared their engaging dream 'of a new international community of justice, democracy and respect for difference'. Working towards the fulfilment of such a radical dream of change would depend upon achieving a long list of policy commitments and practical proposals for action, in which both participatory lifelong learning and popular involvement in governance and democratic decision-making featured.

In a stimulating review and contribution to the debate on the intersection of lifelong learning and democracy, Peter Jarvis (2008, p.219) has suggested that a fifth focus for lifelong learning needs to be added to the four proposed by Delors: 'learning to care for the planet'. This is essential, he argues, because the Earth is much more than a mere resource, important though that is; it constitutes the home for all of us and for the generations to come. In constructing such a lifelong learning, he adds, in addition to emphasising the importance of critical reflection and the key role of teaching and leadership, it will be necessary to move beyond criticism into the more challenging terrain of proposing a 'realistic utopia', as suggested in the writings of John Rawls.

If we are to create active citizens we need a learning people whose learning is also practical: a people prepared to understand the complexities of contemporary society and give time and effort to be involved in helping solve the problems; we need people who understand the risks of today's society. In this sense, we need an open democratic society in which the people regard it as their responsibility to learn and play their role, so that we can all respond to the needs of everybody in social living. The primary aim of the learning society then is to help people learn to love learning – a culture of learning – and regard it as their civic responsibility to continue to learn. In this sense, society has to become reflective as well as reflexive …
(ibid., p. 215)

For Delors, for the Sixth World Assembly and for Jarvis, a primary task for lifelong learning would be to 'restore to education its central place among the forces at work in society [and] to safeguard its functions as a melting pot by combating all forms of exclusion'. Such a function accepts as a core assumption that diversity and people's multiple loyalties and diverse identities constitute 'valuable assets': 'Education for pluralism is not just a safeguard against violence but an active principle for the enrichment of the cultural and civic life of present-day societies' (*ibid.*, pp.58 and 59).

Living and learning

Neither citizenship nor belonging matters most because of its abstract meaning, but rather because each helps shape and provide a context for everyday life – for our hopes and ambitions, our possibilities as well as our disappointments and frustrations (Giroux and Simon, 1989). Mostly, learning about and through citizenship and belonging occurs as part of living in given times and places – tacitly, informally and consequent to being embedded in given ways of life. Sometimes, there is a more conscious inscribing of learning into the construction of citizenship or into people's sense of belonging – to ensure, promote, explain, exemplify or enhance one of them.

Thus, citizenship, identity and belonging, in their sometimes surprising variety of forms and guises, and structured variously by different authorities and contextual influences, inevitably impinge upon each of us in our everyday lives. They might do so more as constraint; they might hold out the prospects of opportunity; or else they might figure mostly as denial and exclusion (Mason, 2000; Lawler, 2008).

196

Given the historical importance and contemporary potential of both citizenship and belonging for impacting upon the everyday lives of individuals, communities and whole countries, there is a convincing case to make that serious intellectual engagement with these matters should feature in the core formation and initial education of all citizens. Confidence and capacity, to consider others' views and express one's own, to assess evidence and, when possible, to participate in decisions on these complex matters might also be expected to sit at the heart of any coherent public policy for both initial education and continuing life-long and life-wide learning.

No matter how it occurs, learning often plays, or is expected to play, its part in helping to clarify people's rights and obligations or their identity, in raising people's awareness of them and communicating their nature and meaning to others. Whether formal or informal, non-formal, tacit or explicit, initial or continuing, all of these different forms and locales of lifelong learning merit attention (Dewey, 1897 and 1916; Hildreth, 2004; Delanty, 2007). Being an effective citizen in the late modern world, declares Keogh, 'requires lifelong learning'. Civic virtue does not develop spontaneously or naturally, but requires development and nurturing through learning. Moreover, society is increasingly characterised by complexity, where citizens must be able to position themselves in relation to exacting political issues and debates, confident in their ability to handle conflicting arguments and critically assess evidence. What is more, learning for citizenship or identity cannot consist only of a kind of abstract or disinterested intellectual curiosity, but also requires direct experience and active involvement, enhanced by critical reflection (Keogh, 2003).

Critical thinking, dialogue and deliberation

It is clear that different perspectives on lifelong learning manifest quite sharp differences of purpose, of modes of engagement, of forms of organisation, of curriculum, of pedagogy and of their varying links with and relevance for citizenship, belonging and identity. Indeed, one valuable function that analysts of lifelong learning can perform is to understand and explain how, to what ends and with what results different narratives of lifelong learning are undertaken. 'Competing discourses shape the kinds of questions that are asked about lifelong learning and so it is important to have an understanding of the different contexts in which discourses are re/produced locally, nationally and internationally, struggling for hegemony' (Burke and Jackson, 2007, p.25).

The advantage of acknowledging the driving narrative or ideology behind any particular version of lifelong learning is not that such recognition, nor any analysis undertaken through such a perspective, can itself help with the choice between competing narratives. That is clearly a question of the value orientation of those required to exercise choice between competing perspectives. Rather, the best thing to do is to turn this weakness into virtue by ensuring always that the underpinning aims and values of any proposed perspective are made explicit and are systematically presented for critical review and debate. To some extent, that may even entail protagonists not simply indicating their own value orientations and preferences, but even, in some circumstances, declaring exactly whose or what side they are on – always provided, of course, that such declarations are open to rigorous scrutiny and debate. There is a tradition of tackling these matters in sociology, so considering them in the context of policies and practices for lifelong learning does not represent an unusual challenge (Gouldner, 1962; Hammersley, 2000).

At the same time, if learning is to enhance the chances of inclusive citizenship, a shared sense of belonging and respect for legitimate but non-divisive differences, it requires a commitment to foster in citizens the capacity for independent critical thinking and the capability in engaging in dialogue with fellow citizens, with political and other representatives, and with those in authority. Brookfield (1987) suggests that there are two central elements to critical thinking or 'critical literacy': identifying and challenging assumptions, and exploring and imagining alternatives. Critical thinking enables people to make some sense of the deep changes occurring in contemporary society, of the complexities of political life and mass communications and in 'trying to feel some sense of control over them' (*ibid.*, p.51).

In an echo of the work of C. Wright Mills, Brookfield invokes critical thinking as a principal means of connecting private lives to public issues in an era when 'people frequently perceive themselves to be helpless in the face of overwhelming social forces. They regard their individual lives as relatively insignificant brush strokes when viewed against the broad canvas of social, economic, and technological changes' (*ibid.*, p.56). Through critical thinking, people can learn to join with others of like mind to seek or influence changes collectively, thereby contributing to

198

the democratic vibrancy of the community, sometimes with unantici-
pated and even destabilising consequences. Critical thinkers and the
teachers who support them must expect to be accused of bias, as they
almost inevitably ruffle the feathers of existing power holders: 'critical
questioning is the last thing those in positions of power who are autocrati-
cally seeking to retain the *status quo* wish to see' (*ibid.*, p.65).

Brookfield's invocation of the virtues of debate and critical thinking
represents a contemporary echo of the arguments in favour of an adult
education to consider differences of opinion, set out in the Ministry of
Reconstruction's '1919 report':

> *Most of the subjects [considered in 'non-vocational', social purpose adult
> education classes] of political, social or industrial interest are highly
> controversial; the very fact that there are conflicts of view upon the
> problems of social life and organisation, so far from being a justification for
> the exclusion of controversial questions, is a strong reason for study and the
> fullest discussion. In the consideration of such problems and the principles
> involved, the students bring to the class a varied and valuable experience
> of life, and in consequence the method of education is largely that of a
> frank exchange of views and mutual criticism rather than that based upon
> the relation usually existing between teacher and taught. (Ministry of
> Reconstruction, 1919, paragraph 203)*

Discussion, debate, the skills of listening and deliberation, and an innovative capacity to find grounds for compromise, communicate ideas and
propositions and take practical action, not only lie at the centre of the best
examples of adult and social purpose learning. They also typify civic
republican conceptions of participative democracy and the engagement
with others' identities and views of the world that are essential for
effective pluralism and genuine multiculturalism to have any chance of
success.

There are many versions of the idea of 'critical pedagogy'. Chief
among its advocates has been Henry Giroux, writing prolifically on
cultural analysis, schooling and education more generally, and on democratic possibility. For Giroux, the task of the critical educator is to help
develop in learners not just the key skills of critical review of dominant
discourse and received 'common sense', scepticism about the prevailing
economic and political rhetoric underpinning public policy, intellectual
challenge to ideas, and how to connect theory with both practice and

199

experience. The task is also to enable learners to imagine other possibilities: critical pedagogy 'makes space available for an argument about the
responsibility for the present for a democratic future' based on the values
of reason, debate, openness, freedom and equality.

Critical pedagogy aims to enable learners to go beyond thinking
and, as citizens, to act as engaged agents in their various worlds, giving
voice to their hopes and ambitions for change and improvement (Giroux,
2007, pp.1–5). It is, in short, about fostering 'a language of critique and
possibility' (*ibid.*, p.211) in which the aim must be 'to provide students
with the knowledge and skills they need to learn how to deliberate, make
judgements and exercise choice' (*ibid.*, p.1). Where it operates properly
and within a genuinely open society, this kind of education promises to
engender what Barber (1998) regards as the true mark of an activist
democracy, a 'noisy and fractious citizenry'.

Giroux insists that critical pedagogy must never degenerate into
propaganda; indeed, he argues that by remaining faithful to its core values
and aims, critical pedagogy rules out any sort of indoctrination. 'The
politics of critical pedagogy are radical but not doctrinaire. That is, critical
pedagogy self-consciously operates from a perspective in which teaching
and learning are committed to expanding rather than restricting the
opportunities for students and others to be social, political and economic
agents' (Giroux, 1997a, p.169). Nor, despite its current concern
vigorously to challenge the orthodoxies of neo-liberal ideology that
Giroux and others claim are distorting education dangerously, does
critical pedagogy not value matters of economy, employment and skills
for work.

> *While we believe that public education should equip students with skills
> to enter the workplace, it should also educate them to contest workplace
> inequalities, imagine democratically organized forms of work, and identify
> and challenge those injustices that contradict and undercut the most
> fundamental principles of freedom, equality and respect for all people who
> constitute the global public sphere.* (Giroux, 2005, p.217)

Without such critical pedagogy, the danger is that learning and citizen-
learners risk exposure to narrowing or deliberately distorted or ideologically based interpretations of social life, and increasingly restricted and
undemocratic policies and practice. Moreover, as Barbagli and Dei (1977)
argued, there can be no escape for either teacher or learner into the refuge

of political neutrality in order to avoid the charge of unwarranted one-sidedness. 'He who ingenuously accepts criticism of "unilaterality" and is not aware of the implications and political consequences of this effectively renounces his freedom to think' (*ibid.*, p.431).

It is important to re-emphasise that this is not an argument in favour of a deliberately biased approach to discussion in learning, nor for any abuse of the power of the teacher. Teaching must be a deeply ethical practice. What Barbagli and Dei called for was the potential exposure of all assumptions, values and perspectives, including those of the learners and teachers themselves, to critical enquiry and debate. Their point is that 'political neutrality leads either to a de-politicisation of consciousness or to more or less blind acceptance of the existing power relationships in society'.

Agency and empowerment

Citizenship, lifelong learning and, perhaps most of all, belonging, also share a commitment to the encouragement and enhancement of *human agency*. Indeed, agency may be deemed to constitute the essential core of all three notions. Adherents to and advocates of citizenship and lifelong learning argue that one of the most positive and direct consequences of either strengthening citizenship or extending lifelong learning is in providing individuals and groups with the resources and opportunity to exercise greater influence or even control over their lives and in giving them opportunities to express their identities. Moreover, as Lister puts it:

> The notion of agency (also) helps knit together the different citizenship traditions. It can also be found implicitly in the idea of 'active citizenship' which has been promoted in the British context from a variety of standpoints. (Lister, 1997, p.22)

This hopeful and appealing conception of human agency is at the centre of all versions of citizenship, although it is more obviously a defining characteristic of civic republicanism and, within limits, of communitarianism. Its appeal lies not just in the promise of counteracting the sense of powerlessness that Bauman, in particular, depicts as the human condition in late modern society. It also underlines the idea that one possible liberating aspect of globalisation is the scope for people to be far more engaged in shaping their lives and defining and re-defining their own identities, freed from some of the oppressive containment of more traditional social organisation, in the ways that Giddens and Beck, among others, have suggested. It is easy to see how lifelong learning might both contribute to this and be an element of its expression.

> *The reflexive project of the self, which consists in the sustaining of coherent, yet continuously revised, biographical narratives, takes place in the context of multiple choice as filtered through abstract systems. In modern social life, the notion of lifestyle takes on a particular significance. The more tradition loses its hold, and the more daily life is reconstituted in terms of the dialectical interplay of the local and the global, the more individuals are forced to negotiate lifestyle choices among a diversity of options (Giddens, 1991, p.5).*

However, it is essential to avoid oversimplification in this matter of agency and the degree to which this entails citizens' freedom to manoeuvre, to settle or help shape the conditions of their lives. As is often recognised, people struggle to make their history but rarely, if ever, in circumstances of their own choosing or making, and often in conflict with others: 'the world is not a passive medium that we can shape at will. There is always resistance from the nature of the institutions people have built and from the actions of others who seek to shape collective practices in different ways' (Reicher and Hopkins, 2001).

Although the world may appear to some agents as largely material, external or objective, Reicher and Hopkins suggest that it is best understood as constructed through the institutionalised subjectivity of other agents and 'sedimented into institutionalised forms'. In this, an agent's identity commonly not only 'determines the values and beliefs which define what counts as a desirable end ... it (also) provides a map of the social topography which shows one how to reach that end' (*ibid.*) The success of any agent's mobilisation, both of a given identity and of a community's sense of how things may be maintained or changed in terms that are consistent with that identity, also depends upon depicting a state of affairs that seems not only desirable but also achievable. This requires first that agents have some shared sense of being able to act successfully in the world; otherwise, invoking agency risks falling somewhere between the illusions of fantasy and the frustrating impossibility of an unachievable ideal. Both represent serious diminutions of the idea of a self-acting citizenry: each may also prefigure the resort to all sorts of illegitimate ways of making reality seemingly accord with the imaginations of agents' minds.

Marjorie Mayo has also pointed out that the idea of community empowerment based on agency, when seen in the context of 'capacity building', can also carry a variety of connotations. Empowerment can mean movement towards consensus 'whereby those with little power can come to share in the fruits of development, alongside those who have already achieved significant power, *without major challenges to the existing order*' (emphasis added). Conversely, empowerment – whether individual or collective – can constitute 'more significant challenges to the vested interests of the status quo' (Mayo, 2000, p.25).

In a study Mayo carried out with colleagues in South London, 50 stakeholders were asked to comment on what the terms 'community empowerment' and 'community capacity building' meant to them. The researchers classified the responses into three categories, from the most constricted to the most expansive. In the first, empowerment meant developing the appropriate knowledge and skills to be able 'to feed their views back to decision makers'. In the second 'more extended version', empowerment meant the fostering of bargaining skills and assertiveness and 'included the promotion of community initiatives, developing local people's abilities to ensure that their own priorities were lodged proactively on the regeneration agenda and sustained subsequently'. The third experience of empowerment and capacity building, incorporating both of the two previous versions and held by only a minority, 'included developing critical understanding to effectively challenge the vested interests of the powerful, identifying the spaces within which to promote strategies for social change' (*ibid.*, p.26).

Against this, in a critical, poststructuralist review of higher education and lifelong learning policies in the UK and Australia, Dudley takes a far more jaundiced view of agency and what it might mean.

> *The language of the learning society is seductively of participation, agency, control over one's own life, independence and empowerment ... Yet the language is also of responsibility and obligation ... learning for life also suggests an unending task, that learning has become a 'life sentence'... Life and citizenship are conflated with work and participation in the economy, particularly in ways that will enhance the competitiveness of the nation's economy in world markets. (Dudley, 1999, pp. 89 and 90)*

Voice

Agency and 'voice' are but sides of the same coin in discussions of empowerment, whether in the expansion of citizenship, in the confident expression of identity, or in learning. Lifelong learning can help people develop the confidence, skills, know-how, knowledge, networks and capacity for agency; citizenship can provide the means, opportunities, rights, processes and relationships through which to express it; a sense of belonging and identity can be its clearest manifestation. Thus, a core part of agency is the development of people's own voice, in which individuals, groups and communities – often those hitherto little heard – can confidently express their views, needs, preferences, priorities and identities. As Cleaver (2004, p.271) indicates, 'active citizenship, the exercise of voice, the championing of interests and the advocacy of rights are seen as the very manifestation of agency'. Thus, the respective contributions of a strengthened citizenship and commitment to lifelong learning often both feature in the declared policies and campaigns designed to tackle social exclusion, or to help counteract examples of perceived inequality, for example in the realms of race, ethnicity, gender, sexual orientation, disability or age.

From here, it is easy to see how both agency and voice are so closely related to the idea of 'empowerment' (yet another slippery concept) in the literature of citizenship, lifelong learning and identity, and especially in their advocacy. Through the processes of debating or deliberating (citizenship) or analysing and reflecting on (learning) a given issue, greater understanding is achieved or rationality replaces ignorance or incomprehension. Any social group that feels excluded, discriminated against, misunderstood or simply not tolerated, can seek and achieve 'voice' to improve its position by changing the understandings of others.

Thus, with some justification, it can be claimed that citizenship and lifelong learning are also at once not only *manifestations* of empowerment and voice, but also serve to *mobilise and strengthen* them. Increased confidence, better know-how, deeper understanding and, no less important, participation, dialogue and working with others can also provide valuable springboards from which to empower those involved and strengthen their voice. Agency is not just about capacity or potential, or even only about articulating views and desires, it is crucially about action and achievement. In a review of the role of the university in contemporary civil society, Maria Slowey (2003, p.150) quotes with approval

Boardman's biography of Patrick Geddes, Edinburgh's celebrated city planner: 'Education is not merely by and for the sake of thought, it is in a still higher degree by and for the sake of action.'

Through citizenship or lifelong learning, or both, people do not just develop the skills to take decisions, but also the ability to make things happen. Similarly, a strong sense of belonging and of feeling free openly to express and celebrate identity not only testifies to people's empowerment, it also provides the strong basis for their actions – cultural, political, communal, defiant or celebratory. For those on the outside, understanding a person's or group's identity and sense of belonging is often the best clue to comprehending their actions or behaviour.

Some of those who want to see agency and empowerment embody an invigorated conception and practice of citizenship also underline the importance of learning in fostering a particular, responsible mind-set, definitive attitudes and a cluster of strong values which, in turn, form the basis of community and belonging.

> Yet even empowerment and opportunity together are not sufficient for the practice of citizenship. What is further required is that a particular attitude of mind be encouraged, an attitude which not only prompts individuals to recognize what their duties are as citizens, but which motivates them to perform them as well .... The solution is education ... Citizens are learners all their lives, and education in the sense of building the appropriate character for willing engagement in the practice of citizenship never ceases ... The argument is therefore that if one creates citizens, one also, and at the same time, creates community. Citizenship, as conceived in civic republicanism, entails community. (Oldfield, 1998, pp. 87 and 88)

Against this understandable but perhaps over-optimistic view, Cleaver's reminder of the often-limiting contexts for agency, voice and empowerment is sobering. 'In defining citizenship as the active manifestation of agency there is a danger of abstracted under-socialization. Agency cannot be exercised in a vacuum and it is the very minutiae of social life and relationships that shape the forms that citizenship can take.' She warns, too, of the temptation for advocates of participation always to emphasise only its positive side. 'We tend to look at social processes and highlight the potential of the bits we like: the transformation rather than the tyranny, the solidarity rather than the conflict, articulation rather than muteness, the enablement of agency rather than the constraint of structure' (Cleaver, 2004).

Cleaver concludes her brief analysis (based on a review of several case studies of, and conceptual papers on, participation in development) in terms that should always be in the minds of would-be enthusiasts for learning as 'participation through engagement and empowerment to achieve beneficial change'.

> *The nature of these social processes is that the duality is inherent in them, and cannot be done away with … Our challenge is to use an understanding of the dynamic nature of such duality to identify opportunities for change. However, we have to reconcile ourselves to these only ever being partial, intermittent, involving winners and losers, not entirely controllable or predictable.* (ibid., p. 272)

Learning and social change

An approach to lifelong learning that stresses critical thinking, action and agency is of particular relevance in circumstances of social change such as those outlined earlier in this monograph, and alluded to by Brookfield (1987). The main functions of learning during rapid and widespread social change have been spelled out clearly by Raymond Williams (Williams, 1990). They are, first, that learning provides people with an opportunity to understand and seek to make sense of social change. This entails accessing a range of information so that people can better address and interpret what is going on in rational terms, rather than responding to change on the basis of prejudice or according to the (sometimes imposed) views of others, or rather than suffering bewilderment and confusion.

Secondly, says Williams, people need to be able to adapt to change so that they can make the most of it for themselves, for their families and loved ones, communities, businesses, or even for the nation or humanity as a whole. Obvious examples of this are in respect of new technologies, or questions concerning ecology, the environment or climate change.

Thirdly – and for Williams most importantly and most closely connected with some core aspects of citizenship – learning opens up the possibility of people becoming in part the authors and shapers of social change, rather than its victims. For some authors, this calls for new kinds of learning – what Bauman (2001) refers to as 'tertiary' learning – rarely provided through established channels of education.

206

Competencies, mentalities and capabilities

If lifelong learning is successfully to fulfil the tasks suggested by the advocates of learning for social purpose, critical thinking and learning to help shape social change, both the learners themselves and those charged with teaching or with devising the programmes of learning need to develop the skills required as well as the appropriate mentalities. Writing in 1995, Karen Evans suggested that differing notions of citizenship carry quite different implications for education, particularly in respect of 'thick' or 'maximal' notions of citizenship and democracy and their opposites. 'Education for citizenship in its minimal interpretation requires only induction into basic knowledge of institutional rules covering rights and obligations. Maximal interpretations require education which develops critical and reflective abilities and capacities for self determination and autonomy' (Evans, 1995, p.17).

In this connection, drawing on a comparative study of the transition to adulthood in Britain and Germany, Evans observed that in Britain, at the time of writing (1995), 'transition structures are weakly institutional-ised, and post-compulsory education and training arrangements reflect historically embedded narrowness and divisions, with the elite A level and the narrowly based NVQ exemplifying the academic/vocational divide' (*ibid.*, p.23). As she rightly added, while a competence-based curriculum may help to promote economic independence in an individualistic sense, alone it still contradicts a 'thicker' development of citizenship in which critical skills and a shared sense of autonomy contribute to citizens' biographical projects.

'Active citizenship' for the first Crick Advisory Group report on schools also meant that people would be able 'to think for themselves', to be 'willing, able and equipped to have an influence in public life' and to manifest 'the critical capacities to weigh evidence before speaking and acting' (Crick, 1998, p.7). These are the qualities of mind that all education and learning should seek to develop, and the skills of thought-ful independence to encourage people to cherish and extend. These skills move learning from simple acts of transmission, memorisation and repetition to those of reflection, deliberation, analysis and consideration.

Amartya Sen (1985), following his earlier work on welfare economics, and the philosopher Martha Nussbaum (2000 and 2001), have developed a 'capabilities approach' to deal with questions of poverty, inequality, and opportunities to change or transform social conditions,

the quality of life and ideas of human well-being. This approach emphasises the real freedoms open to people, as against what is provided for only
in formal terms. Nussbaum (2000) has suggested that, for democracy to
thrive, ten capabilities require fostering and operate as 'part of a minimum
account of social justice: a society that does not guarantee these to all its
citizens, at some threshold level, falls short of being a fully just society,
whatever its level of opulence' (Nussbaum, 2001, p.10).

Nussbaum's capabilities overlap with the contiguous notions of
human rights and universal citizenship entitlements, although she claims
superiority for the idea of capabilities over the legal and philosophical
notion of rights, which she sees as too much related to 'negative' freedom.
For Nussbaum, the critical difference between the human rights approach
and her emphasis on capability lies in the latter's emphasis not on any
nominal, 'pre-political' rights, determined according to the precepts of
social justice, but on the extent to which those rights have been fully
achieved and effectively implemented so that people can function with
them in the everyday world, always bearing in mind that progress towards
the fulfilment of people's capabilities will necessarily vary from context to
context. In that sense, especially, capabilities are affirmative rather than
emphasising the negative aspects of many human rights which, in effect,
are advocated in order to protect citizens from undue interference or
restriction, especially by the State or its agents. 'To secure a capability to a
citizen it is not enough to create a sphere of non-interference: the public
conception must design the material and institutional environment so
that it provides the requisite affirmative support for all the relevant
capabilities' (*ibid.*, p.27).

Nussbaum's ten key capabilities, which determine 'what people
actually are and what they are able to be', are:

- life – being able to live a full human life of normal length;
- bodily health – being able to enjoy bodily health, including adequate
  nourishment and capacity for reproduction;
- bodily integrity – being able to move freely and safely from place to
  place;
- sense, imagination and thought – being able to make full use of the
  senses to experience, think, reason, imagine and create;
- emotion – being able to experience attachment to people, things and
  experiences and to express feelings of love, longing, grieving and
  justifiable anger;

208

- practical reasoning – being able to conceive of the good life and to engage in critical reflection;
- affiliation – being able to live with others in mutual respect, understanding the position and worth of others, and establishing the basis of self-respect and non-discrimination;
- other species – having respect for animals and plants;
- play – the ability to laugh and enjoy recreational and playful activity; and
- environmental control – being able to engage with the processes and choices that affect our political and material lives, including rights of political participation, property holding and employment.

In 2005, the Center for Multicultural Education at the University of Washington convened an international panel of experts to develop principles and guidelines that educators – especially schools – could use in citizenship education in order to achieve balance between diversity and unity and to enable people to become effective citizens in a global context. The experts made their proposals in the context of a major political challenge: 'Multi-cultural societies are faced with the challenge of creating nation-states that recognize and incorporate the diversity of their citizens *and* embrace an overarching set of shared values, ideals, and goals to which all citizens are committed' (Banks *et al.*, 2005, p.5).

The experts suggested a framework of four core principles and ten concepts. The principles were first that students should learn about the complex relationships between unity and diversity in their local communities, the nation and the world. Secondly, students should learn about the increasing interdependence of people in their community, nation and the world in terms of economy, politics, culture, environment and technology. Thirdly, the teaching of human rights should underpin citizenship education. Fourthly, students should be provided with knowledge and practical experience of democracy, including democracy in the life of the school and developing the skills of deliberation, weighing alternatives as a prelude to decision-making. The ten concepts requiring attention in citizenship education were, they suggested: democracy; diversity; globalisation; sustainable development; empire, imperialism and power; prejudice, discrimination and racism; migration; identity/diversity; multiple perspectives; and patriotism and cosmopolitanism.

Multiple sites, forms and purposes of learning

Citizenship and belonging revolve around their social dimensions. That is to say, the interest centres on the various forms, functions, quality and effects of the people involved in particular activities, organisations and localities, and their patterns of interaction and sociability. Seen from the perspective of this monograph, such forms of behaviour invite a consideration of situated learning, in which people's involvement in different tasks and activities, and the acquisition and application of knowledge and skills, occur in particular social contexts, with their own peculiar meanings and understandings (Lave and Wenger, 1991). Such 'communities of practice' can both instantiate citizenship or belonging and support the realisation and development of their practical manifestations, thus further deserving comment in this review.

It is clear from all of the foregoing that learning in relation to both citizenship and belonging can occur in many ways. It may be manifest in a variety of different sites, through various modes and mechanisms, in all sorts of different forms, and for a variety of purposes. The learning thus involved may take the form of focused and formal study and scholarship, be largely informal or non-formal, be oriented to the accomplishment of practical tasks, or be incidental to or embedded in other activities. Learning may also be implicit, be dialogic, reflective, reactive or deliberative, or be a normal yet significant by-product of everyday living and experience (Eraut, 2000). Most often, learning will consist of a mixture of several of these different types.

Whatever form it takes, lifelong learning takes place in a wide variety of sites and settings. Most obviously, it is the main business of specialist organisations whose purposes centre on education, training, learning and research – a whole variety of schools, colleges, academies, institutes, libraries, laboratories, dedicated study centres, and universities. Mostly, these are found in particular places and buildings, but learning has been provided at a distance for many years and, increasingly, information technology and the Internet have provided opportunities for 'virtual' learning.

In addition, as we have seen, learning also occurs at home, in families, at work, in the community, in leisure activities, in a variety of voluntary associations and in the many walks of everyday life. Most importantly, the learning that happens in all of these different forms and locales can, and often does, include learning for, about and through citizenship and to define, explain, promote or enhance belonging and identity.

One particularly effective and increasingly accessible site for learning connected to citizenship and belonging is the museum. As the Inquiry was told, museums in the UK and throughout Europe offer a variety of opportunities for insight – into other times, other peoples, other places, other cultures, and other conceptions of the beautiful, valuable or sacred. Critical engagement with museums also provides chances for understanding how British collectors and curators – past and present – have understood and sought to present the meaning and implications of key artefacts from elsewhere (Gibbs *et al.*, 2007).

Beyond formal education

Most striking about the materials and issues covered by this monograph is that the learning involved not only concerns all the formal domains of learning, especially initial education in school, but also that it is manifest in so many other locales in civil society. This certainly requires that any attempt systematically to trace the links between citizenship, belonging and lifelong learning must embrace a broad conception of life-*long* and life-*wide* learning, including not only the various domains of informal and non-formal learning in adult life that shape citizens in contemporary Britain, but also the learning environments that constitute childhood and schooling. Given the vastness of this enterprise, it is perhaps not surprising that the work of the Inquiry did not extend to such a complete analysis. That remains to be undertaken.

Most importantly, as the research by Holford and his colleagues (2003) reported, the exploration of citizenship and belonging in civil society especially underlines that much of the learning involved is not formal. Non-formal and informal learning, and the more elusive notion of tacit knowledge, play important parts in constructing citizenship and people's identities and sense of belonging. The challenge now is to determine how both to recognise this range of learning's manifestations and possibilities and also to ask what sorts of educational interventions and initiatives – not only from public authorities but also from educational bodies, community groups, trades unions, employers and voluntary organisations – may strengthen citizenship and engender respect for difference within a broad and inclusive sense of belonging.

In the light of this, and by way of constructing a framework for lifelong learning in relation to citizenship, belonging and identity, I offer in the final section of this monograph a first attempt to map out some guiding principles. These are proposed for consideration and critical debate by the wider community of scholars, practitioners, activists and policy makers who are striving to understand better, and to make better connections between, the three themes addressed in this monograph.[19]

---

19 This framework of principles was originally prepared for the independent Commission of Inquiry into the Future for Lifelong Learning.

CHAPTER TWELVE

Underpinning citizenship and belonging: some principles for lifelong learning

First principle: focus on learners' interests, needs and priorities

As a minimum, any approach advocated for underpinning citizenship and belonging with lifelong learning will have to demonstrate its capability of serving principally as an enabling and empowerment framework, likely to help learners advance their interests as citizens. It will need to show that it can be applied in ways that meet learners' needs, interests and priorities, and which facilitate the full expression of their identities and sense of belonging. In that respect, the issues raised throughout this book indicate that the promise of lifelong learning has to extend beyond merely advancing understanding, providing greater insight, or enhancing people's skills, important though these outcomes are.

Needless to say, turning this first principle into effective practice is extraordinarily challenging. First, learners may need some educative assistance in working out exactly what constitutes their interests, needs and priorities. This will require the exercise of supreme professional and technical skill, an uncompromising airing of all relevant arguments, and openness in respect of any values endorsed on the part of any educator involved or leader of the learning initiative, as well as strict adherence to the highest standards of ethical practice. All of this is essential to ensure that it is the learners' desires that are so expressed and not those of the educator, leader or some other powerful or influential third party, even if physically absent.

Secondly, in any given group or setting, there is always the chance that there will be differences of opinion or changes of priority when considering issues that touch upon one or other dimension of citizenship, identity or belonging, or their associated ideas and institutions. This will occur whether these cleavages are about the topic to be addressed, how best to address it, or what to conclude from the debate. In many respects, this might be said to be the very stuff not just of vibrant lifelong learning but, equally, of genuine pluralism and deliberative citizenship, and expressive of the essential dynamism of emergent and possibly shifting identities and forms of belonging. Such a celebration of difference within a given group does not make the tasks of lifelong learning any easier, and this is the whole point of Habermas's insistence on the importance of communication at the heart of democracy and citizenship.

Second principle: begin with people's own experiences and their 'definitions of the situation'[20]

A useful corrective to the risk of imposing needs and priorities on learners is to start with their own experiences and their own views of what they want in respect of, for example, their entitlements, obligations and opportunities as citizens, the pros and cons of different institutions and other social mechanisms for achieving their goals, or the manner in which their identities or sense of belonging might best be expressed. This will entail exploring learners' own definitions of the situation and of what matters, and validating them – not in the sense of constituting absolute truths, but as valid expressions and interpretations of those experiences. A good example of this is what has been referred to in American adult education practice as the development of a 'culturally relevant curriculum' – a curriculum that 'speaks' to learners' 'personal experiences and ways of knowing' by validating their language, fostering learners' positive self and group identities and helping to affirm their goals (Sealey–Ruiz, 2007, p.44).

Once such a useful start has been made with citizens/learners, further skilful exploration may then be necessary – perhaps with the aid of the experience of others or with the help of comparative, conceptual or theoretical perspectives – to see whether other interpretations are possible or perhaps even preferred. At the very least, this will entail teachers

---

20 For a valuable discussion of experience in relation to learning, see Jarvis (2004).

practising, and developing in their students, the skills and appreciation of the core educative value of challenge, critique, debate, reflection and revue (Giroux, 1989 and Giroux and Simon, 1989).

Where matters of citizenship are involved, with the inevitable connection to matters of rights, responsibilities and duties, and the contested matters of fairness, equality and power, this second phase of exploration and its comparison with what might be called learners' 'first stage expression' of their own experiences and definitions is a defining feature of effective lifelong learning. In the case of identity or belonging, the implementation of this second principle requires great sensitivity, always bearing in mind that people's expressions or interpretations of their identity or sense of belonging may be mediated through their levels of self-confidence or certainty, and may be tentative or even fearful. Ironically, it may only be when they feel quite secure socially as well as secure in their own identity that people will be free to give it full and public expression. Where they feel that such expression is under threat or meets with hostile disapproval, they may be more reluctant to demonstrate or give voice to their true sense of belonging.

On the other hand, the successful operation of the principle of 'starting where people are' often endows any subsequent discussion or debate with great richness and opens up the possibility of considering the many influences upon people's experiences and the ways in which they strive to make sense of them – in language, imagery, metaphor, memory, biography and so on. Just to illustrate how rich this can be, people's own narratives of their experiences as migrants, immigrants or refugees can throw light not only on the orientations and behaviour of the people among whom their migration located them, but also upon any subsequent claims in respect of their identity and sense of belonging. Knowing, for example, just what it is like to be a young second- or third-generation woman of Bangladeshi origin in, say, Bradford or Southall today, and of some of the potential conflicts and tensions in the lives of such young women, would provide a powerful basis for their further learning.

Third principle: be genuinely life-long and life-wide

From all that has been considered so far with regard to citizenship and belonging, it is evident that learning itself should not be confined to any one domain or single stage of life. Just as an approach to learning should be as concerned with what happens pre-school, in the years of schooling

215

and other formal education and in the various phases of adult life, so too should it embrace family, community, work, leisure and politics, as well as what might normally be thought of as more intimate and personal aspects of people's identities.

There is an understandable tendency for writers on education for citizenship and for policy makers to focus most of their attention on schooling and the education of young people – tomorrow's citizens. After all, it is partly in the formation of young people that the future limits and possibilities of citizenship, and people's aspirations, will be determined. However understandable it might be, such a narrow concentration needs to be rejected for at least three reasons. First, the learning that is part of citizenship finds its expression at all stages in people's lives and in a multiplicity of locales, not just in, or as a product of, school days. Secondly, learning about, for or through citizenship, and the expression of identity, occur in a wide range of forms and modes, and not just in the relatively structured nature of school-based education. Thirdly, school pupils are not just 'future' citizens, they have concerns and priorities, rights and entitlements, duties and obligations, hopes and fears in their lives as young people.

It goes without saying that this principle is firmly against the kind of narrowing of lifelong learning's focus that was indicted earlier by a variety of authors. It also goes beyond those assumptions and distortions that rule out the experiences and world views of whole social groups and interests and their own conceptions of what constitutes the good life and what should figure as genuinely inclusive citizenship.

Positioning lifelong learning in connection with citizenship and people's sense of belonging in terms of the life course in all of its aspects is essential. If lifelong learning is confined only to certain periods in people's lives, or just to particular environments where learning occurs, it is likely that understanding will be restricted and learning constrained. Moreover, people's own scope for determining their needs and priorities and developing their own worked-through interpretations of their situations will be, more than likely, artificially constrained. So, too, will any sense of the essentially dynamic character that people may have of who they are and what they want from citizenship, or from a recognition of their developing or changing identities, or from their feelings of belonging as they shift through life and across its various institutional boundaries.

As an example, such an approach is not simply vital in understanding young people's or young adult's burgeoning sense of themselves; it is also

216

full of insight for the experiences of elderly people, especially as they move into greater dependence on others and risk losses of effectiveness, personal dignity or respect. For those frail older people who may feel forgotten or abandoned, perhaps especially when their uses in the markets of production and consumption are thought to be mostly finished, it is important not just to understand what citizenship or belonging means to them. The promise and task of lifelong learning are also to help them maintain or reassert some control in their worlds – at home, in the family, in response to welfare policies, in hospital or in social care.

Fourth principle: embrace all modes and forms of learning, including formal education, informal and non-formal learning, and incidental learning

Learning that connects to citizenship, identity and belonging occurs in all sorts of ways, both directly and indirectly. Many countries, the UK included, now include learning about and for citizenship as part of their schools' curriculum, or in the offer made to young people in further and higher education. In addition, other formal learning in these settings contributes to young people's understanding of the development or characteristics of some of the key features of citizenship or belonging – questions of suffrage, legal rights, national or cultural identity, rights to a degree of self-determination, issues of privacy, tolerance, respect, mutuality, responsibility, and so on. Similarly, non-citizens seeking admission to citizenship may be required to go through some kind of formal learning or to demonstrate some formal knowledge and understanding as part of the procedures laid down as an element of that process.

That by no means exhausts all of the forms and milieux of learning in relation to citizenship or belonging. Both research and practice demonstrate that not only does a great deal of learning occur that is far from being formal or explicitly designed as learning, but also that much informal and non-formal learning is preferred, most effective and engaged in by people who do not normally think of themselves as 'learners' or consider that they are engaged in 'learning'. Many simply benefit from such learning as an incidental but valuable element of some other activity. Unfortunately, according to the researchers leading the study of lifelong learning and citizenship in Europe, 'little attention has been paid to informal, non-formal and incidental learning of attitudes, values and skills relevant to citizenship, governance and forms of social

217

regulation'. In the view of the researchers, citizens are not born but made, and this 'not simply – nor even primarily – through formal or targeted educational provision', but largely in the incidental learning gained 'in socio-institutional and cultural processes' (Holford *et al.*, 2003, p.29).

Of course, it is not always easy to draw a line between these different forms of learning: often they intermingle and may complement or contradict each other. Moreover, it is, in an important sense, quite difficult to legislate or plan for some sorts of informal, non-formal or incidental learning, at least with any certainty, for in doing so they inevitably shift towards aspects of formality. Mostly, however, as the European study's authors argue, in quoting from Coombs's and Ahmad's definition, 'generally informal education is unorganized, unsystematic and even unintentional at times, yet it accounts for the great bulk of any person's total lifetime learning – including that of a highly "schooled" person' (Coombs and Ahmed, 1974, p.8, cited in Holford *et al.*, 2003, p.30).[21]

Fifth principle: develop learners' skills in independent and critical thinking

At the heart of any notion of citizenship, and especially of the republican model, stand the twin ideas of independence and autonomy. As we have already seen, for citizens to operate freely in the world, they must be free from undue interference – whether that be from the State, from the incursions of others into their independence, and from restrictions upon their rights of expression, independent voting, assembly and belief. In exchange for such rights, and for the opportunities to take advantages of these freedoms in order to be able to act according to their own decisions and priorities, citizens also need to attend to their duties and obligations as citizens. These may be the minimal ones of respecting the same rights of other citizens, paying their taxes and helping to defend the state from which those rights are derived, or else they may extend to include the presumed responsibility for sharing in the life and governance of the community through participation.

In either case, independence of mind – the ability and confidence to assess situations, review evidence and argument, weigh opinion and express a point of view – is of crucial importance. It is worth quoting

---

21 See also Eraut *et al.* (1998 and 2000).

again the words of the Crick advisory group on the teaching of citizenship in schools. Active citizenship for the group meant that people would be able 'to think for themselves', to be 'willing, able and equipped to have an influence in public life' and to manifest 'the critical capacities to weigh evidence before speaking and acting' (Crick, 1998, p.7). These, it may be said, are the qualities of mind that all education and learning should seek to develop and constitute the skills of thoughtful independence to encourage people to cherish and extend. They move learning from simple acts of transmission, memorisation and repetition to those of reflection, deliberation, analysis and consideration. They enable people to engage with others in debate, listening to other points of view and ideas, thinking through proposals, anticipating implications and judging how vision and reality measure up. In this connection, Tom Lovett and his colleagues (1983, p.127) reminded readers of C. Wright Mills' suggestion that, alongside the matters of values and skills in adult learning, 'we ought to put sensibility, which includes them both and more besides. It includes a sort of therapy in the ancient sense of clarifying one's knowledge of one's self, including the imparting of all of those skills of controversy with oneself which we call thinking, and with others which we call debate.'

Another valuable aspect of this mental independence is the capacity for reflexivity. That is to say that, increasingly in the conditions of what Bauman among others calls 'late modernity', people need to be able to make, shape and, if needs be, reshape their own identities. That requires a capacity to actively review one's life, to give it meaning and direction in a self-directed narrative that integrates the person successfully with the unfolding events of the world. In practice, as Giddens (1991) has insisted, this invests reflexivity and identity simultaneously with both robustness and fragility. Reflexivity requires confidence, an ability to consider and live with risk, uncertainty, change and choice, and the capability to plan for the future, as well as to interpret the past. Reflexivity might even add up to an ability to counter some of the worst material circumstances of everyday existence, or at least a capability of visualising alternative possibilities – a palpable advantage for citizens struggling to bring about change or improvement in their lives. Reflexive capacity is also essential for any sense of belonging that is more than one imposed either from within a group or from outside; it is central to the very idea of people sharing in the authorship of their own identities.

219

Sixth principle: connect learning with action

In line with much good practice in adult education, part of lifelong learning's promise must be its potential connection with action. That means linking learning to the lives of citizens as they struggle with, achieve, and enjoy forms of citizenship and action through which they hope to realise their ambitions, express their identities, give meaning to their lives, and exercise greater influence over their worlds. The observation by Oldfield that citizenship is not a spectator sport, places action at the centre of a citizenship that is lived and shaped rather than just given, and, ideally, links learning and activity in a reciprocal and continuing relationship.

The chosen domains of action based on lifelong learning can be almost infinitely varied. Action may centre on people's personal life plans or those of a group; it may concern activity to contribute to community regeneration or to enhance social inclusion. Learning may also drive the deployment of new skills for work or for entrepreneurial initiative; it may entail planning and executing a campaign to secure recognition for a particular way of life from the State or others, or to secure a material improvement in housing or the environment. And, just as learning may drive action, so action in turn may be the stimulus to further learning. In either case, what is envisaged in connecting learning with action is providing, or enhancing, through learning channels, opportunities for people to engage in self-activity – making a contribution to people's sense of the possibilities of their own agency (as well, perhaps, as of its limitations).

Above all, perhaps, lifelong learning connects with citizenship and belonging in the practices of learning for active citizenship for social improvement in the honourable tradition of socially purposive learning, in which people's learning is oriented to achievement of their own priorities, their own needs and the enhancement of their citizenship and identities. The learning element of this triptych may be called, in the Crick-ian vocabulary, 'political literacy', although its components may vary considerably from practitioner to practitioner, from issue to issue, from locale to locale and from purpose to purpose. The actions following may be far-reaching and radical, maybe even adding up to a challenge to some or other aspect of the status quo, or they may be limited, modest and generally fairly conservative in intent or effect. That would all be a matter of determination by those most closely involved. What these different instantiations of action have in common, however, is upholding the connection between learning and participation, between learning and doing, and between learning and practice in everyday life.

Seventh principle: link learning to the possibilities and prospects of increased autonomy for learners and citizens

One of the principal objectives of learning is to free individuals and groups from circumstances or conditions that restrict them – whether such restrictions are mental, physical, organisational, social, cultural or political. Challenging ignorance, prejudice and irrationality have always been central to educational initiatives, but what is envisaged here goes further. It entails the encouragement and provision of learning opportunities that open up wider possibilities for citizens to gain more control over their lives, and for those who suffer from unfair constraints or exclusions to enhance their chances of emancipation or greater freedom through learning.

The learning involved could consist of raising consciousness, enhancing self-esteem and self-confidence, or developing better understanding of the barriers to autonomy, or a consideration of tactics and strategy. Needless to say, this could also include opportunities for individuals and groups to advance, through discussion and debate (not mere assertion), their claims for recognition of the legitimacy of their particular identities or cultures of belonging, within the wider spheres of polity and social life.

In line with this approach, Henry Giroux portrays a key, demanding, role for teachers as 'transformative intellectuals' in promoting an explicitly emancipatory conception of education and authority in which learners are encouraged to take critical democracy and active citizenship seriously. In this, his objective is the development of 'a citizenry capable of genuine public thinking, political debate and social action'.

> Such a view of authority endorses a concept of the citizen as more than a simple 'bearer of abstract rights, privileges, and immunities'; it sees the citizen as a member of any one of a diverse number of public spheres that provides a sense of communal vision and civic courage. (Giroux, 1989, p. 137)

221

David Held (1995, p.207) has suggested that, in an 'ideal' political community, autonomy can be measured against five criteria. The first is 'effective participation', in which all citizens must be equally free to engage in public life and to express their own views and preferences. Second comes 'enlightened understanding', meaning that all citizens should enjoy equal opportunities and the necessary knowledge in order to be able to express and pursue their own interests. Thirdly, citizens must be able to express 'control over the agenda', deciding the public matters to be debated and determined. Fourthly, there must be 'voting equality at decisive stages', in which each citizen's judgement weighs equally. Fifthly, the system of citizenship should manifest full 'inclusiveness', whereby all mature adults are granted the full rights of citizenship, with no exclusions, along with the associated responsibilities. It is clear that lifelong learning can contribute to each of these five in the expansion of autonomy and in relation to the key seven 'sites of power' through which people live their daily lives and which together constitute the overall quality of life: their bodies and health; in welfare provision; in cultural expressions, including beliefs; through civic associations; in the economy; in relation to coercion and the use of force; and in the operation of all legal, political and regulatory arrangements (*ibid.*, pp.191–193).

Increasing learner and citizen autonomy does not simply mean 'more rights and fewer responsibilities', or a licence for all just to do as they please without regard for the lives of other citizens. In an important sense, this means that more independence and greater freedom both *from* constraints and *to do* new things will always be conditional on acceptance of, and active subscription to, a set of open and commonly agreed rules of behaviour, which themselves result from the deliberations and decisions of autonomous citizens.

Eighth principle: base learning on the principles and practices of equity and social justice

One of the most serious indictments of learning is that too often it can be a site not just for the *manifestation* of social injustice, but worse, for its *reinforcement*, *perpetuation* and *legitimation*. Sadly, all too frequently this has been true of schooling, of learning for work, of further and higher education and, even, of some instances of adult and community education. If lifelong learning is to fulfil its promise for the enhancement of citizenship and to bring any sort of understanding and mutual respect to people's different identities and senses of belonging, neither its philosophy nor its forms of organisation and practice can be founded on arrangements that in themselves *automatically and systematically disadvantage* some participants or groups, and privilege others, or which allow for the perpetuation of palpable social inequality.

In this, it needs to be clearly understood that there will continue to be claims from individuals and from new social groups that they are denied full and equitable citizenship by virtue of their treatment – by the State, by powerful interests, by other social groups, or by the organisation and institutions of learning – or that aspects of their lives are accorded insufficient regard, and that, perhaps, learning has failed so far to challenge what is felt to be wrong and unfair. There will, no doubt, also be new claims to difference, and maybe for some sorts of special treatment, in order to secure social justice. In that respect, the search for full citizenship and for a true sense of belonging by a great plurality of individual and social groups is bound to be a continuous political and educational process.

My suggestion is not that there should simply be imposed some absolute external set of standards for social justice in lifelong learning regardless of context, but that the aims, values and the practices of learning should be open to scrutiny and radical challenge in relation to the core principles and central spirit of the ideas of equality and social justice. This approach will enable learners themselves, as well as the providers and funders of learning, to measure any proposed provision against the tests of fairness and equity and, if necessary change what is on offer or how it is to be provided or organised.

Bearing in mind, as already considered, that any programme of learning has inscribed within it certain assumptions, principles and values, even where these are not acknowledged, the suggestion here is that these should be openly stated and, equally, be open to critical review. There are four kinds of assumption or value judgement that need to be clarified for debate. They are, first, *who* is to be educated or given opportunities to learn, and with what sorts of *entitlement*, including especially questions of fairness and the provision of resources to move entitlement from *formal* to *substantive* opportunity. Secondly, there needs to be openness and clarity about *the aims and purposes* of that education or learning, and about how those are to be determined and by whom. Thirdly, there should be agreed ground rules about how the *processes of teaching and learning* are to be conducted, especially with regard to tolerance and respect and what

223

Gallacher (2004) terms the principle of 'non-repression' of difference, as well as through reference to what standards of evidence or proof are to prevail.[22] Fourthly, there needs to be consideration of the *nature of knowledge*, and especially what is to be considered worthwhile knowledge, and how engagement with it is to be accomplished.

Ninth principle: engage learners for citizenship and democracy through inclusive and democratic methods

The kind of learning that is likely to stimulate the development of active citizenship and facilitate the democratic exploration of diversity of identity and culture will need itself to incorporate active engagement and exploration on the part of learners, rather than mere reception of authoritative transmission. It should also aim to include all of the learners in debate, and in this respect be genuinely inclusive, ensuring that learners of whatever provenance, with whatever prior learning or achievement, and manifesting whatever sorts of difficulties or disabilities are enabled to engage.

This will also mean encouraging and supporting the sorts of learning that promote learners' own sense of independence and of educational responsibility for exploring ideas – their own and those of others – through open discussion and debate. Much excellent adult education has long exemplified this principle, in which the role of teacher is to act as guide, informer, expert (at least in some respects), mediator, questioner, challenger and critic, but not as the hierarchical first and last word. This is a most demanding role – organisationally, intellectually, professionally and ethically, especially where the education of young people is involved.

As indicated earlier, the educational philosopher and pragmatist John Dewey (1916) advocated that schools should also be embryonic democratic communities in which children experience early examples of participation in decision-making and contribute to the communal life of the school. The idea of the school as a kind of 'miniature democratic state' has not, however, enjoyed much popularity in the UK (with the notable exception of Summerhill School in Suffolk, founded by A. S. Neil), or

---

22 See also Gutmann (1987) on the notion of a 'democratic threshold' that should obtain in relation to respect for differences of identity and Howe (1997) on how this principle could be deployed through dialogue to ensure that otherwise marginalised or excluded identities might be afforded recognition.

indeed in Europe or in other parts of the world (Levin, 1998; Dürr, 2005). As the Council of Europe research suggested, the idea of fully democratising schooling in all its aspects can be misleading, as has also been pointed out by the Citizenship Foundation (2001). But even within the recognised limitations of the scope for full democracy in schools, pupils can still contribute to and participate in the governance of their schools, as well as learning through genuinely 'investigative curriculum projects' that are deliberately oriented towards their own school's governance.

The Council of Europe report, prepared by Dürr (2005, p.56), concludes by setting out a rationale and the objectives for learning democracy in and through school and beyond with the aim of promoting stability in a Europe that is notable for its cultural variety. This could represent a valuable way of carrying forward the ninth principle proposed here. Such learning, suggests Dürr, should be oriented towards the promotion of social cohesion, solidarity and social inclusion. Its purposes should be the development and sustenance of a dynamic democratic culture, with commitment to shared values in respect of human rights, responsibilities, equality and the rule of law. It should embody the idea that the school has a key part to play in both learning and practicing democracy from an early age.

In form, learning democracy should be multi-faceted, multiple-dimensional, innovative and bottom up; it should stimulate active, creative and responsible participation in decision-making; and it should provide lifelong opportunities for acquiring and applying information and values in a broad range of formal and non-formal contexts. Further, learning democracy should cross the boundaries between school and the community, transcending divisions between formal, informal and non-formal learning, and it should promote reciprocity in teaching and learning, encouraging the idea that learning is always a two-way process.

Another aspect of this democratic approach to learning is to engage learners themselves in helping to determine the content of the curriculum or subject matter of enquiry. As Lovett and colleagues (1983, pp.148 and 149) insist, 'if democratic education is to have any sense, students must be consulted about the programmes they enter, both in terms of curriculum and standard procedures and in relation to particular incidences and grievances. Teachers have a responsibility to open up courses to that kind of discussion. They also have a responsibility to promote what generations of democrats and scholars and others have bequeathed them: namely

225

bodies of knowledge and principles of practice'. This sort of 'negotiation' of the curriculum often features in community education and, in the organisation and constitution of the WEA and in much adult education, is a long-institutionalised feature of good practice.

This approach both allows learners to connect any planned learning activity with their own life priorities or intended practical initiatives, including through a 'constructivist' genesis of topics to be studied, and also helps to de-mystify the issue of designing a curriculum. The role of any teacher, organiser, facilitator or leader in this is not to be passive or the mere instigator of any agreed curriculum or content, still less to pay undue respect to the views of adult or lifelong learners when they choose to espouse irrational, irrelevant or inconsistent views, or where opinion flies in the face of robust evidence, or where they adopt positions or endorse behaviours that stand in contradiction to the core principles of liberal democracy, such as equality. Tutors have a professional and moral obligation to scrutinise, challenge and criticise, within an overall ethic of support for learners and always eschewing the use of humiliation. At the same time, when it comes to determining a focus for study or debate, the approach being advocated here also needs to open opportunities for learners to understand the many different ways in which power, status, class, gender or identity can be extremely influential in shaping concepts, theories and knowledge.

This is an arena in which the professionalism and pedagogic exper-tise of the teacher or tutor needs to be fully exercised. As Mary Stuart (1995, p.205) has written, the complex interplay of individual, institu-tional, organisational, community and professional identities within the operation of wider structures of power, culture and social relations 'make the idea of democratic learning more difficult to implement'. This calls for new approaches to pedagogy, such as the model of the Swedish study circle, and new conceptions of what constitutes the knowledge that learning needs to address, in which learners engage more in what she prefers to call 'investigation' than traditional and more conventional modes of 'learning'. In this connection, Jane Thompson (2000) has produced a most useful explanatory lexicon of, and guide to, the key elements of a radical tradition of 'emancipatory learning'. This 'is con-cerned with how learning, knowledge and education can be used to assist individuals and groups to overcome educational disadvantage, combat social exclusion and discrimination, and challenge economic and political inequalities – with a view to securing their own emancipation and promoting progressive social change'.

In all of this, it is important to emphasise that it is not being proposed, for example, that claims for truth or validity should be simply subjected to some reductive test of what is favoured by the majority in any given instance. Rather, the idea is that learning should not be conducted in ways that are predicated on the assumption of an always all-knowing teacher transmitting absolute and uncontested knowledge to all-accepting and subordinated learners. Just as ideas, evidence, concepts, propositions and so on should be subject to rigorous debate and review, so too all learners should be able to share in that debate, to voice opinions and concerns, and to state their own priorities – both for *what* to learn and in respect of any *conclusions* reached. The only major condition for adopting such an approach should be learners' willingness for those opinions, concerns, priorities and conclusions also to be subject to challenge and review.

Tenth principle: enable discursive consideration of claims for recognition of difference

If lifelong learning is to contribute to the creation of satisfactory milieux in which claims for recognition of difference or for the legitimacy of particular identities can be considered, it will be necessary first to establish a framework of agreed ground rules through which discursive deliberation should occur, including the criteria against which such claims are to be assessed. A first element of such a framework would need to be the agreed minimum common elements of citizenship that should apply to all participants. This would perform four functions. First, it would provide a basis of shared rights, norms and values, enabling people to understand what elements of citizenship they share, irrespective of any other differentiating characteristics. Secondly, on the basis of such a common platform, the rules of engagement could then be agreed for considering all claims for difference or recognition. Thirdly, the framework would stand as an initial reminder that nobody can, with any fairness or completeness, be wholly allocated to some singular category for purposes of his or her identity. Finally, by definition, such ground rules would completely rule out of order any claims of difference whose principal objective was the wholesale denial or obliteration of alternative or opposing claims, or which sought to undermine the core principle that even where recognition is accorded to diversity there still subsist some elements of commonality.

These matters need to be broached with great sensitivity, especially in the light of recent indications in the UK of some heightening of tension where matters of immigration and multiculturalism are in question. However, they are better addressed through the approach suggested rather than either in an arena of mutual confrontation or from entirely segregated islands of separate belonging. These are difficult times for retaining any acceptable version of multiculturalism, as fears grow that the ways in which it has hitherto been adopted have reinforced division and provided no basis for the creation of a genuine pluralism, embodying mutual respect, tolerance and acceptance. In a review of the possibilities of multicultural education in American schools, 'that is faithful to our form of liberal democracy and that can assist citizens in flourishing as human beings within our society', Wendy Turgeon observes that:

> *Recent events in the US and worldwide have precipitated intense examination of the spectrum of multicultural methods and programs and have sharpened our focus on the immediate need to protect the concept of diversity while we still negotiate its limits. (Turgeon, 2004)*

In the light of this controversy, the political theorist Bhikhu Parekh (2000) provides a new approach to multiculturalism. His re-conception is based on the simple recognition that human beings are at once both 'natural' – as formed by their birth, bodies and genetic code – and 'cultural' – as shaped by the environment of their family, upbringing, beliefs, relationships, actions and preferences. People's naturalness constitutes their common humanity, and their cultures constitute their differences. In such circumstances, argues Parekh, we cannot base a system of equality merely on what people have in common and the qualities that are uniform among them. What is needed is to reject any approach to equality grounded entirely on people's uniformity and that treats 'human beings equally in those respects in which they are similar and not in those in which they are different'.

> *Human beings do share several capacities and needs in common, but different cultures define and structure these differently and develop new ones of their own. Since human beings are at once both similar and different, they should be treated equally because of both. Such a view, which grounds equality not in human uniformity but in the interplay of uniformity and difference, builds difference into the very concept of*

228

equality, breaks the traditional equation of equality with similarity, and is immune to monist distortion. Once the basis of equality changes so does its content. Equality involves equal freedom or opportunity to be different, and treating human beings equally requires us to take into account both their similarities and differences. (ibid., pp.234 and 235)

In noting that multicultural education touches not just upon race and ethnicity but also on issues concerning gender, sexual orientation and disability, Turgeon describes an ascending scale of acceptance, moving from recognition, to tolerance and through respect to support. The study of diversity – in terms of an exploration of different cultures, languages, histories, mores, religions, forms of social and political organisation and everyday lives, including family and kinship relations, food, clothing and popular rituals – opens up the possibility of achieving 'imaginative empathy'. Encountering other people's narratives of their histories and identities enables us to learn from comparison, to see the world through the eyes of others and, thereby, also to reflect more deeply upon our own lives. It also facilitates the development of appropriate criteria for judging the legitimacy of claims for recognition of difference and the appropriate forms and limits within which such difference should reasonably be manifest, rather than proceeding from either an assumption of absolute homogeneity or a presumption of the dominance of our own or a 'majority' identity and sense of belonging. This way, multiculturalist learning should be able to avoid what Martha Nussbaum (1997) refers to as 'cultural romanticism' on the one hand and 'cultural chauvinism' on the other.

Eleventh principle: provide all adults with an lifelong annual 'entitlement' to post-school learning

If the above principles are to have any influence in people's lives, it is essential that all people should have a real opportunity to take advantage of instances of lifelong learning that meet their own interests, desires and priorities, and in forms and modes, and in times and through mechanisms which they choose for themselves. There may be a need for some general rules covering the sorts of learning activity for which the new entitlement could properly be used. Any such rules should be drawn as widely and generously as possible, with scope for individuals or groups to make a case

229

to a prescribed authority for any more 'idiosyncratic' uses that are not covered by the core rules.

In recognition of the public interest in fostering a learning citizenry, one way of facilitating people's access to such learning would be for all adults to enjoy a publicly funded 'learning entitlement'. This could be expressed in terms of a financial value or be measured in time, but would be a common basic entitlement for all people beyond school age (the matter of entitlement for school-age pupils and students having already been covered).

A new adult lifelong learning entitlement could be administered in a number of different ways – for example, by local authorities, possibly in connection with their responsibilities for council taxes and/or the electoral register, and could take the form either of some sort of personalised voucher system, or be incorporated into one of the kinds of electronic local services card that some local authorities now provide. An alternative arrangement may be to link the administration of such a system with the new NHS electronic patient record system, which would have the advantage of moving around the country with the learner. Again, this is an area of public policy in which a network of community-based and voluntary organisations, trades unions, churches and online communities could assist the formal bodies of the national and local state.

Clearly, it would be necessary to set the cash equivalent value of such a new entitlement. It would also be necessary to consider any rules that may be required for individuals wishing to accumulate their annual entitlements as being used at their own convenience, or for any individuals wishing to combine their respective entitlements to purchase some collective learning provision. There may even be circumstances in which individuals could 'overdraw' against future anticipated entitlements for particular approved educational activities (for instance in relation to certain approved qualifications).

In all of these situations, if responsibility for leading the administration of the scheme were to be lodged with local authorities, its funding could be covered by the authorities' annual financial settlement – maybe even with powers for local authorities to supplement the basic 'national' entitlement, in accordance with agreed rules and procedures. Needless to say, it would also be open for individuals or organisations such as employers, trades unions or voluntary bodies to supplement the annual lifelong learning entitlement from their own funds.

Twelfth principle: provide public investment through a 'community fund' to build and sustain an infrastructure to underpin lifelong learning for citizenship

Providing an adult entitlement to funding, even if some people chose (under agreed rules) to join entitlements together for their collective use and benefit, will still not be enough to ensure a healthy and vigorous moral economy of involvement, discourse, debate and learning. For individuals and groups to survive and thrive, and to breathe new life into lifelong learning for citizenship, there will need to be a structure of opportunities, information and support. This will be especially important for drawing in and sustaining those individuals, groups and communities who have been excluded from learning or have lacked the self-confidence to engage.

Building and servicing such an infrastructure will not be easy and, as well as requiring the dedication of protected finance and other resources, will need to be preceded by public debate on what should be the main elements of such an infrastructure. Some sorts of resource may be more necessary in some milieux or for some categories of citizen than others – for example, outreach, information and advice, and physical resources, including access to information technology, specialist educational support, and so on.

This is another delicate area, and one to be broached with professional care, but not one to be shirked. Debate will be essential if inequalities are not to be reproduced in the new system, and to ensure that, if any additional facilitation is to be provided to any category of individual or to any particular group, that such provision either meets with wider approval or is made in accordance with agreed rules. Once more, serious public debate cannot be avoided if a challenge to inequality and unfairness is to be accomplished, and some agreed way found of auditing and assessing the provision and impact of any additional infrastructural resources thus made available.

There are four other matters to resolve, or at least to think of alternatives for, in respect of the creation of a 'community fund' to support an infrastructure for citizens' lifelong learning. First, what should be the level of, and from where should come, the funding and other resources for such an endeavour? Secondly, who should administer and generally oversee the proper and efficient use of such funds and other resources? Thirdly, should a centrally fixed, dedicated contribution to the community chest be collected through local taxation – the council tax and business rates? Fourthly, what mechanisms would be needed to ensure that either public authorities or private interests cannot intervene in the operations of the infrastructure to distort them or bend them to their own desires, irrespective of informed public opinion?

This is not the place to rehearse all of the possible answers to these questions, but they all entail a key role for public authorities, private contributions, democratic control and the involvement of learners or their representatives in the machinery established to create, administer and review both the proposed 'community chest' and the working of the infrastructure. In line with earlier suggestions, as well as implicating central government funds, this may entail a key role for local authorities, supplemented by contributions from others providing funding or resources (including businesses, voluntary groups and other organisations) and involving learners in agreed ways.

Thirteenth principle: the goals of social improvement, the strengthening of citizenship and an enlargement of belonging cannot be secured by an expansion and deepening of learning alone

This brings us, finally, to a veritable 'baker's dozen' in my proposals. This whole monograph and the principles suggested for guiding the future development of lifelong learning have consistently looked, in hope, to the main ingredients of learning for progress – to openness, discussion, debate, challenge, critique, rigour, deliberation, reflection, knowledge, skills, wisdom and action. But learning alone, however expansive, diverse and involving, can never expect to secure the parallel promises of citizenship and belonging, and of freedom, social justice and democracy.

A little humility and a lot of political realism is required from the advocates, such as myself, regarding the potential contribution of lifelong learning to the creation of the good life and a 'just learning society' in the continuing struggle for enhanced citizenship and a richer sense of belonging. Social improvement and the ever-enlarging, but never fin-ished, horizon of achievement will also call for the commitment of resources of all kinds; it will require the mobilisation of collective and political will, and a determination to overcome opposition; and it will need diffusion through civil society. It cannot proceed without a determined reinvigoration of popular democratic participation and accountability at all levels and in a multiplicity of milieux; and it will depend upon an expansion and diversification of public space, the physical locales of social interaction and shared learning. It will both require and contribute to the democratisation of the various media and technologies of communication. Finally, it will also call for the patient construction of new sorts of alliance and innovative kinds of partnership and expressions of social solidarity, many of which will need to cut across some of the traditional social cleavages that have helped to frustrate the enhancement of citizenship, the fearless expression of identity, and the chances of everyone reaching out for freedom.

From principles to practice

Although these principles were first produced for consideration by the members of the independent commission of Inquiry into the Future for Lifelong Learning, they are offered here as a contribution towards a new vision for the role that lifelong learning should play in relation to citizenship and belonging, especially in the UK. The next steps require that the principles be widely and fully discussed and, no doubt, amended in the light of debate, before then being used to inform policy and practice.

A first move in that could be for organisations such as NIACE, the WEA, the Campaign for Learning and trades unions to publish the principles outlined here, disseminating them for wider debate. The intended audiences for such a wider debate would first be all those individuals, organisations and institutions that are either self-consciously or by their declared objectives concerned with education, training or learning at whatever level or stage of life, and in every milieu in which learning is acknowledged as occurring. Thus the debate should be taken to all governmental and public institutions with responsibility for learning. The debate would include government departments, local authorities, educational funding and regulatory bodies, schools, colleges, universities and training organisations, and all of the representative and professional bodies responsible for organising the staff working in education, training or with responsibility for some aspect of learning. It would also seek the views of professional staff working with learning in the press, broadcasting and publishing, and those responsible for the governance of such bodies.

233

The debate on the principles or a new vision for lifelong learning should include learners themselves, both as individuals – insofar as that is practicable – and through organisations and representative institutions. This would again include learners in schools, colleges, universities and training organisations, but also learners located in community groups, voluntary associations, trades unions and other bodies.

An invitation to take part in the debate should include political representatives and political parties at local, regional, national and European levels, especially those whose representative responsibilities include learning – as ministers, on select or specialist committees, or in overseeing programmes of learning or the funding for them.

The agreed principles or vision should be shared for debate with all those organisations and individuals concerned with matters to do with citizenship. As well as public authorities, this would include any organisation whose aims and objectives have to do with the advance or defence of citizenship, or are engaged in arguing for or reviewing questions of identity and its recognition. In particular, this would include organisations whose concerns touch upon the rights, status and responsibilities of groups (in respect of gender, race, ethnicity, religious belief, geographic location, sexual orientation, disability, age and so on) who feel that their claims have been overlooked or limited.

Finally, the idea behind generating such an ambitious and demanding debate, the organisation of which may be both costly and daunting, would be to arrive at a major public statement on the aims, values and purposes of lifelong learning, and the associated rights and responsibilities of citizens, that should apply in the UK and, maybe, even further afield.

References and further reading

Advisory Council of Teaching and Learning in Scotland (2001) *Education for Citizenship in Scotland: A Paper for Discussion and Development*. Glasgow: ACTLS

Albrow, M. (1996) *The Global Age*. Cambridge: Polity

Alibhai-Brown, Y. (2001) 'After multiculturalism', in Crick, B. (Ed.) (2001) *Citizens: Towards a Citizenship Culture*. Oxford: Blackwell

Andrews, G. (Ed.) (1991) *Citizenship*. London: Lawrence and Wishart

Anwar, M. (Ed.) (1998) *Ethnic Minorities and the British Electoral System*. Coventry: University of Warwick. Subsequently published in 2001 as 'Participation of ethnic minorities in British politics', in *Journal of Ethnic and Migration Studies*, Vol. 27, No. 3

Apple, M. W. (2002) *Power, Meaning and Identity: Monographs in Critical Education Studies*. New York: Peter Lang

Aspin, D. and Chapman, J. (2001) 'Lifelong learning: Concepts, theories and values', paper presented at SCUTREA, 31st Annual Conference, 3–5 July 2001

Audigier, F. (2000) 'Education for democratic citizenship', in *Basic Concepts and Core Competences for Democratic Citizenship*. Strasbourg: Council of Europe

Avinerni, S. and de Shalit. A. (Eds) (1992) *Communitarianism and Individualism*. Oxford: Oxford University Press

Bachrach, P. and Baratz, M. S. (1962) 'Two faces of power', *American Political Science Review*, Issue 56

Bakhtin, M. (1965) *Rabelais and his World*. Cambridge MA: MIT Press

Ball, M. and Hampton, W. (2004) (Eds) *The Northern College: Twenty-five Years of Adult Learning*. Leicester: NIACE

Ball, S. J. (2003) *Class Strategies and the Education Market*. London: Routledge Falmer

Banks, J. A. *et al.* (2005) *Democracy and Diversity: Principles and Concepts for Educating Citizens in a Global Age.* Seattle: Center for Multicultural Education

Barbagli, M. and Dei, M. (1977), 'Socialization into apathy and political subordination', in Karabel, J. and Halsey, A. H. (Eds) (1977) *Power and Ideology in Education.* Oxford: Oxford University Press

Barber, B. (2004) *Strong Democracy: Participatory Politics for a New Age.* Berkeley: University of California Press

Barber, B. (1998) *A Passion for Democracy: American Monographs.* Princeton, NJ: Princeton University Press

Baron, S., Field, J. and Schuller, T. (Eds) (2000) *Social Capital: Critical Perspectives.* Oxford: Oxford University Press

Barratt Brown, M. (1998) *'Bugger Bognor!' Education Needs the Money.* Nottingham: Spokesman

Barton, L. (1996) 'Citizenship and disabled people: A cause for concern', in Demaine, J. and Entwistle. H. (Eds) (1996), *Beyond Communitarianism: Citizenship, Politics and Education.* New York: St Martin's Press

Bauman, Z. (1997) *Postmodernity and its Discontents.* Cambridge: Polity

Bauman, Z. (2001) *The Individualized Society.* Cambridge: Polity

Bauman, Z. (2002) *Society Under Siege.* Cambridge: Polity

Bauman, Z. (2004) *Identity.* Cambridge: Polity

Bauman, Z. (2005) *Liquid Life.* Cambridge: Polity

Bauman, Z. (2007) *Liquid Times: Living in an Age of Uncertainty.* Cambridge: Polity

BBC/MORI (2005) *Multiculturalism Poll.*
Available at: http://news.bbc.co.uk/i/shared/bsp/hi/pdfs/multi_culturalism_poll. (Last accessed 30 September 2010)

BBC/IPSOS MORI (2008) *Britons Fear Race Violence.* London: BBC/IPSOS MORI

Beck, J. (1998) *Morality and Citizenship in Education.* London: Cassell

Beck, U. (1992) *Risk Society: Towards a New Modernity.* London: Sage

Beck, U. (1997) *The Reinvention of Politics: Rethinking Modernity in the Global Social Order.* Cambridge: Polity

Beck, U. (1998) *Democracy Without Enemies.* Cambridge: Polity

Beck, U. (1999) *World Risk Society.* Cambridge: Polity

Beck, U. (2000) *The Brave New World of Work.* Cambridge: Polity

Beck, U. (2003) 'Towards a New Critical Theory with a Cosmopolitan Intent', in *Constellations,* Vol. 10

Beck, U. and Beck-Gernshein, E. (2001) *Individualization.* London: Sage

Beiner, R. (Ed.) (1995) *Theorizing Citizenship*. Albany, NY: SUNY Press

Bellamy, R. (2008) *Citizenship: A Very Short Introduction*. Oxford: Oxford University Press

Bendix, R. (1956) *Work and Authority in Industry: Ideologies of Management in the Course of Industrialization*. Berkeley, CA: University of California Press

Benhabib, S. (2002) *The Claims of Culture: Equality and Diversity in the Global Era*. Princeton, NJ: Princeton University Press

Benhabib, S., Shapiro, I. and Petranovic, D. (Eds) (2007) *Identities, Affiliations and Allegiances*. Cambridge: Cambridge University Press

Benn, R. (2000a) *Including Citizenship in the Adult Curriculum,* Paper presented at SCUTREA Annual Conference, July 2000

Benn, R. (2000b) 'The genesis of active citizenship in the learning society', *Studies in the Education of Adults,* Vol. 32, No. 2

Berlin, I. (1969) 'Two Concepts of Liberty' in Berlin, I. (1969) *Four Monographs on Liberty*. Oxford: Oxford University Press

Bhabha, H. K. and Parekh, B. (1989) 'Identities on parade: A conversation', in *Marxism Today*, June 1989

Birch, A. H. (2007) *The Concepts and Theories of Modern Democracy*. London: Routledge

Blunkett, D. (2001) *Politics and Progress: Renewing Democracy and Civil Society*. London: Politico's Publishing

Blunkett, D. (2003a) *Active Citizens, Strong Communities: Progressing Civil Renewal*. London: Home Office

Blunkett, D. (2003b) *Civil Renewal: A New Agenda*. London: CFSV/Home Office

Blunkett, D. and Crick, B. (1991) *The Labour Party's Aims and Values*. Nottingham: Spokesman Books

Bourdieu, P. (1986), 'Forms of capital' in Richardson, J. (Ed.), 1986, *Handbook of Theory and Research for the Sociology of Education*. New York: Greenwood Press

Bourdieu, P. (2003) *Firing Back: Against the Tyranny of the Market*. London: Verso

Bradburn, D. (2009) *The Citizenship Revolution: Politics and the Creation of the American Union*. Charlottesville, VA: University of Virginia Press

Bron, A. and Malewski, M. (1996) *Adult Education and Democratic Citizenship*. Wroclaw: Wroclaw University Press

Brookfield, S. (1987) *Developing Critical Thinkers: Challenging Adults to Explore Alternative Ways of Thinking and Action*. Milton Keynes: Open University Press

Brookfield, S. (2003) 'Racializing criticality in adult education,' in *Adult Education Quarterly*, Vol. 53, No. 3

Brown, C. (2006) *Religion and Society in Twentieth-Century Britain*. London: Longman Pearson

Brown, J., Britton, A., Sigauke, A., Priestly, A. and Livingston, K. (2008) *Citizenship and Democracy in Scottish Schools*, Research Briefing Paper 4, AERS Universities of Edinburgh Stirling and Strathclyde

Brown, P. and Lauder, H. (1996) 'Education, Globalization, and Economic Development', in *Journal of Education Policy*, Vol. 11, reproduced in Halsey *et al.* (1997)

Burbules, N. C. and Torres, C. A., (Eds) (2000) *Globalization and Education: Critical Perspectives*. London: Routledge

Burke, P. (2000) *A Social History of Knowledge: From Gutenberg to Diderot*. Cambridge: Polity

Burke, P. J. and Jackson, S. (2007) *Reconceptualising Lifelong Learning*. London: Routledge

Butler, J. (1990) *Gender Trouble: Feminism and the Subversion of Identity*. London: Routledge

Byrne, D. (2005) *Social Exclusion*. Maidenhead: Open University Press

Calder, G. (2003) 'Communitarianism and New Labour'. Available at: www.whb.co.uk/socialissues/vol2gc.htm (last accessed 30 September 2010)

Calhoun, C. (Ed.) (1992) *Habermas and the Public Sphere*. Cambridge, MA: MIT Press

Calhoun, C. (2007) 'Social solidarity as a problem for cosmopolitan democracy', in Benhabib *et al.* (2007)

Cantle, T. (2008) *Community Cohesion: A New Framework for Race and Diversity*. Basingstoke: Palgrave Macmillan

Carr, W. and Hartnett, A. (1996) *Education and the Struggle for Democracy*. Buckingham: Open University Press

Carter, A. and Stokes, G. (Eds) (2001) *Democratic Theory Today: Challenges for the 21st Century*. Cambridge: Polity

Castells, M. (1996) *The Rise of the Network Society, The Information Age: Economy, Society and Culture Vol. I*. Oxford: Blackwell

Castells, M. (1997) *The Power of Identity, The Information Age: Economy, Society and Culture Vol. II*. Oxford: Blackwell

Castells, M. (1998) *End of Millennium, The Information Age: Economy, Society and Culture Vol. III.* Oxford: Blackwell

Castells, M. (2004) *The Networked Society: A Cross-cultural Perspective.* Chapter 1, London: Edward Elgar

Chambers, S. and Kymlicka, W. (Eds) (2002) *Alternative Conceptions of Civil Society.* Princeton, NJ: Princeton University Press

Child, J. (1964) 'Quaker employers and industrial relations', in *Sociological Review*, Vol. 12, pp.293–315

Citizenship Foundation (2001) *Democracy in Schools and the Local Community: A Brief Guide.* London: Citizenship Foundation

Civil Renewal Unit (2005) *Together We Can: The Government Action Plan for Civil Renewal.* London: Home Office

Clarke, J., Newman, J., Smith, N., Vidler, E. and Westmarland, L. (2007) *Creating Citizen-Consumers: Changing Identities in the Remaking of Public Services.* London: Sage

Cleaver, F. (2004) 'The social embeddedness of agency and decision-making', in Hickey, S. and Mohan, G., (Eds) (2004) *Participation: From Tyranny to Transformation?* London: Zed Books

Cockburn, C. (1983) *Brothers.* London: Pluto

Coffield, F. (Ed.) (2000) *The Necessity of Informal Learning.* Bristol: Policy Press

Coffield, F. (2007) 'Running ever faster down the wrong road: An alternative future for education and skills', Professorial lecture, London: IoE, University of London

Cohen, A. P. (1985) *The Symbolic Construction of Community.* London: Tavistock

Cohen, J. L. and Arato, A. (1992) *Civil Society and Political Theory.* London: MIT Press

Coleman, A. and Higgins, W. (2000) 'Racial and cultural diversity in contemporary citizenship', in Vandenberg, A. (Ed.) (2000) *Citizenship and Democracy in a Global Era.* London: Macmillan

Coleman, J. S. (1988) 'Social capital and the creation of human capital', in *American Journal of Sociology*, Vol. 94

Coleman, J. S. (1990) *Equality and Achievement in Education.* Boulder, C O: Westview Press

Coombs, P. H. and Ahmed, M. (1974) *Attacking Rural Poverty: How Non-formal Education can Help*, a research report for the World Bank, edited by Barbara Baird Israel

239

Cooper, Z. and Lodge, G. (Eds) (2008) *Faith in the Nation: Religion, Identity and the Public Realm in Britain Today*. London: IPPR

Cowburn, C. (1983) *Brothers: Male Dominance and Technological Change*. London: Pluto

Cranton, P. (2006) *Understanding and Promoting Transformative Learning*. San Francisco: Jossey-Bass

Crick, B. (1998) *Education for Citizenship and the Teaching of Democracy in Schools*. Final report of the Advisory Group on Citizenship. London: QCA

Crick, B. (2000) *Citizenship for 16–19 Year Olds in Education and Training*. London: DfES/LSC

Crick, B. (Ed.) (2001) *Citizens: Towards a Citizenship Culture*. Oxford: Blackwell

Crick, B. (2002a) 'A note on what is and what is not active citizenship.' Available at: www.excellencegateway.org.uk/media/post16/files/033_BernardCrick_what_is_citizenship.pdf (last accessed 30 September 2010)

Crick, B. (2002b) *Democracy: A Very Short Introduction*. Oxford: Oxford University Press

Crick, B. (2002c) 'Democracy and Citizenship', in *Teaching Citizenship*, Autumn 2002

Croucher, S. (2004) *Globalization and Belonging: The Politics of Identity in a Changing World*. Oxford: Rowman and Littlefield

Crow, G. (2002) *Social Solidarities: Theories, Identities and Social Change*. Buckingham: Open University Press

Cruikshank, M. (1992) *The Gay and Lesbian Liberation Movement*. London: Routledge

Dagger, R. (1997) *Civic Virtues: Rights, Citizenship, and Republican Liberalism*. Oxford: Oxford University Press

Dahl, R. (1961) *Who Governs?* New Haven, CT: Yale University Press

Dahl, R. (2000) *Democracy*. London: Yale University Press

Davies, D. (2001) 'Freedom and progress through lifelong learning', in *Widening Participation and Lifelong Learning*, Vol. 3, No. 1

Davis Smith, J. and Locke, M. (2008) (Eds) *Volunteering and the Test of Time*. London: Institute for Volunteering Research

DCMS/BERR (2009) *Digital Britain: The Interim Report*. Norwich: TSO

Dean, K. (2003) *Capitalism and Citizenship: The Impossible Partnership*. London: Routledge

Dearing, R. (Chair) (1997) *Higher Education in the Learning Society*. Report of the National Committee of Inquiry into Higher Education. London: Crown Copyright

Delanty, G. (2000) *Citizenship in a Global Age*. Buckingham: Open University Press

Delanty, G. (2003) 'Citizenship as a learning process: Disciplinary citizenship versus cultural citizenship', in *International Journal of Lifelong Education*, Vol. 22, No. 6

Delanty, G. (2007) 'European Citizenship: A critical assessment', in *Citizenship Studies*, Vol. 11, No. 3

Delors, J. *et al.* (1998) *Learning: The Treasure Within*. Paris: UNESCO

Demaine, J. (1996) 'Beyond communitarianism: Citizenship, politics and education', in Demaine, J. and Entwistle, H. (Eds) (1996) *Beyond Communitarianism: Citizenship, Politics and Education*. Basingstoke: Macmillan

Department of Communities and Local Government (no date) The *National Framework for Active Learning for Active Citizenship*. London: DCLG

Department of Communities and Local Government (2006) *2005 Citizenship Survey: Active Communities Report*. London: DCLG

Department of Health (2005) *Choosing Health*. London: DH

De Tocqueville, A. (2003) *Democracy in America*. London: Penguin Books

Dewey, J. (1897) 'My pedagogic creed', in *The School Journal*, Vol. LIV, No. 3

Dewey, J. (1916) *Democracy and Education*. New York: Free Press

Dewey, J. (1929) *Experience and Nature*. New York: Dover

Dewey, J. (1933) *How We Think: A Restatement of the Relation of Reflective Thinking to the Educative Process*. Boston: DC Heath

Dewey, J. (1938) *Experience and Education*. New York: Collier Books

Dirkx, J. M. (1998) 'Transformative learning theory in the practice of adult education: An overview', in *PAACE Journal of Lifelong Learning*, Vol. 7, pp.1–14

Dower, N. and Williams, J. (Eds) (2002) *Global Citizenship: A Critical Reader*. Edinburgh: Edinburgh University Press

Driver, S., and Martell, L. (2006) *New Labour*. Cambridge: Polity

Dryzek, J. H. (2000) *Deliberative Democracy and Beyond*. Oxford: Oxford University Press

Dudley, J. (1999) 'Higher education policy and the learning citizen', in Petersen, A., Barns, I., Dudley, J. and Harris, P. (Eds) (1999) *Poststructuralism, Citizenship and Social Policy.* London: Routledge

Duke, C. and Layer, G. (Eds) (2005) *Widening Participation: Which Way Forward for English Higher Education?* Leicester: NIACE

Dunant, S. and Porter, R. (Eds) (1996) *The Age of Anxiety.* London: Virago

Dürr, K. (2005) *The School: A Democratic Learning Community, the All-European Study on Pupils' Participation in School,* part of the Education for Democratic Citizenship Project 2001–2004. Strasbourg: Council of Europe

Eagleton, T. (1996) *The Illusions of Postmodernism.* Oxford: Blackwell

Edwards, R. and Usher, R. (2001) 'Lifelong learning: A postmodern condition of education?', in *Adult Education Quarterly,* Vol. 51, No. 4

Elliot, L. and Atkinson, D. (1999) *The Age of Insecurity.* London: Verso

Ellis, A. (2004) *Generation V – Young People Speak Out on Volunteering.* London: IVR

Elsdon, K. T., Reynolds, J. and Stewart, S. (1995) *Voluntary Organisations, Citizenship Learning and Change.* Leicester: NIACE

Eraut, M. (2000) 'Non-formal learning, implicit learning, and tacit knowledge in professional work', in Coffield, F. (Ed.) (2000) *The Necessity of Informal Learning.* Bristol: Policy Press

Etzioni, A. (1993) *The Spirit of Community.* New York: Crown

Etzioni, A. (1996) *The New Golden Rule: Community and Morality in a Democratic Society.* New York: Basic Books

European Union (2004) *Citizenship and Sense of Belonging.* Strasbourg: EU Commission

Evans, K. (1995) 'Competence and citizenship: Towards a complementary model for times of critical social change', *British Journal of Education and Work.* Vol. 8, No. 2

Evans, K. (1998) *Shaping Futures: Learning for Competence and Citizenship.* Aldershot: Ashgate

Evans, K. (1999) 'Beyond the work-related curriculum: Citizenship and learning after 16', in Leicester, M., Modgil, C. and Modgil, S. (Ed.) (1999) *Politics, Education and Society.* London: Falmer Press

Evans, W. G. (1990) *Education and Female Emancipation: The Welsh Experience.* Cardiff: University of Wales Press

Fahrmeir, A. (2007) *Citizenship: The Rise and Fall of a Modern Concept.* London: Yale University Press

Faulks, K. (1998) *Citizenship in Modern Britain*. Edinburgh: Edinburgh University Press

Faulks, K. (2000) *Citizenship*. London: Routledge

Fejes, A. and Nicoll, K. (Eds) (2008) *Foucault and Lifelong Learning: Governing the Subject*. London: Routledge

Fenwick, T. (2008) 'Women learning in garment work: Solidarity and sociality', *Adult Education Quarterly,* Vol. 58, No. 2

Ferri, E., Bynner, J. and Wadsworth, M. (2003) *Changing Britain, Changing Lives*. London: Institute of Education

Field, J. (2002) *Lifelong Learning and the New Educational Order*. Stoke on Trent: Trentham Books

Field, J. (2003) *Social Capital*. London: Routledge

Field, J. (2004) 'Forming public policy: Trends and prospects for residential adult education in an era of lifelong learning', in Ball, M. and Hampton, W. (Eds) (2004) *The Northern College: Twenty-five years of adult learning*. Leicester: NIACE

Field, J. (2005a) *Social Capital and Lifelong Learning*. Bristol: Polity Press

Field, J. (2005b) 'Civic engagement and lifelong learning', in *Studies in the Education of Adults,* Vol. 3, No. 2

Field, J. (2006) *Lifelong Learning and the New Educational Order*. New Revised Edition. Stoke on Trent: Trentham Books

Finlayson, J. G. (2005) *Habermas: A Very Short Introduction*. Oxford: Oxford University Press

Fletcher, S. (2000) *Education and Emancipation: Theory and Practice in a New Constellation*. New York: Teachers' College Press

Foley, G. (1999) *Learning in Social Action: A Contribution to Understanding Informal Education*. London: Zed Books

Foner, E. (1983) *Nothing but Freedom: Emancipation and its Legacy*. Baton Rouge: Louisiana State University Press

Foner, E. (1994) 'The meaning of freedom in the age of emancipation', in *Journal of American History*, September 1994, pp. 435–460

Fraser, N. (1992) 'Rethinking the Public Sphere', in Calhoun (1992)

Freire, P. (1973) *Education: The Practice of Freedom*. London: Writers and Readers Publishing Cooperative

Freire, P. (1982) *The Pedagogy of the Oppressed*. Harmondsworth: Penguin

Freire, P. (1986) *The Politics of Education*. Massachusetts: Bergin and Garvey

Freire, P. (1998) *Pedagogy of Freedom: Ethics, Democracy and Civil Courage*. Oxford: Rowman and Littlefield

243

Freire, P. (1999) *Pedagogy of Hope*. New York: Continuum

Freire, P. (2007) *Education for Critical Consciousness*. London: Continuum

Fryer, R. H. (1973a) 'The myths of the Redundancy Payments Act', in *Industrial Law Journal*, Vol. 2, No. 1, pp.1–16

Fryer, R. H. (1973b) 'Redundancy, values and public policy', in *Industrial Relations Journal*, Vol. 4, Issue 2, pp.2–19

Fryer, R. H. (1990) 'The challenge to working class education', in Simon, B. (1990) (Ed.) *The Search for Enlightenment: The Working Class and Adult Education in the Twentieth Century*. Leicester: London: Lawrence and Wishart

Fryer, R. H. *et al.* (1997) *Learning for the Twenty-first Century*. First report of the National Advisory Group for Continuing Education and Lifelong Learning. London: DfEE

Fryer, R. H. *et al.* (1998) *Creating Learning Cultures*. Second report of the National Advisory Group for Continuing Education and Lifelong Learning. London: DfEE

Fryer, R. H. (2008) *Inclusive Learning in Liquid Society*. Second John Tomlinson Memorial Lecture. Leicester: NIACE

Gallacher, T. (2004) *Education in Divided Societies*. Basingstoke: Palgrave

Garforth, F. W. (1962) *Education and Social Purpose*. London: Oldbourne

Gaskin, K. (2004) *Young People, Volunteering and Civil Service*. London: IVR

Gellner, E. (1994) *Conditions of Liberty: Civil Society and its Rivals*. London: Hamish Hamilton

Gibbs, K., Sani, M. and Thompson, J. (Eds) (2007) *Lifelong Learning in Museums: A European Handbook*. Ferrara: EDISAI

Giddens, A. (1990) *The Consequences of Modernity*. Cambridge: Polity

Giddens, A. (1991) *Modernity and Self-Identity: Self and Society in the Late Modern Age*. Cambridge: Polity

Giddens, A. (1994) *Beyond Left and Right: The Future of Radical Politics*. Cambridge: Polity

Giddens, A. (1998) *The Third Way: The Renewal of Social Democracy*. Cambridge: Polity

Giddens, A. (1999) *Runaway World*. London: Profile Books

Giddens, A. (2000) *The Third Way and its Critics*. Cambridge: Polity

Gilchrist, P. (2007) 'Sport under the shadow of industry: Paternalism at Alfred Herbert Ltd' in Tomlinson, A. and Woodham, M., in *Image, Power and Space: Studies in Consumption and Identity*. Maidenhead: Meyer and Meyer Sport

Giroux, H. A. (1989) 'Schooling as a form of cultural politics: Toward a pedagogy of and for difference', in Giroux, H. A. and McLaren, P. (Eds) (1989) in *Critical Pedagogy, the State and Cultural Struggle*. New York: State University of New York Press

Giroux, H. A. (1992) *Border Crossings: Cultural Workers and the Politics of Education*. London: Routledge

Giroux, H. A. (1997a) *Pedagogy and the Politics of Hope*. Oxford: Westview Press

Giroux, H. A. (1997b) 'Crossing the boundaries of educational discourse: Modernism, post-modernism and feminism' in Halsey *et al.* (1997)

Giroux, H. A. (2007) 'Democracy, education and the politics of critical pedagogy', in McLaren, P. and Kincheloe, J. (2007) *Critical Pedagogy: Where are we now?* New York: Peter Lang

Giroux, H. A. and Simon, R. (1989) 'Popular culture and critical pedagogy: Everyday life as a basis for curriculum knowledge', in Giroux, H. A. and McLaren, P. (Eds) (1989) *Critical Pedagogy, the State and Cultural Struggle*. New York: State University of New York Press

Gleeson, D. (1994) 'Open for business? Knowledge, rhetoric and reality', in *International Journal of Training Research*, Vol. 2, No. 2

Goldsmith, Lord (2008) *Citizenship: Our Common Bond*. London: Citizenship Inquiry/Justice Ministry

Gorman, J. (1973) *Banner Bright*. London: Allen Lane

Gorman, J. (1985) *Images of Labour*. London: Scorpion

Gouldner, Alvin (1962) 'Anti-Minotaur: The myth of a value free sociology', in *Social Problems*, Vol. 9, No. 3

Grayson, J. and Jackson, K. (2004) 'Engagement with the community', in Ball and Hampton, 2004

Green, A., Preston, J. and Janmat, J. G. (2006) *Education, Equality and Social Cohesion*. Basingstoke: Palgrave Macmillan

Griffith, R. (2000) *National Curriculum: National Disaster, Education and Citizenship*. London: Routledge Falmer

Guijt, I. and Shah, M. K. (Eds) (1998) *The Myth of Community*. London: ITP

Gunderson, J. (1987) 'Independence, citizenship and the American Revolution', in *Signs*, Vol. 13

Gustavsson, B. (1997) 'Lifelong learning reconsidered' in Walters, S. (Ed.), *Globalization, Adult Education and Training*. London: Zed Books

245

Gutmann, A. (1987) *Democratic Education*. Princeton, NJ: Princeton University Press

Gutmann, A. (Ed.) (1994) *Multiculturalism: Examining the Politics of Recognition*. Princeton, NJ: Princeton University Press

Gutmann, A. (Ed.) (1998) *Freedom of Association*. Princeton, NJ: Princeton University Press

Gutmann, A. (2003) *Identity in Democracy*. Princeton, NJ: Princeton University Press

Gutmann, A. and Thompson, D. (2004) *Why Deliberative Democracy?* Oxford: Princeton University Press

Habermas, J. (1996) *Between Facts and Norms: Contributions to a Discourse Theory of Law and Democracy*. Cambridge: Polity

Hale, S. (2006) *Blair's Community: Communitarian Thought and New Labour*. Manchester: Manchester University Press

Hale, S., Leggett, W. and Martell, L. (Eds) (2004) *The Third Way and Beyond: Criticisms, Futures, Alternatives*. Manchester: Manchester University Press

Hall, S. and Held. D. (1989) 'Citizens and citizenship', in Jacques, M. (Ed.) (1989) *New Times*. London: Lawrence and Wishart

Halsey, A. H., Lauder, H., Brown, P. and Stuart Wells, A. (Eds) (1997) *Education, Culture, Economy, Society*. Oxford: Oxford University Press

Hammersley, M. (2000) *Taking Sides in Social Research*. London: Routledge

Hampson, N. (1982) *The Enlightenment*. London: Penguin

Hanley, L. (2007) *Estates: An Intimate History*. London: Granta

Hansard Society (2008) *Audit of Political Engagement 5: The 2008 Report*. London: Hansard Society

Harvey, D. (2005) *A Brief History of Neoliberalism*. Oxford: Oxford University Press

Hayward, C. R. (2007) 'Binding problems, boundary problems: The trouble with "democratic citizenship" ', in Benhabib *et al.* (2007)

Heater, D. (1999) *What is Citizenship?* Cambridge: Polity

Heath, A. and Roberts (2008) *British Identity: Its Sources and Possible Implications for Civic Attitudes and Behaviour*.
Available at: www.justice.gov.uk/docs/british.identity.pdf (last accessed 30 September 2010)

Heath, P. (1999) 'Citizenship/transformative pedagogy: A critical space', in *Higher Education Research and Development,* Vol. 19, No. 1

Held, D. (1987) *Models of Democracy*. Cambridge: Polity

Held, D. (1995) *Democracy and the Global Order: From the Modern State to Cosmopolitan Governance.* Cambridge: Polity

Held, D. and McGrew, A. (Eds) (2003) *The Global Transformations Reader: An Introduction to the Globalization Debate.* Cambridge: Polity

Held, D. and McGrew, A. (2007) *Globalization/Anti-Globalization: Beyond the Great Divide.* Cambridge: Polity

Held, D., McGrew, A., Goldblatt, D. and Perraton, J. (1999) *Global Transformations: Politics, Economics and Culture.* Cambridge: Polity

Hickey, S. and Mohan, G. (Eds) (2004) *Participation: From Tyranny to Transformation?* London: Zed Books

Hildreth, R. W. (2004) 'John Dewey on experience: A critical resource for the theory and practice of youth engagement', annual meeting of Midwest Political Science Association, April 2004

Hill, R. J. (2006) 'The War on Democratic Public Space', *Convergence,* Vol. XXXIX, No. 2–3

Hills, J., Sefton, T. and Stewart, K. (Eds) (2009) *Towards a More Equal Society? Poverty, Inequality and Policy since 1997.* Bristol: Policy Press

Hirst, P. (2001) *War and Power in the 21st Century.* Cambridge: Polity

Hirst P. and Thompson, G. (1999) *Globalization in Question.* Second Edition. Cambridge: Polity

Hoban, M. (2008) 'Blair's community: Communitarian thought and New Labour', in *Community Development Journal,* Vol. 43, No. 2

Hobsbawm, E. (1997) *Globalization, Democracy and Terrorism.* London: Little Brown

Hobson, B. (Ed.) (2000) *Gender and Citizenship in Transition.* London: Macmillan

Holford, J. *et al.* (2003) *Lifelong Learning, Governance and Active Citizenship in Europe.* Final report of the ETGACE Research Project. Guildford: University of Surrey

Howe, K. R. (1997) *Understanding Equal Educational Opportunity: Social Justice, Democracy and Schooling.* New York: Teachers' College Press

Ichilov, O. (Ed.) (1990) *Political Socialization, Citizenship and Democracy.* New York: Teachers' College Press

Ichilov, O. (Ed.) (1998) *Citizenship and Citizenship Education in a Changing World.* London: Routledge

IES (2003) *New Learners, New Learning: A Strategic Evaluation of Ufi.* Sheffield: Ufi

International Council for Adult Education (2001) *The Ochos Rios Declaration.* Toronto: ICAE

247

Isin, E. F. and Wood, K. (1999) *Citizenship and Identity*. London: Sage

Jackson, K. (1995) 'Popular education and the State' in Mayo M. and Thompson, J. (Eds), (1995) *Adult Education, Critical Intelligence and Social Change*. Leicester: NIACE

Jarvis, P. (no date) 'Lifelong learning, active citizenship, social capital and the human condition.'
Available at: http://llw.acs.si/ac/09/cd/full_papers_plenary/Jarvis.pdf (Last accessed 30 September 2010)

Jarvis, P. (1987) *Adult Education in the Social Context*. London: Croom Helm

Jarvis, P. (1997) *Ethics and the Education of Adults in Late Modern Society*. Leicester: NIACE

Jarvis, P. (2004) *Adult Education and Lifelong Learning: Theory and Practice* (Third Edition). London: Routledge Falmer

Jarvis, P. (2007) *Globalisation, Lifelong Learning and the Learning Society*. London; Routledge

Jarvis, P. (2008) *Democracy, Lifelong Learning and the Learning Society: Active Citizenship in a Late Modern Age*. London: Routledge

Jenkins, R. (2004) *Social Identity*. London: Routledge

Jochum, V., Pratten, B. and Wilding, K. (2005) *Civil Renewal and Active Citizenship: A Guide to the Debate*. London: NCVO

Johnston, R. (1999) 'Adult learning for citizenship: Towards a reconstruction of the social purpose tradition', in *International Journal of Lifelong Education*, Vol. 18, No. 3

Johnston, R. and Usher, R. (1997) 'Re-theorising experience: Adult learning in contemporary social practices', in *Studies in the Education of Adults*, Vol. 29, No. 2

Jones, Kathleen B. (1998) 'Citizenship in a woman-friendly polity', in Gershon, S., Ed. (1998) *The Citizenship Debates*. Minneapolis: University of Minnesota Press

Kabeer, N., (Ed.) (2005) *Inclusive Citizenship*. London: Zed Books

Kane, J. (2002) 'Democracy and group rights', in Carter, A. and Stokes, G. (Eds) (2002) *Democratic Theory Today*. Cambridge: Polity

Keane, J. (1998) *Civil Society: Old Images, New Visions*. Oxford: Oxford University Press

Keane, J. (2003) *Global Civil Society?* Cambridge: Cambridge University Press

Keane, J. (2009) *The Life and Death of Democracy*. London: Simon and Schuster

Kellner, D. (2000) 'Globalization and the New Social Movements', in Burbules and Torres (2000)

Kennedy, H. (Chair) (1997) *Learning Works*. Coventry: FEFC

Kennedy, K. (Ed.) (1997) *Citizenship Education and the Modern State*. London: Routledge Falmer

Kenny, M. (2004) *The Politics of Identity: Liberal Theory and the Dilemmas of Difference*. Cambridge: Polity

Keogh, H. (2003) 'Learning citizenship in Ireland', in Medel-Anonuevo, C. and Gordon, M. (2003)

Kerr, D. (1999) *Citizenship Education: An International Comparison*. London: QCA

Kerr, D. (2003) 'Citizenship education in England: The making of a new subject', in *Journal of Social Science Education*

Kerr, D., Cleaver, E. M., White, G. and Judkins, M. (2005) *DCA Connecting with Citizenship Education: A Mapping Study*. Slough: NFER

Kerr, D., McCarthy, S. and Smith, A. (2002) 'Citizenship education in England, Ireland and Northern Ireland', in *European Journal of Education*, Vol. 37, Issue 2

Kettner, J. H. (1978) *The Development of American Citizenship*. Chapel Hill: University of North Carolina University Press

Keum, H., Devanathan, N., Deshpande, S., Nelson, M. R. and Shah, D. V. (2004) 'The Citizen-consumer: Media effects at the intersection of consumer and civic culture', in *Political Communication*, Vol. 21, No. 3

Kiwan, D. (2007) *Becoming a British citizen: A Learning Journey*. Discussion paper prepared for the Citizenship Review (citizenshipreview@justice.gsi.gov.uk). London: Citizenship Review, Ministry of Justice

Kiwan, D. (2008) *Education for Inclusive Citizenship*. London: Routledge

Klein, M. (2001) *No Logo*. London: Flamingo

Korsgaard, O. (1997) 'The impact of globalization on adult education', in Walters, S. (Ed.) (1997), *Globalization, Adult Education and Training: Impacts and Issues*, London: Zed Books

Kraemer, S. and Roberts, J. (Eds) (1996) *The Politics of Attachment*. London: Free Association Books

Kymlicka, W. (1995a) *Multicultural Citizenship*. Oxford: Oxford University Press

Kymlicka, W. (Ed.) (1995b) *The Rights of Minority Cultures.* Oxford: Clarendon Press

Kymlicka, W. (2007) *Multicultural Odysses.* Oxford: Clarendon Press

Laclau, E. (1996) 'Universalism, particularlism and the question of identity', in Laclau (1996) *Emancipation(s).* London: Verso

Laden, A. S. and Owen, D. (2007) *Multiculturalism and Political Theory.* Cambridge: Cambridge University Press

Larsson, S. (1997) 'The meaning of life-long learning' in Walters, S. (Ed.) (1997) pp. 250–261

Lave, J., and Wenger, E. (1991) *Situated Learning.* Cambridge: Cambridge University Press

Lawler, S. (2008) *Identity: Sociological Perspectives.* Cambridge: Polity

Lawson, J. (2001) 'Disability as a cultural identity', in *International Studies in Sociology of Education,* Vol. 11, No. 3

Lawton, D. (1977) *Education and Social Justice.* London: Sage

Lawton, D., Cairns, J. and Gardner, R. (Eds) (2000) *Education for Citizenship.* London: Continuum

Layer, G. (Ed.) (2005) *Closing the Equity Gap: The Impact of Widening Participation Strategies in the UK and the USA.* Leicester: NIACE

Leggett, W. (2005) *After New Labour: Social Theory and Centre-Left Politics.* Basingstoke: Palgrave Macmillan

Leitch, Lord (Chair) (2006) *Prosperity for All in the Global Economy – World Class Skills.* London: TSO

Levin, B. (1998) 'The educational requirement for democracy', in *Curriculum Inquiry,* Vol. 28, No. 1

Levitas, R. (1998) 'The concept of social exclusion and the new Durkheimian hegemony', *Critical Social Policy,* Vol. 16, No. 1

Linton, S. (1998) *Claiming Disability: Knowledge and Identity.* New York: New York University Press

Lister, R., (Ed.) 1997, *Citizenship: Feminist Perspectives.* London: Macmillan

Lister, R. (1998) 'Citizenship and difference: Towards a differentiated universalism', in *European Journal of Social Theory,* Vol. 1, No. 1

Lister, R. (2000) 'Dilemmas in engendering citizenship', in Hobson, B. (Ed.) (2000) *Gender and Citizenship in Transition.* London: Macmillan

Livingstone, S., Lunt, P. and Miller, L. (2007) 'Citizens, consumers and the citizen-consumer', in *Discourse and Communication,* Vol. 1, No. 1

Lockyer, A., Crick, B. and Annette, J. (2003) *Education for Democratic Citizenship: Issues of Theory and Practice.* Aldershot: Ashgate

Lovett, T. (1975) *Adult Education, Community Development and the Working Class*. London: Ward Lock

Lovett, T., Clarke, C. and Kilmurray, A. (1983) *Adult Education and Community Action*. Beckenham: Croom Helm

Lovett, W. (1840) 'Chartism: a new organization of the people', in Simon, B. (Ed.) (1972) *The Radical Tradition in Education in Britain*. London: Lawrence and Wishart

Low, N., Butt, S., Ellis Paine, A. and Davis Smith, J. (2007) *Helping Out: A National Survey of Volunteering Charitable Giving*. London: The Cabinet Office

Lukes, S. (1974) *Power: A Radical View*. London: Macmillan

Lukes, S. (2004) *Power: A Radical View*. (Revised Edition). Basingstoke: Palgrave Macmillan

Lyon, D. (1988) *The Information Society*. Cambridge: Polity

Lyon, D. (1994) *Postmodernity*. Buckingham; Open University

Macedo, Donald (1998) 'Foreword', in Freire, P. (1998) *Pedagogy of Freedom: Ethics, Democracy, and Civic Courage*. Oxford: Rowman and Littlefield

Macedo, S. (1990) *Liberal Virtues*. Oxford: Clarendon Press

MacIntyre, A. (1985) *After Virtue*. London: Duckworth

Maier, C. S. (2007) ' "Being there": Place, territory and identity', in Benhabib *et al.*, 2007

Mann, M. (2005) *The Dark Side of Democracy: Explaining Ethnic Cleansing*. Cambridge: Cambridge University Press

Mansbridge, J. (1995) 'Does participation make better citizens?', paper delivered at the PEGS Conference, 11–12 February, 1995. Available at: www.bsos.umd.edu/pegs/mansbrid.html (last accessed 30 September 2010)

Marquand, D. (2004) *The Decline of the Public: The Hollowing Out of Citizenship*. Cambridge: Polity

Marshall, T. H. (1950) *Citizenship and Social Class*. Cambridge: Cambridge University Press

Marshall, T. H. and Bottomore, T. (1992) *Citizenship and Social Class*. London: Pluto Press

Martell, L. and Driver, S. (1997) 'New Labour's communitarians', in *Critical Social Policy*, Vol. 17, No. 3

Martin, I. (1999) 'Adult education, lifelong learning and active citizenship', in *Adults Learning*, Vol. 11, No. 2

Martin, I. (2000) 'Reconstituting the Agora: Towards an alternative politics of lifelong learning', paper presented at the AER Conference 2000.
Available at www.adulterc.org/Proceedings/2000/martini-final.pdf (last accessed 30 September 2010)

Martin, I. (2002) 'Citizenship debate asks some awkward questions', in *Adults Learning*, Vol. 13, No. 19

Martin, I. (2003) 'Adult education, lifelong learning and citizenship: some ifs and buts', in *International Journal of Lifelong Education,* Vol. 22, No. 6

Martin, R. and Fryer, R. H. (1973) *Redundancy and Paternalist Capitalism*. London: Geo Allen and Unwin

Mason, A. (2000) *Community, Solidarity and Belonging*. Cambridge: Cambridge University Press

Mayo, M. (2000) 'Learning for active citizenship: Training for and learning from participation in area regeneration', in *Studies in the Education of Adults*, Vol. 32, No. 1

Mayo, M. (2005) *Global Citizens: Social Movements and the Challenge of Globalization*. London: Zed Books

McGrew, A. (2001) 'Transnational democracy', in Carter, A. and Stokes, G (Eds) (2001)

McIlroy, J. and Westwood, S. (1993) *Border Country: Raymond Williams in Adult Education*. Leicester: NIACE

McLaughlin, T. H. (1992) 'Citizenship, diversity and education: A philosophical perspective', in *Journal of Moral Education*, Vol. 21, No. 3

Medel-Anonuevo, C. and Gordon, M. (Eds) (2003) *Citizenship, Democracy and Lifelong Learning*. Philippines: UNESCO

Miliband, D. (Ed.) (1994) *Reinventing the Left*. Cambridge: Polity

Mill, John S. (1861) *On Liberty*. London: Folio Edition 2008

Mill, John S. (1982) *On Liberty*. Harmondsworth: Penguin

Miller, D. (2000) *Citizenship and National Identity*. Cambridge: Polity

Mills, C. Wright (1959) *The Sociological Imagination*. Oxford: Oxford University Press

Ministry of Reconstruction (1919) *Final Report of the Adult Education Committee*. London: HMSO

Mitchell, Juliet (1966), 'Women: The longest revolution', in *New Left Review* (November–December), Vol. 26

Modood, T., Berthoud, R., Lakey, J., Nazroo, J., Smith, P., Virdee, S. and Beishon, S. (1997) *Ethnic Minorities in Britain: Diversity and Disadvantage*. London: PSI

Mouffe, C. (Ed.) (1993) *Dimensions of Radical Democracy*. London: Verso

Mouffe, C. (2004) 'Pluralism, dissensus and democratic citizenship', in Inglis, F. (Ed.) (2004) *Education and the Good Society*. Basingstoke: Palgrave Macmillan

Munt, S. (1998) *Heroic Desire: Lesbian Identity and Cultural Space*. New York: New York University Press

Needham, C. (2003) *Citizen-Consumers: New Labour's Marketplace Democracy*. London: Catalyst

Nelson, J. and Kerr, D. (2006) *Active Citizenship in INCA Countries*. London: QCA/NFER

Newby, H. (1977) 'Paternalism and capitalism', in Scase, R. (Ed.) (1977) *Industrial Society: Class, Cleavage and Control*. London: Allen and Unwin

Newby, H., Bell, C., Rose, D. and Saunders, P. (1978) *Property, Paternalism and Power: Class and Control in Rural England*. London: Hutchinson

Nicholson, G. (1996) 'Place and local identity' in Kraemer, S. and Roberts, J. (Eds) (1996) *The Politics of Attachment*. London: Free Association Books

Nicoll, K. (2006) *Flexibility and Lifelong Learning: Policy, Discourse and Politics*. London: Routledge Falmer

Nozik, R. (1974) *Anarchy, State and Utopia*. New York: Basic Books

Nussbaum, M. (1997) *Cultivating Humanity*. Cambridge: Harvard University Press

Nussbaum, M. (2000) *Women and Human Development: The Capabilities Approach*. Cambridge: Cambridge University Press

Nussbaum, M. (2001) 'Capabilities as fundamental entitlements: Sen and social justice.' Paper given at conference on Sen's work at the University of Bielefield and in a revised form at the London School of Economics in March 2002. Later reprinted in revised form in 2003 in *Feminist Economics*, Vol. 9, No. 2/3

Nussbaum, M. (2010) *Not for Profit: Why Democracy Needs the Humanities*. Oxford: Princeton University Press

Nussbaum, M. and Sen, A., (Eds) (1993) *The Quality of Life*. Oxford: Clarendon Press

Ofsted (2006) *Towards Consensus? Citizenship in Secondary Schools*. London: Crown Copyright

Okin, S. (1979) *Women in Western Political Thought*. Princeton, NJ: Princeton University Press

Oldfield, A. (1990) *Citizenship and Community: Civic Republicanism and the Modern World*. London: Routledge

Oldfield, A. (1998) 'Citizenship and community: Civic republicanism and the modern world', in Shafir, G. (Ed.) (1998) *The Citizenship Debates: A Reader*. Minneapolis: University of Minnesota Press

Olin Wright, E. (2010) *Envisioning Real Utopias*. London: Verso

Oliver, D. and Heater, D. (1994) *The Foundations of Citizenship*. London: Harvester Wheatsheaf

Osler, A. and Starkey, H. (2005) *Education for Democratic Citizenship: A Review of Research, Policy and Practice 1995–2005*.
Available at: www.bera.ac.uk/files/reviews/
oslerstarkeyberareview2005.pdf (last accessed 30 September 2010)

Osler, A. and Vincent, K. (2002) *Citizenship and the Challenge of Global Education*. Stoke-on-Trent: Trentham

Parekh, B. (1991) 'British citizenship and cultural difference', in Andrews, G., (Ed.) (1991) *Citizenship*. London: Lawrence and Wishart

Parekh, B. (2000) *The Future of Multi-Ethnic Britain: Report of the Commission on the Future of Multi-Ethnic Britain*. London: Profile Books

Parekh, B. (2002) *Rethinking Multiculturalism: Cultural Diversity and Political Theory*. Harvard: University Press

Parekh, B. (2007) *Europe and the Muslim Question: Does Intercultural Dialogue Make Sense?* (ISIM Papers) Amsterdam: University Press

Parekh, B. (2008) *A New Politics of Identity: Political Principles for an Interdependent World*. Basingstoke: Palgrave Macmillan

Parkin, A. (1996) 'Building Civil Society "From the Ground Up": The Halifax People's Summit,' presented at the conference on the *Emergence of Civil Society: A Precondition or a Problem for Democracy*. Centre for Studies in Democratisation, University of Warwick, February 16–17, 1996

Pateman, C. (1970) *Participation and Democratic Theory*. Cambridge: Cambridge University Press

Pateman, C. and Mills, C. (2007) *Contract and Domination*. Cambridge: Polity

Payne, J. (2001) 'Lifelong learning: A national trade union strategy in a global economy.' *International Journal of Lifelong Education*, Vol. 20, No. 5

Phillips, A. (1991) *Engendering Democracy*. Cambridge: Polity

Phillips, A. (1995) 'Democracy and difference: Some problems for feminist theory' in Kymlicka, W. (Ed.) (1995b)

Phillips, A. and Putnam, T. (1980) 'Education for emancipation: The movement for independent working class education 1908–1928', in *Capital and Class*, No. 10

Phillips, T. (2005) 'Sleepwalking to Segregation', in *The Times*, 23 September 2005

Pieterse, J. (Ed.) (2000) *Global Futures: Shaping Globalization*. London: Zed Books

Porter, J. (1987) *The Measure of Canadian Society*. Ottawa: Carleton University Press

Porter, M. and Kramer, M. (2004) 'The link between competitive advantage and corporate social responsibility,' in *Howard Business Review*, December, 2006

Portes, A. (1998) 'Social capital: Its origins and applications in modern sociology', in *Review of Sociology*, Vol. 24

Prideaux, S. (2005) *Not So New Labour: A Sociological Critique of New Labour's Policy and Practice*. Bristol: Policy Press

Purvis, J. and Holton, S. (Eds) (2000) *Votes for Women*. London: Routledge

Putnam, R. D. (1993) *Making Democracy Work: Civic Traditions in Modern Italy*. Princeton, NJ: Princeton University Press

Putnam, R. D. (2000) *Bowling Alone: Civic Disengagement in America*. New York; Simon and Schuster

QCA/DfEE (1999) *The National Curriculum for England: Key Stages 3–4*. London: QCA/DfEE

Ranson, S. (1994) *Towards the Learning Society*. London: Cassell

Rees, T. (1992) *Women and the Labour Market*. London: Routledge

Reich, R. (2008) *Supercapitalism: The Battle for Democracy in an Age of Big Business*. Cambridge: Icon Books

Reicher, S. and Hopkins, N. (2001) *Self and Nation: Categorization, Contestation and Mobilization*. London: Sage

Rex, J. (Ed.) (1991) *Ethnic Identity and Ethnic Mobilisation in Britain*. Research Monograph No. 5. Coventry: Centre for Research in Ethnic Relations, University of Warwick

Rex, J. and Moore, R. (1967) *Race, Community and Conflict*. Oxford: Oxford University Press

Riddell, S. and Watson, N. (2003) *Disability, Culture and Identity*. London: Pearson Education

Robertson, R. (1992) *Globalization*. London: Sage

Rogers, A. (2004) 'Looking again at non-formal and informal education –
Towards a new paradigm', in *The Encyclopaedia of Informal Education*
Available at: www.infed.org/biblio/non_formal_paradigm.htm
(last accessed 30 September 2010)

Rosenberg, J. (2005) 'Globalization theory: A post-mortem', in
International Politics, Vol. 42, No. 2

Rowbotham, S. (1969) *Women's Liberation and the New Politics*.
Nottingham: Spokesman

Rowbotham, S. (1973) *Hidden From History*. London: Pluto Press

Rowbotham, S. (1989) *The Past is Before Us*. London: Pandora

Rowbotham, S. (1997) *A Century of Women*. London: Viking

Rowbotham, S. and Wollstonecraft, M. (2010) *Sheila Rowbotham Presents
Mary Wollstonecraft*. London: Verso

Rowe, D. (1995) 'Education for citizenship in Europe', in Bell, G. (Ed.)
(1995) *Educating European Citizens: Citizenship Values and the
European Dimension*. London: David Fulton Publishers

Rowe, J. (2005) 'Corporate social responsibility as business strategy.' UC
Santa Cruz: Center for Global, International and Regional Studies

Russell, I. (2005) *Russell Commission Report: A National Framework for Youth
Action and Engagement*. London: Crown Copyright

Ryan, A. (2001) 'Staunchly modern, non-bourgeois liberalism', in
Simhony, A. and Weinstein, D. (2001) *The New Liberalism: Reconciling Liberty and Community*. Cambridge: Cambridge University Press

Saggar, S. and Heath, A. (1999) 'Race: Towards a multicultural electorate',
in Evans, G. and Norris, P. (Eds) (1995), *Critical Elections: British
Parties and Voters in Long-term Perspective*. London: Sage

Sandel, M. (1982) *Liberation and the Limits of Justice*. Cambridge:
Cambridge University Press

Sarachild, Kathie (1978) 'Consciousness-raising: A radical weapon', in
Sarachild, K., Hanisch, C., Levine, F., *et al*. (Eds) (1978) *Feminist
Revolution*. New York: Random House

Schlosberg, D. (1998) 'Resurrecting the pluralist universe', in *Political
Research Quarterly*, Vol. 51, No. 3

Schugerensky, D. (2003) *Citizenship Learning and Participatory Democracy*.
Ontario: Canada

Schuk, P. H. and Smith, R. M (1985) *Citizenship Without Consent*.
Cambridge: Cambridge University Press

Schuller, T. and Bengtsson, J. (1977) 'A strategy for equity: Recurrent education and industrial democracy', in Karabel, J. and Halsey, A. H. (Eds) (1977) *Power and Ideology in Education*. Oxford: Oxford University Press

Schuller, T. and Watson, D. (2009) *Learning Through Life: Inquiry into the Future for Lifelong Learning*. Leicester: NIACE

Scottish Executive (2003) *Think Global, Act Local*. Edinburgh: Crown Copyright

Sealey-Ruiz, Y. (2007) 'Wrapping the curriculum around their lives; using a culturally relevant curriculum with African American women', in *Adult Education Quarterly*, Vol. 58, No. 1

Seidman, S. (Ed.) (1994) *The Postmodern Turn*. Cambridge: Cambridge University Press

Sen, A. (1985) *Commodities and Capabilities*. Oxford: Oxford University Press

Sen, A. (2006) *Identity and Violence: The Illusion of Destiny*. London: Penguin

Shafir, G., (Ed.) (1998) *The Citizenship Debates: A Reader*. Minneapolis: University of Minnesota Press

Shotter, J. (1993) 'Psychology and citizenship: Identity and belonging', in Turner, 1995

Skinner, Q. (2003) 'States and the freedom of citizens', in Strath, B. and Skinner, Q. (Eds) (2003) *States and Citizens*. Cambridge: Cambridge University Press

Slowey, M. (2003) 'Higher education and civil society', in Slowey, M. and Watson, D. (Eds) *Higher Education and the Lifecourse*. Maidenhead: Open University Press/McGraw hill

Smith, M. K. (1996 and 2001) 'Lifelong learning', in *The Encyclopaedia of Informal Education*
Available at: www.infed.org/lifelonglearning/b-life.htm (last accessed 30 September 2010)

Solomos, J. (1989) *Race and Racism in Contemporary Britain*. London: Macmillan

Spellman, W. M. (2008) *Uncertain Identity: International Migration since 1945*. Chicago: Chicago University Press

Stedman Jones, G. (2004) *An End to Poverty?* London: Profile Books

Steger, M. B. (2009) *Globalization: A Very Short Introduction*. Oxford: Oxford University Press

Stiglitz, J. (2002) *Globalization and its Discontents*. London: Penguin

Stiglitz, J. (2007) *Making Globalization Work*. London: Penguin

Stuart, M. (1995) 'Education and self-identity: A process of inclusion and exclusion', in Stuart, M. and Thomson, A. (Eds) (1995) *Engaging with Difference*. Leicester: NIACE

Taylor, C. (1994) *Multiculturalism: Examining the Politics of Recognition*. Princeton, NJ: Princeton University Press

Taylor, C. (1989) *Sources of the Self*. Cambridge: Cambridge University Press

Taylor, R. (1998) 'Lifelong learning in the liberal tradition', in *Journal of Moral Education*, Vol. 27, Issue 3

Thompson, J. (2000) *Emancipatory Learning: NIACE Briefing Sheet No. 11*. Leicester: NIACE

Tomlinson, J. (Chair) (1996) *Inclusive Learning*. London: HMSO

Torney-Purta, J. *et al.* (2001) *Citizenship and Education in Twenty-eight Countries*. Amsterdam: IAEEA

Turgeon, W. (2004) 'Multiculturalism: Politics of difference, education and philosophy for children', in *Analytical Teaching*, Vol. 24, No. 2

Turnbull, J. (2002) 'Values in educating for citizenship', in *Pedagogy, Culture and Society*, Vol. 10, No. 1

Turner, B. S. (Ed.) (1993) *Citizenship and Social Theory*. London: Sage

Ufi Ltd (2008) *Economic Benefits of Digital Inclusion: Building the Evidence*. Sheffield: Ufi

Van Dyke, V. (1995) 'The individual, the State and ethnic communities in political theory', in W. Kymlicka (Ed.), *The Rights of Minority Cultures*. Oxford: Oxford University Press

Vidler, E. and Clarke, J. (2005) 'Creating citizen–consumers: New Labour and the remaking of public services', in *Public Policy and Administration*, Vol. 20, No. 2

Vincent, D. (1981) *Bread, Knowledge and Freedom: A Study of Nineteenth-Century Working Class Autobiography*. London: Methuen

Walzer, M. (1983) *Spheres of Justice*. New York: Basic Books

Walzer, M. (1994) *Thick and Thin: Moral Argument at Home and Abroad*. Notre Dame, IN: University of Notre Dame Press

Walzer, M. (1995) 'Pluralism and political perspectives', in Kymlicka (1995b)

Waters, M. (1995) *Globalization*. London: Routledge

Watson, D. (2005a) 'What I think I know and don't know about widening participation', in Duke and Layer (2005)

Watson (2005b) 'Overview: Telling the truth about widening participation', in Layer (2005)

Webster, F. (1995) *Theories of the Information Society.* London: Routledge

Welsh Assembly Government (2006) *Education for Sustainable Development and Global Citizenship – A Strategy for Action.* Cardiff: Welsh Assembly Government

Welton, M. R. (Ed.) (1995) *In Defense of the Lifeworld: Critical Perspectives on Adult Learning.* Albany, NY: SUNY Press

Welton, M. (2005) *Designing the Just Learning Society.* Leicester: NIACE

Wernik, A. (1991) *Promotion Culture: Culture, Advertising Ideology and Symbolic Expression.* London: Sage

Wikipedia (2010) 'Corporate Social Responsibility.' Available at: http://wikipedia.org/wki/corporate_social/responsibility (last accessed 30 September 2010)

Williams, J., Morrissette, A. S. and Vazquez, A. M. (2004) *Tales of the City: The Experience of REAL Learning.* Glasgow: Scottish Enterprise

Williams, R. (1976 and 1984) *Keywords.* London: Fontana

Williams, R. (1983) *Towards 2000.* London: Chatto and Windus

Williams, R. (1989) *Resources of Hope: Culture, Democracy, Socialism,* London: Verso

Williams, R. (1990) 'Adult education and social change', in Williams, R. (1990) *What I Came to Say.* London: Hutchinson Radius

Wolin, S. (1989) *The Presence of the Past: Essays on the State and the Constitution.* Baltimore: John Hopkins University Press

Wolf, A. (2002) *Does Education Matter? Myths about Education and Economic Growth.* London: Penguin

Woodin, T. (2007) 'Working class education and social change in nineteenth-and twentieth-century Britain', in *History of Education*, Vol. 36, Issue 4 and 5

Woodward, V. (2004) *Active Learning for Active Citizenship.* London: Civil Renewal Unit/Home Office

Young, I. M. (1995) 'Polity and group difference: A critique of the ideal of universal citizenship', in Beiner, R. (Ed.) (1995) *Theorizing Citizenship.* Albany: State University of New York Press

Young, Iris M. (1998), 'Polity and group difference: A critique of the ideal of universal citizenship', in Shafir, G., (Ed.) (1998) *The Citizenship Debates: A Reader.* Minneapolis: University of Minnesota Press

Yuval-Davis, N. and Werbner, P. (1999) *Women, Citizenship and Difference.* London: Zed Books

Index

269